An Overview of the Old Testament and How it Relates to the New Testament

An Overview of the Old Testament and How it Relates to the New Testament

Jim McKeehan

Writer's Showcase
San Jose New York Lincoln Shanghai

An Overview of the Old Testament and How it Relates to the New Testament

All Rights Reserved © 2002 by James McKeehan

No part of this book may be reproduced or transmitted in any form or by any means, graphic, electronic, or mechanical, including photocopying, recording, taping, or by any information storage retrieval system, without the permission in writing from the publisher.

Writer's Showcase
an imprint of iUniverse, Inc.

For information address:
iUniverse, Inc.
5220 S. 16th St., Suite 200
Lincoln, NE 68512
www.iuniverse.com

ISBN: 0-595-20758-8

Printed in the United States of America

To my wife Marian

Contents

Foreword ix
Editorial Method xi
Faith Overview and The Present Day Church 1
   Chapter 1: Faith Overview 3
   Chapter 2: The Present Day Church 19
   Chapter 3: Overview of the Bible 31
   Chapter 4: Reading the Bible 46
The Old Testament 49
   Chapter 1: The Pentateuch: The First Five Books of the Bible 51
   Chapter 2: Genesis 1 through Genesis 11 57
      Fig Trees: An Overview of Israel 64
      Genealogies Used as Messages 68
      Wickedness of Man, the Flood and the New Covenant 70
   Chapter 3: The Bible Account of the Great Flood 74
   Chapter 4: The Books of Genesis, and Exodus with Judges, and Kings 82
      Sinai 83
      The Ancient Near East (Not drawn to scale) 85
      The Iron Age 91
      Moses 94
      The Ten Plagues 105
      Covenants and Laws 108
      Slavery: 111
      Capital Punishment (An Eye for an Eye) 113
      Jubilee or Kinsman Redemption 121
      A Summary of the Law and the Kinsman Redeemer 124
   Chapter 5: Entering the Promised Land 126
      I. Military Conquest of the Land of Canaan 127
      II. Theory of Israel Emerging From Within the Land of Canaan 129
      III. Theory of a Social Revolution with the Word of God 130

Chapter 6: The Book of Kings 135
   A King was chosen for Judah and Israel. *139*
   The Book of Numbers (The 12 Tribes) *141*
Chapter 7: The Book of Numbers (The 12 Tribes) 158
   Covenants *158*
Sub Section: Wisdom Literature 179
   Chapter 8: Overview of the Wisdom Literature 181
     The Cultural Context of Wisdom Literature: *183*
     The Culture of Marriage *188*
     Overview of the Wisdom Literature: *188*
     A. Book of Proverbs: *197*
     B. The Book of Sirach *201*
     C. The Book of Ecclesiastes *204*
   Chapter 9: Song of Songs (Solomon's Canticle of Canticles) 210
   Chapter 10: The Book of Wisdom (of Solomon) 216
   Chapter 11: The Book of Job 226
   Chapter 12: The Book of Hosea 230
     Marriage to God (Romans 7:1 to 13) *237*
   Chapter 13: Isaiah 241
Bibliography 273
Notes 275
Index 289
About the Author 297

Foreword

The gospel is the message for today and it teaches us how to live with God and in Him as His children. The gospel is also the memory we offer in God's name. These memories consist of the realities of heaven that come to earth and are given to us. We use our experiences and love to continue through time as the Church that Jesus established. Our Church is historical but it transcends our time and lives on in God's time.

God is patient and He judges slowly. He gives us a chance to change and to mature because God is a lover of souls.

This book is a compilation of many years of scripture study. Many books and many scholars have influenced me. Many times, I have written something and then I find that an early Church Father had already written about the matter. I have referenced everything as accurately as possible. Similarities of my work compared to others may exist because so many writers meditate on the same subjects.

Most of the scripture quotations are those of the author. Many were adapted from a version of The King James Bible that is no longer under copyright protection.

Deutero canonical Books are quoted from the New International Version.

The Scripture quotations contained herein are from the New Revised Standard Version Bible, copyright 1989 by the Division of Christian Education of the National Council of the Churches in Christ in the USA, and are used by permission. All rights reserved.

Editorial Method

The word Church is capitalized when the word refers to the universal Church. It is not capitalized when it refers to a local church. Whenever scripture is written in the present tense it is because the scripture citation refers to the book.

Section 1

Faith Overview and The Present Day Church

Chapter 1: Faith Overview

Scripture is alive, we are alive, and we share as a community. We write to reflect on the work of our hearts and how the word of God is affecting us, transforming us, and converting us. We study scripture because this is our story, and we are God's people.

Christianity is the living out of our faith as expressed in our family values, ethnic values, and social values. Actual religion is not an American dream; instead it is two thousand years of wisdom in living out the gospel so that we can see the connection of this world with eternity. We need to stay in touch with our rich tradition, and the truths that are taught by the Church. The Church has gone through many steps of spiritual growth. We have experienced a lot as a Church, but we are still maturing. Some concepts take hundreds, or thousands, of years before they can be full understood. Consequently, doctrine is still being more fully understood.

1. Jesus is the cornerstone of the Church and the Apostles formed the foundation of the Church around Jesus. How we live out our faith determines whether or not we have the spark of God within us, just as a house can be a home, the Church can be the body of Christ. Our Church life, our prayer life, our scripture studies, our marriages, our families, and our relationship to the peoples of the world reflect on who we are. We view creation, God, and the world as follows:

Creation is good and the primeval views of God and family are contained in creation stories written in the Book of Genesis. We have an optimistic approach to original blessing, and to original sin. God saw that creation was good. Man and woman were created on the sixth day, and it was very good. Elohim is the Hebrew word for God, and tov is the Hebrew word for good and these words were repeated throughout the story of creation. Creation is a reflection of the glory of God. We are wounded but are not corrupt. All of nature leans toward the cross and the resurrection of Jesus. When someone questions Christianity we should recognize that his soul is yearning to experience truth.

The early Reformation Father Martin Luther taught that human beings were corrupt from birth. The grace of Jesus covered our souls, but underneath the grace of Jesus, we were still corrupt. Luther taught that the communion of saints was first a communion of sinners, and that we had to cry out about our evil desires and the weakness of our flesh. Paul does write in the Book of Romans 7:18 to 19, "For I know that in me, that is in my flesh, dwells no good thing. For to will is present with me; but I cannot find how to perform that which is good." Martin Luther taught that the law of God in the spirit is at war with the law of sin in the person. He spoke as if there were two people inside of each of us.

Martin Luther wrote that a person is always a sinner, always penitent, and always right with God.

Paul, Peter, and the Gospel writers tell us that we each share in Jesus' relationship with the Father. We were created in the image of God, and we are children of God. 1John 3:1 says, "Look what love the father has given us that we may be called children of God."[1]

The Son was sent by the Father to redeem us. Jesus taught us how to become righteous so we could be justified before God. The Greek word dikaiosune means both righteousness and justification. We become more righteous through obeying the commandments and the teachings of the Sermon on the Mount. We become more righteous so that we can become more fully children of God.

The Holy Spirit brings the love of the Father and the son. The Holy Spirit guides the Church and the members of the Church. The Church is holy only because the Holy Spirit is in the Church. We can become more holy like Jesus commanded us to be, only through the grace of the Holy Spirit that lives with us. The Holy Spirit sanctifies us, which means to make us more holy.

God is a family where Jesus is eternally begotten through the love of the Father. There never was a time that the Father was not sending Jesus forth, and we are to imitate the family of the Trinity. There is one God who created the Universe who continually shows us His love through Jesus. The Holy Spirit unifies us to the Father and the Son by being perfect Love. God is Trinitarian because God is a family and we too are families.

2. Bread, wine, oil, and healing touch are used to show that the earthly and heavenly realities are related and connected. At his baptism by John, Jesus went into the water and all water became part of him. "Stuff" became divine when Jesus was baptized. We must breathe in creation because all of creation is good. We praise all of creation when we use vestments, candles, incense, water, music, art, stained glass, and dancing. Creation is messy, it is inviting, and it touches us. We come away grounded and blessed after a good service, and we come out knowing we are good. If a connection is not happening in church, it could be because our spiritual lives are The Gift of God is mediated through His gift of creation. Sacraments are signs of God's giving, caring, and just way of not what they should be at home.

All of creation is a gift and a blessing and we use it judiciously to reflect on our God. Sacraments come from heaven through God and these heavenly gifts are given to us. God calls us, we respond, and He gives us His Live. Isaiah 66 describes God who gives us life through the Church, Zion. Mount Zion is described as a mother who is feeding her child. We rejoice and are glad because we come from God and are nourished by Him. Just as a baby comes from the mother and feeds from her body, Jesus says come and eat of my body. Marriage is a covenant to teach us how to become one with the Trinity. The Holy Spirit sanctifies us to help make us holy, and only Christ can carry us to the Father where we can be one with Him. Healthy theology helps us to be happy with ourselves so that we can look forward to when we will join God when we die.

Marriage can be explained from an excerpt of a letter I wrote to a friend. I wrote to him right after his wife had died of cancer.

Dear Bill;

Pope John Paul II wrote a theological work, which a reviewer says is a writing that will stand the test of time. It is now his least known writing, but will eventually be his most read, according to the reviewer. He writes about the theology of the body, beginning with the creation of Adam and Eve and progressing to their nakedness. It is a total vision of man. It is written from the bible. He describes how everything God wants to tell us on earth about the meaning of life is contained somehow in the meaning of the human body. Mostly through the call of male and female to become "one body" in marriage. After all, the message of scripture is the message of a marriage between Jesus and the Church. It was God's plan to draw us into a marriage with him. In The Book of Ephesians, Paul writes about the union of man and wife, but then he says that he is talking about Christ and the Church. In this passage, it gets fuzzy whether it is about man and woman or about Jesus' relationship with us.

This is a great mystery, but I speak in reference to Christ and the church.

In any case, each one of you should love his wife as himself, and the wife should respect her husband.

I thought about this when I heard your wonderful admonishment to men, when you said, "Men, love your wives". The Pope wrote, "In our marriage, we love and our bodies become a gift and by means of this gift fulfills the very meaning of being and existence." We men can only find ourselves by making a gift of ourselves. Love is the source of God's creation being a gift.

The message I am trying to convey is that you had a wonderful wife, a person that I dearly love. The messages contained on the tape you sent to us, sounds like everyone who came in contact with her, also loved her. The fulfillment of our marriages is when we enter into Jesus who is the resurrection. When we die, we enter into the communion of saints who are in communion with the Communion of the Trinity. Heaven is the eternal marriage of Christ's Church with the Trinity. Jesus said there is no marriage in heaven because as John Paul II says, "Heaven is the rediscovery of a new and perfect communion of persons, redeemed and glorified in Christ, and consolidated by complete concentration on God himself." Our marriage is a sign and heaven is the reality. Bette is where we want to be, and it is sad that she is not here, but it is joyous that she is where we want to be.

God forgives us again and again; He heals us all of the way to our family tree. The crucifixion of Jesus shows us real power in his suffering and death. His obedience to the Father and his love for us is where real power is. God became incarnate to show us that money, control of others, social status, power, and worship of the world is the type of success that is condemned on the cross. Jesus rose on the third day to show us that his power is real. Jesus showed us that power does not come from violence and killing, instead power comes from wafers of bread, and a chalice of wine.[2] Matthew wrote that than all of the money on earth does not compare to the treasures in heaven. Matthew's Gospel asks us, "Would you take the world in exchange for eternal life?" Jesus said, do not worry about what we will eat, what we will drink, or what clothes we are to wear, "But seek first the kingdom (of God) and his righteousness, and all these things will be given you besides."[3] A flower that blooms for one day is more beautiful than the richest and finest garments that can be made. God loves us because God created the world and He said that it is good.

Many Protestant congregations have a theology that emphasizes words and ideas. Many Protestant churches are dynamic, and they reach out to the hungry and downtrodden. They emphasize memorizing verses of the bible and it is good to do this. We also see the good and the beauty in all that the world through the sacraments. Christians can enjoy a sacramental form of worship that includes God created because we yearn to worship God. Society does not understand the real beauty of nature, and many people think that things in nature are here to just satisfy the material needs of human beings. It is sad when people develop a conscience that is worldly, and they have communities that do not appreciate the sacred.

God can show the good that is in a healing touch, smell, eternal water, bread of life, and wine of remembrance. We cannot abandon these practices. To remember means to bring heavenly events upon us.

Even a funeral service is a final act that closes our life on earth, so that there is closure to the community. We begin our life with baptism and we begin our eternal life in heaven with the community coming to celebrate together. We love God and all that He has given us to live in Him and with Him. For instance, a baptismal service is something beautiful and it allows the community to participate in a connection with God. It is the opposite of many of the things that the world has to offer. The beauty of the practices in the Church is what we use to counteract the world's ugliness, its loneliness, its dislike for minorities, its lack of respect for all life, its media propaganda, and the corrupt governmental power of the local communities and the world.

3. The Communion of Saints

We are communal; we are a family working together. Jesus is our Lord and Savior and we cannot separate the two. We live in an environment that teaches us that we should do everything by ourselves, but we have a framework of living together and we call this the Communion of Saints. The communion of Saints is in both this life and the next life. We find God in the community, and we must remain in the community. Even death cannot separate us. We carry both the death and rising of Christ and the death and rising of all the saints who have gone before us.

Purgatory is a place where God's love and forgiveness is the last word. God forgives and makes us complete to dwell in heaven. Purgatory can be thought of as not a place, but as a state of being. It is the final preparation to meet the King of Kings. We cannot go to heaven as sinners, so purgatory is where we change so we can live in the presence of God.

There is a great power in shared life, and to be a Catholic means belonging together. If you were the last person on earth, you could be a Christian but you could not be a Jew or a Catholic Christian. We need to trust in God and live as a family. Prayer groups and retreats try to renew what the scriptures try to teach us. When we dream together it becomes a reality, alone it remains just a dream. We must share to be fully Catholic. There are many ways of living out our faith. We experience God's love through diversity because God cannot be contained in one image. We can only live out the mystery of God. God is love.

Saints are moral examples of people who reveal God's grace, and His saving power to us. God uses saints to reveal Himself, but we must remember that they are totally dependent of God's mercy. Saints are models who show us how perseverance for good can be attained by us. We need models to show us how to struggle, how to live, and how to worship God. The Church is a community of believers who are not only living in the present, but also lived in the past and will live in the future. We cannot allow ourselves to think only of the present. The world is telling us not to be concerned about the future and to forget our connection to the past. This attitude affects our morals and our walk with God.

Our God is a God of the living, and consequently we all pray for each other. We continue to live when we are with God and we can pray even more fervently. Saints do not take away from Jesus, they add to him because his Church is a Church of all ages. Our lives do not stop when we die. Mark 12:26 to 27 says, "God told him, 'I am the God of Abraham, (the) God of Isaac, and (the) God of Jacob.' He is not God of the dead but of the living." And, Saint Paul wrote in Hebrews 12:1, "Therefore, rid ourselves of everything that weighs us down and sin that easily waylay us and let us run with perseverance the race that is set before us."

The Communion of Saints can be summarized through another letter that I wrote to my friend Bill. I had spoken to his wife, on her deathbed.

Dear Bill:

I am writing to express my sorrow at your wife's death. At the same time, I rejoice that she is where we all want to be.

I am so glad that I got to speak to Bette before she died. When we become Christians, we become living and active members in the Mystical Body of Christ. Followers of Jesus are part of the Mystical Body of Christ.[4] And that is why Jesus says that anyone who does this to the least of my brothers, does it to me. We are children of God and this revelation is a true reality while we are on earth and it is also part of the life to come.[5] As Christians, we transcend the relationships we have with our countries and with our families, we are no longer Jew, Greek, or another nationality; nor are we free or slave. The entire assembly of the new covenant is described in the book of Hebrews.[6] Jesus is the first born "for those he fore knew he also predestined to be conformed to the image of his Son, so that he might be the firstborn among many brothers."[7]

When I spoke to Bette, I explained to her that Catholics and other Christians believe in the Communion of Saints. I told her that it is part of our belief as expressed in the last line of the ancient Apostles' Creed, "I believe in the communion of saints, the forgiveness of sins, and life everlasting, Amen."[8] I then mentioned that God is a God of the living and not of the dead.[9] Jesus then said that when you are with God, you are closer to Him than people on earth are, because you are perfected when you are in heaven. I said to Bette that in the Book of Revelation, there is a description of our prayers being taken to God. Both the elders and the angels take our prayers to God.[10] I then asked, "When you are with Jesus, will you pray for me? I really need prayer."

Bette replied, Well, I don't know if I really agree with what you just said." Her voice indicated that this was not the time to get into the subject. She continued, "But when I see Jesus, I will ask him if I can pray for you. And, I will if he says it is okay."

I was not trying to convince her that she should agree with the concept of the communion of saints, but I knew that once she was in heaven that she would see how much more effective her prayers would be. In other words, she would see that I knew what I was talking about. And, I do feel that she is helping me. Things that are bothering me, she has helped to resolve through intercession.

The communion of saints is something that I did not really comprehend until just a few years ago. I never thought I could talk to a relative who died. But, just as I can ask a friend or relative on earth to pray for me; I can also ask someone who has died to pray for me. The Church is on earth but it continues in heaven, now and throughout history. There is one mediator, but we share in God's divine life. For instance, we know that only God is good[11] but we share in that absolute Goodness. When Jesus saw Bette, I'm sure he said, "Well done, my good and faithful servant" Mt. 22:23. So, I can feel the presence of Bette. Hebrews 12:1 tells us that we are "surrounded by so great a cloud of witnesses, let us rid ourselves of every burden and sin that cling to us and persevere in running the race that lies before us." And of course those who are watching us, have to be concerned about us.

So, what I am trying to say is this. I am happy that I got to speak to Bette, and to ask her to pray for me to Jesus. And I feel that she is praying for me. I just want you to know that my views on this are biblically grounded. How wonderful it was to speak to someone so close to the true rest that can only be had in Jesus. When I spoke to her, I thought, "Blessed are the clean in heart for they shall see God. She was so encouraging, even while lying in her deathbed. She even said that she can hardly wait to see me, and that it won't be long.

I told her that I knew she would be with Jesus, but that I was not good like she is. She really thought it was not true. Now that she is in heaven, she can see what I mean. I feel that her prayers will help me to get to the entrance into the heavenly sanctuary,[12] the eternal inheritance.[13] I have faith that Jesus will give me the grace to make if. If Bette helps me so much, I can only imagine how much her life had done for others.

4. God is the initiator and we respond to His call of salvation. We cannot put limits on God and that is why we baptize babies. Sacramental grace is not encapsulated at one moment. We receive grace before the ritual and the grace continues after the ritual. Baptism is not something we do to get grace, but something that God does in us. John 1:12 and 13 says, "But to those who did receive him he gave power to become children of God, to those who believe in his name, who were born not by blood nor the will of the flesh, nor the will of man, but of God."

5. We have a deep sense of tradition and history.

We have a tradition of acting but we did not always take full advantage of it. It took a century of Catholic reformation so that we could get back to where we had been. Vatican II asked us to look at our roots, to look at the early Church and find out what we are missing from our past.

Many people reacted instead of acting responsibly during the Reformation. We need to have dialogue, and a meaningful dialogue was taking place. We are moving toward being an adult Church where we are a people of God. We are disciples of Jesus and we should move together, not separately. The Church has been under capitalism, communism, kings, and presidents as it continued forward in history. We find truth somewhere in the middle of social justice and political economic issues. There can be idolatry in both socialism and in capitalism. The scriptures were written through life experiences of the people of God and are illuminated through the Holy Spirit. The bible is given to us and not us to the bible. The bible is the word of God and was given to us. The Church is the pillar and foundation of truth[14] and is the primary authority of our lives on earth.

6. The Church is open to social sciences because we respect reason and promote understanding. We respect reason in order to understand knowledge. Through our faith we seek understanding. When we are firmly grounded in our faith, we do not have to worry about science. We can learn from others and others can learn from us when we have an ongoing dialogue. All truth comes from God whether it is revealed to us or discovered by us through the sciences. Science can be an important tool in describing truth.

7. We respect our bodies and sexuality. Sex is beautiful in marriage and we know that there are positive aspects of our bodies, and to sex. The Church has always condemned negative views of the body. The Puritans said that the body was evil, sex was bad, and marriage was not good because it resulted in bringing more bodies into the world. This is not a healthy concept of life because our bodies are beautiful. Collectively, we make up the Temple of God; God has chosen the tent of our beings to dwell in.

8. We are rooted in present life situations. God cooperates with us, we do not stand to a side and let Him do everything for us. We also pray for the transformation of economic, political and cultural structures; and for the growth and transformation of individuals. The Gospel message is to be taught at all levels of life. The Church helps us in communal discernment to understand so we can see what is Truth and what is Love. The leaders questioned Jesus when he asked why are people oppressed, and why are people in poverty in such a rich world? Then many people rebelled against him. The world only wants Jesus' blessings, they do not want to hear of social justice.

It took almost one hundred years after Jesus' death to recognize that the Jewish people and the Greek people were equal. Issues involving slavery, social status, and sexual equality took much longer.

God wants everyone to have full potential. The bishops write that basic needs must first be met for this to occur. Catholicism is cosmic and holistic, and we feed the soul to help the body (1 Thes 5:23 and 24). The Church encourages us to choose our careers so that we work in healthy and life giving areas. We need to be a truly whole and holy people. We must be in an environment that promotes wholeness. If we are not living our lives in justice, we will find ourselves trying to possess others, or to possess things.

The crucifix is the focus of our faith. The wooden cross did not save us, Jesus saved us by dying on the cross. The wooden crucifix is a constant reminder that Jesus died for us and he wants us to live lives that are unselfish. We cannot wear a crown if we do not carry the cross. Suffering is a necessary component of Christianity, because there is no life without death. Paul wrote, "I am now rejoicing in my sufferings for your sake. I fill up in my flesh that which is lacking in Christ's afflictions for his body's sake, which is, the church."[15] The Church suffers for Christ when it suffers because the Church is the body of Christ.

It is important that we have compassion for those who are suffering around us. Compassion needs to be real and meaningful, and we must reach out to others with a healing touch so that the hurting will know that they are love. We are to serve and to help others as Jesus directed us. The Book of Hebrews says when we are walking in darkness and Jesus calls, our response to the call is the realness of our faith. Our prayers come from deep inside of us. Our prayers are of laughter, of loves, of our pains, and our angers from not understanding.

9. The Church is Episcopal. We have a universal or global outlook of the world as we try to see the world through God's perspective God sees the world without boundaries made of walls, fences, and lines drawn on the ground. Prophets had dreams

and visions of changing each of us. They were killed because people wanted to keep things the same because change bothers us. Unity is not easy but God has the universal outlook that all people are His people. If a person really loves God it is shown through the love we have given to one another.

10. Liturgy is an expression of an internal reality where we express what is inside of us. We have scripture services, prayer services, and prayer at meals and at other times of the day. Our main expression of faith is experienced together at Church. God has true vision and sees what is developing and it will come into perfection in God's time. In liturgy we celebrate by participating in the liturgy of heaven. Liturgy has been handed down from revelation of the bible, and from tradition handed on to us through the Apostles.

An example of developed liturgy is shown in chapter eight of the Book of Nehemiah. There is a description of the whole people gathered together as one, they gathered together in one accord. Ezra stood on a wooden pulpit and opened the book of scripture so all of the people could see him do so. Then verse six described everyone prostrated themselves to the ground and said Amen.

> And Ezra blessed the Lord, the Great God. And all the people answered, Amen, Amen with lifting up of their hands: they bowed their heads, and worshipped the Lord with their faces to the ground.

We call this the Great Amen to signify that we are in one accord as the Gospel is about to be read. The great Amen is acclaimed throughout the world. The liturgy presented in the Book of Nehemiah continues throughout the bible to the Book of Revelation where we see the liturgy in heaven. In the Book of Revelation 5:14 and 19:4, the writer describes the priests (or elders) in heaven in worship of God with the same liturgy found in the Book of Nehemiah.

This is the same liturgy used in Church Services through the world. The reader stands on a pulpit, opens the book of scripture and reads. We later praise (or bless) the Lord and acclaim the Great Amen. Everyone in the world gives Jesus, the slain lamb, blessings and honor. They prostrate themselves to the ground and say the great Amen.

> And the twenty-four elders and the four beasts (angels) fell down and worshipped God that sat on the throne and said Amen.

Liturgy is serious because it represents heavenly worship. During the worship service of the mass we also worship god, and we kneel as we say Amen in unison. We do not prostrate ourselves with our face to the ground, but we do kneel in honor or God.

11. There is a hierarchy of holy orders that begin with Baptism.

All of us are priests but some of us have our baptisms focused through holy orders into a special ministry of God. We are all ministers to share the word of God, but there is a distinction between a person who is a priest through baptisms and a person who had had hands laid upon him so that he can do things like consecrate bread and wine. The Book of Jude verse 11 reminds us that many are perishing in the rebellion of Korah as described in chapter 16 of the Book of Numbers. Many were killed who thought that their universal priesthood allowed them to do the things reserved for God's ministerial priesthood. We must understand the things of heaven that are here on earth.

12. The Church has Dogmas and doctrines.

Doctrines are the central core beliefs of our faith. Dogmas are taught by the Church to be central to our salvation. The main Dogmas are written in the Nicene Creed as taught by the councils of the Church. The Father sent the son to redeem us and this is still being acted out. Verse one through five of chapter one of the Gospel of John is an echo to remind us of this great gift.

> In the beginning was the Word, and the Word was with God, and the Word was God. He was in the beginning with God. He made all things, and without him was not any thing made that was made. In him was life, and the life was the light of men. And the light shines in darkness and the darkness comprehends it not.

Darkness cannot overcome the light of Christ. The act of redemption is continuously being acted out. We see God in His creations, but we must always remember that the Creator is infinitely greater than his creations.

Ordinary teachings do not bind us like doctrines but should be received by everyone with respect and in the spirit of faith. We take the teachings and we study them, reflect, struggle, argue with them, then we pray, share, and grow with them. We as a people are part of the Way, the Light, and the Truth of Jesus. Ordinary teachings should be adhered t[16]o.

Church disciplines can change over time with growth of understanding, but Doctrines never change. Church disciplines are not important matters like the Divinity of Jesus, God being Trinitarian, or items contained in the Nicene Creed. A discipline could be the way we pray, whether we kneel or stand while receiving communion, or how often we are allowed to receive communion in one day. The Church is thought by many to be Provincial and not open to change like the American way of doing things. The Church is universal and is not limited to the United States or other individual countries. The bible also restricts what we can or cannot do. Some changes that people want may not be in agreement with scripture, so these changes can not be made.

Sometimes the soul is neglected to the whole person. We can even mistakenly think that conformity is community. Fundamentalism and anti dogmatic views have come into the Church, so the members of the Church are far from perfect. We find the most blessed people in the Church, but we also find wicked people in the Church.

The Church is centered on the Eucharist and the Church proclaims the mystery of the Pascal Feast. Paul wrote, "for our Pascal lamb Christ has been sacrificed," he does not say amen, but writes, "let us celebrate the feast."[17] The feast is the Passover Feast, which is the sacrifice of Jesus that Paul writes we still celebrate. The Church is a sacrament and the Church is for the sanctification of all. The Church was fully manifested at Pentecost and is guided by the Holy Spirit. The Church has a baptismal priesthood and a ministerial priesthood that are in tension but not in opposition to each other. There are things we can do with the grace of baptism, but there are things we can only do with the grace of holy orders.

Jesus prayed that the Church should have a visible unity and it is a great scandal that the Christian Churches are not united.[18] The Church must be holy, catholic, and apostolic. Jesus established his Church and it was one in faith, one in purpose, and one in him. To understand the Church is important. When someone fully understands what the Church is, he will be willing to die for the Church.

Descriptions of the Church are varied and complex. There are different ways of describing the Church. Avery Dulles, in his book *Models of the Church* describes the Church as having many models. It is an institution with a common creed and doctrine. The Church is a servant church that cares for the needy in the world; and it is the body of Christ. It is the herald of good news where we evangelize the world. The Church is sacramental to be a visible sign of the redeeming grace for the world. It also consists of models of a community church of believers; a disciple's church; and believers in perfection of the church at the end of times. Avery Dulles says that the Church must be a combination of all the models.

I think a Universal Church has always existed and it is a continuation of the present day Church. My model of the Church is presented on the following pages.

CHAPTER 2: THE PRESENT DAY CHURCH

The Church is alive today as the physical body of Christ.[19] The Church is a dynamic interaction of three main churches that are part of the One Church and are contained in the One Church. There is the Catholic Church that consists of the Roman Church, the Easter Orthodox, and other catholic Churches. The second church is the Church of believers or the individual churches. Third is the Church of the Jews.

To a Catholic, faith in Christ and faith in the church is the same; and the Church is sacramental as a visible sign of Emanuel, God being with us. The liturgy of the mass and the liturgy of the seasons are part of the Catholic Church. To Evangelical Christians, faith is a commitment to Christ an their faith is usually filled with emotions. Other Christian faiths strive to follow Christ by saying *yes* to God and they do it with their whole heart. Jews follow their conscience and strive to maintain their relationship with God and the biblical promises of Abraham, Isaac, Jacob and the other Fathers and prophets. These three bodies of the Church are found in scripture.

First the Catholic Church declares that Jesus started his Church and it was built upon Peter as the visible head of the Church. Jesus told Peter in Matthew 16:18 to 19, "And I say unto you, you are Peter, and upon this rock I will build my church, and the gates of hell shall not prevail against it. I will give you the keys to the kingdom of heaven Whatsoever you bind on earth shall be bound in heaven; and whatsoever you loose on earth shall be loosed in heaven." Jesus gave an authority to Peter that was connected to authority in heaven. The Church continues on through succession of the seat of Peter as is described in the parallel passage of Isaiah 22.

In Luke 22:31, Jesus prayed for Peter's faith not to weaken to Satan so that Peter would come back to lead the other apostles. "Simon, Simon, behold Satan has demanded to have you so that he can sift all of you like wheat, but I have prayed that your won faith many not fail; and once you have turned back, you must strengthen your brothers."

The Gospels of Matthew and of John were most likely written in the ancient Aramaic language. Jesus called Peter by his Aramaic name *Kephas,* which means *Rock.*[20] The Gospel of John tells us that Jesus sanctified the apostles in truth. This is a priestly ordination in truth. Jesus sent them into the world as apostles with the same authority that he has.[21] In the Gospel of John, Jesus tells us that the Church is visible and is an organization that the world can see.[22] Jesus prayed for unity of his followers who believe in him through his apostles and their successors. In our unity we witness to the world that the Father sent Jesus.

The people of the Church travel through time and space in union with the will of our bishops. The bishops send forth the priests to do the will of Jesus and they are an integral part of the bishop just like the strings on a violin are matched to produce a sound that transcends our earthly bounds. Together, all of the people of the world perform a concert and as a choir the love of Jesus abounds throughout the lands. Individual by individual, nation by nation, age by age, we all sing, "Holy, holy, holy"[23] and our voices are lifted in unison with the angels and saints so that we can eternally give Glory to God. When we are in one accord with the precepts of Jesus, we give honor to our Father in heaven.

We live by our faith because we are faithful to Him We show our faith through our works, and the Father can see that we are truly members of the Church that Jesus established. Like those who stay in the protection of the shade of a fig tree, we live in unity with Jesus by staying in his Church. We believe the words of Jesus who said for us to stay in communion with him because we must stay grafted to the vine. Jesus is the vine and we are the branches grafted to him. Jesus told us that whoever remains in him will bear much fruit.[24] Jesus also told how to remain in him, whoever eats my flesh, and drinks my blood remains in me and I in him."[25]

Christians travel through time with the grace of God who bestows upon us sacraments to replenish us. When we worship in remembrance of

Jesus, we know that this defines the realities of heaven that come to earth and are given to us individually as a fellowship of Christians. Catholics find Christ in the community, in the word, and in the Eucharist. The Holy Spirit guides the Church, this is evident now and has been evident throughout history.

Understanding the primacy of Peter is important to the Church that was built upon Peter. In Luke 5:1 to 11, Jesus saw two boats and one of them belonged to Simon Peter. It was not coincidental that one of the boats belonged to Simon, or that a boat is spoken of. Peter and other fishermen had a miraculous catch of fish, and in the Gospel of Matthew, Jesus told to Peter to become a fisher of men. Peter understood that Jesus was calling him to be someone special, and like the prophets of the Old Testament, he fell to his knees and said, "Depart from me Lord because I am a sinful man."

Peter was afraid but he followed Jesus. He matured into the man that is described in the Book of Acts of the Apostles. In Acts chapter fifteen, there is a written account of the first Church Council. Paul and Barnabas could not come to an agreement on salvation. Matthew in chapter eighteen writes what to do when you cannot agree. "If he refuses to listen to them, tell the church. If he refuses to listen even to the church, then treat him as you would a Gentile or a tax collector." Matthew wrote that the Church has the final authority. Paul and Barnabas and others were quite capable, but they took their problem to the Church.

There had been much discussion among the Apostles and the Presbyters to understand salvation. When Peter spoke, the assembly fell silent. He had spoken with authority of the Holy Spirit and his statement ended the discussion. The Apostles then spoke in agreement. James acknowledged the authority of Peter, "Simon hath declared," and then James spoke to all those assembled. James spoke in union with the whole body of bishops.

Cyprian wrote, in 251 A.D. that Jesus gave primacy to Peter.[26] He wrote, "And again He says to him after His resurrection: 'Feed my sheep.'

On him He builds the church, and to him He gives the command to feed the sheep; and although he assigns a like power to all the Apostles, yet He founded a single chair, and He established by His own authority a source and an intrinsic reason for that unity. Indeed, the others were that also which Peter was; but a primacy is given to Peter, whereby it is made clear that there is but one Church and one chair. So too, all are shepherds, and the flock is shown to be one, fed on all the apostles in one accord. If someone does not hold fast to this unity of Peter, can he imagine that he still holds the faith? If he deserts the chair of Peter upon whom the Church was built, can he still be confident that he is in the Church?"

The early writings detailed the presence of bishops and an established Church. The Didache[27] spoke of bishops and so did Clement who in 80 AD. Wrote, the Apostles "appointed the earliest converts, testing them by the spirit, to be the bishops and deacons of future believers."[28]

The Apostolic tradition and the Church of history cannot be given up by a true believer. Jesus wanted unity, certainty of truths, correct teachings, and not contradictory views. Jesus wanted a new church to come forward. First, Jesus told his disciples to beware of teachings that are not correct and are misleading. He even told them to beware of the teachings of the religious leaders of their time.[29] At Philippi, Jesus asked his Apostles, "Who do men say that I am?"[30] He asked the question to find out what the majority of people interpreted as the truth. The various views of the people showed that the general opinion was not consistent. Some thought Jesus was John the Baptist, Elijah, Jeremiah, or one of the prophets. Jesus asked the question to teach that you cannot leave the Church to individual interpretation Incorrect views were displayed on something as important as Jesus being the Messiah, the Son of the Living God.

None of the teachings of Jesus can be changed, so he knew that he had to build the Church on one leader. When Jesus asked the apostles, "But who do you say that I am?" Peter was the one who stepped forward as the head of the mystical body on earth. The Church was built on Peter. Jesus spoke to Peter in the second person pronoun singular with phrases like

"Blessed are you Simon …," "I say to you …," and "I will give to you …." Jesus wanted one person who could be directed and inspired by God. God chose Peter as head of the Church. This is evident from the words spoken by Jesus when he said to Peter, "Blessed blood has not revealed this to you, but my heavenly Father."

Jesus said to Peter, "Blessed are you." Jesus blessed Peter because he was the Vicar of Christ and head of the mystical body of Christ. When Peter told Jesus who he was, Jesus replied that only the Father could have revealed this to him. Jesus then told Peter that he, Peter, is "*Petras*" or rock and upon him Jesus would build his Church. The word Church is singular and not plural because the Church is Jesus' body. The same way that Eve was formed out of Adam, is the same way that the Church is built upon Peter from Jesus. Adam was made full when Eve was created, and Jesus' body is made full through his Church filled with the Holy Spirit.

Peter was chosen to be the leader of the new Church as a rock to the visible world. Of course, God is the invisible rock. "Petras" is a word that means rock. Christ is always our eternal rock that made Peter as the rock that his Church was built upon. When Jesus gave the keys to the kingdom of heaven, he gave his authority to Peter. The image of the keys of heaven is drawn from Isaiah 22:15 to 25 where Eliakin who succeeded Shebnah "the key of the house of David is placed on his shoulder." Keys symbolize authority, and the Jewish understanding of the first century is that this authority would be passed on to a successor. The promise of the keys was given to Peter alone and his authority is confirmed in heaven. The power of the Church would never fail throughout the ages.[31] The Keys of the Church were given to Peter. Only prejudice in thought would prevent someone from accepting Peter as the head of the visible Church, and that his authority continues in history through apostolic succession.

In Matthew 16:26, Jesus implied that when we are willing to lose our life for him, then we will begin to live. When they entered Capernum, the subject of Temple Tax came up when the collectors approached Peter.[32] Jesus told Peter to get a coin from the mouth of a fish and then he said,

"Give to them for me and for you." Jesus associated himself with a human being, Peter. Jesus, then used the personal pronoun *we*, when he said, "so that we will not be scandalized." This was the only time that Jesus associated himself with someone else. Jesus associated himself with Peter, and Jesus *the invisible rock* still has an association with Peter *the visible rock*.

The primacy of Peter was brought up again in Luke 22:31 and 32 on the night of the Last Supper when Jesus said, "Simon, Simon, behold Satan has demanded to sift all of you like wheat. But I have prayed that your own faith may not fail: and once you have turned back, you must strengthen your brothers." Jesus prayed for Peter alone (in the second person singular) because Peter is the cornerstone of Jesus' Church. Even when Peter failed, he came back in power with the Holy Spirit. Peter's name means rock. Kephas is the Aramaic word for "Rock" and the name Kephas is used in John 1:42 for Peter. Kephas means large rock and the name was used to establish Peter as the Rock sent forth from Jesus. Throughout the Gospels, the Greek word *Lithos* is the word used for small rock. Jesus named Simon, *Kephas*, and not *Lithos*.

1 John 4:6 says, "We (the Apostles) belong to God and anyone who knows God listens to us, while anyone who does not know God refuses to hear us. This is how we know the spirit of truth and spirit of deceit."

The primacy of Peter was first, clearly established in the Book of Acts so that credence would be given to Paul and to the Church. Jesus ushered in the Church that was spoken of by Isaiah as being the people of Mount Zion. Eventually, in Acts, Peter became an image equivalent to the Church on earth. He traveled throughout the land curing the sick and those who were possessed. This image of Peter is an image of the Church. Acts 5:15 and 16, "They brought forth the sick into the street, and laid them on beds and couches that at least the shadow of Peter passing by might overshadow some of them."

The sick and possessed were cured by the Church through the authority of Peter. Luke wrote that the shadow of Peter was passing by to signify that the Church was coming forth through Peter. Luke then wrote of the

Church blooming forth. Stephen in chapter six said that the Temple was only for transition into the new covenant. God always points forward and He brought forth the Messiah through David. Luke wrote in Acts 14:22 and 23 that we will enter the Kingdom through tribulations. The Church is the Kingdom of God and has a hierarchy from above; the Kingdom of heaven and earth are united.

Once Peter is established as the visible Church, Luke wrote in the Book of Acts that Paul did everything that Peter had done. In the Book of Acts 15:7, Peter says that God had chosen him, so that through his mouth the Gentiles would hear the word of God and believe. Paul continued what Peter had begun with the Gentiles. Peter cured a cripple and so did Paul, Peter raised someone from the dead and so did Paul.

Peter was chosen to bring the Gentiles to believe in Jesus and to bring them into the Church. Later, Paul took up the mission of bringing Gentiles into the Church. It was through Peter's mouth that God wanted the Gentiles to believe. God's plan was to bring all of the scattered Jews into the Church and at the same time to bring the Gentiles into the Church. Those who accepted the message were baptized[33] into the Church and were forgiven of sins. They received the Holy Spirit as promised by Jesus.

The Church of Believers, or the Individual churches

The second church is what I call the Church of Mary, or the church of believers. When Mary said yes[34], the greatest work of the Holy Spirit was begun. The incarnation is the greatest work of the Holy Spirit that was ever accomplished in history. For a short time in history God stepped upon the earth to dwell with us in the person of Jesus. Those who worship God with their whole hearts belong to this Church. They pronounce the words of Luke 1:38, "My soul proclaims the greatness of the Lord, and my spirit rejoices in God my savior." Their faith is expressed in their actions, and emerging forth from scripture they sing in one voice, "Holy, holy, holy is his name."

To Protestants, faith is a personal commitment to Christ. Some faiths emphasize works, some emphasize tradition, some emphasize sacraments, and some emphasize the bible. There is a different emphasis on the worship in each congregation or local church. To Evangelical Christians, faith is a personal commitment to Christ and their faith is usually filled with emotions. They continue to love with a love that is never complete because the soul is never at rest until it rests in Jesus. They declare themselves sinners but they know that His mercy is from generation to generation to those who love and fear Him.

Mary is often though of as the model of the Church because God came and took her as His bride. As such, many Christians anxiously wait for the end of time when Christ will come for his bride the Church.

The church includes all believers in God. The New Testament church of believers was started when Mary said, "Not every word shall be impossible with God. Behold the handmaid of the Lord; be it done to me according to thy word."[35] This church of believers is part of the Church of God and is under His protection.

The Church of the Jews:

The New Testament Church received the power of the Holy Spirit on Pentecost Sunday. The Church is described as the people who are *called out*. The Early Greeks defined the people of Exodus as the people *called out*. The Greek word *ekklesia* means *called out* and is the word used for church in Thessalonians 1:1, 1 Corinthians 1:1, 2 Corinthians 1:1, Galatians 1:13, and Philippians 3:6.

The *ekklesia* were first called out on Pentecost Sunday on Mount Sinai. God gave Moses the ten words (Ten Commandments) which offered mankind a radical new way of living. The people of the called out are built on the promises of God that were given to the Fathers and the prophets. To the people of the Sinai covenant, belief in God allowed the early Fathers to perform worthwhile acts. The Fathers and the prophets were obedient to faith. They may be said to be faith full. Their actions were meaningful and they performed God's will to bring the faithful into a deeper relationship with God. The called out have a faith that is linked to faithful obedience of God's law. God is trustworthy, and God is good.

The Church Universal:

The Christian Church consists of the *ekklesia* (called out) who were organized as a church at Mount Sinai. The Christian Church consists of the Church of believers who say yes to God because God came to his people. We worship Him with all of our hearts and our spirits rejoice in Him. The Church links its faith to Jesus who tells us that a person who believes in him is also empowered to do what Jesus does. Through our faith in Jesus we receive the Holy Spirit but we also have a responsibility to bear witness to Jesus and keep his commandments.[36] Christians must have high Christology and high Ecclesiology (Church) because they are necessary elements of a Christian. We have a strong belief in Christ but we also believe that the Church is the body of Christ. Our God is the God of the past, of the present, and of the future.

The Woman described in chapter twelve of the Book of Revelation gave birth to Jesus; consequently it is a reference to Mary. In the Book of Revelation 12:17 and 18, the evil force is described as going off to wage war against her offspring, the remnant of her seed. Mary also is synonymous with representing the Church, because her offspring are those who keep God's commandments and have the testimony (bear witness) to Jesus Christ. Paul wrote that God shall bruise Satan under the feet of Christians[37] and this echoes Genesis 3:15. Paul describes Christians as those who do good works in their lives and are obedient. They will accomplish their work with the grace of Jesus.

The Universal Church has actually always been present. Paul wrote about the relationship of Christ to the Church and husband to his wife in Ephesians 5:25 to 32. Paul wrote that Christ loves the Church and even gave his life for her, "that he might sanctify and cleanse her by the washing of the water through the word."[38] Paul wrote that men should love their wives as Christ loves the Church. Christ would never leave the Church. Paul says, "This is a great mystery, I speak of Christ and the Church."[39]

This mystery is the Church, which he says teaches angels in heaven. Ephesians 3 says that the mystery of the Church was hidden. The Apostles revealed to us the Church. Paul wrote that he was to reveal this mystery to the Gentiles, and actually to everyone. Paul said,

> To make all see what is the plan of the mystery hidden from ages past in God who created all things by Jesus Christ, to the intent that now unto the principalities and authorities in the heavens, the manifold wisdom of God might be made known by the Church. According to the eternal purpose that he brought forth in Christ Jesus our Lord (Ephesians 3:9 to 11).

There has always been a Universal Church of the *Ekklesia* (called out). Paul described our mother the Church as the Jerusalem above[40] and we are the children of the promise. We are part of the Church that is free through our Fathers Abraham, Isaac, and Jacob. We are not slaves who live outside of the Church.

Augustine critiqued Galatians 4:22. Augustine wrote that the Church gives birth to everyone, whether we are inside of the Church or outside of it. The sons of Isaac are allegories of the Church. Esau was born of the lawful wife but he quarreled with his brother and consequently, he was separated from the *Ekklesia*. Esau was separated from the *called out people* of God. Aser was admitted to the *called out people* of God because he was born of the seed of the bridegroom and submitted to the authority of his wife who symbolized the Church. Ishamael was born like Aser but he quarreled with his brother and so he was not taken in by the wife and thus did not receive any of her power.

Augustine warns us not to quarrel. Jesus and the Apostles told us to be of one accord. If we are not careful, we could find ourselves outside of the Church.

Justin Martyr wrote that the marriages of Jacob were fulfilling prophecies of the Church. The marriages were types of what Christ would accomplish; they were not sanctions of multiple marriages. God never sanctioned marriage to more than one person. The number seven represents completeness, and the number seven means covenant. So, Jacob served Laban for seven years before he married Leah. Leah represented the old covenant and Justin says that she represented the Jewish people of the synagogue[41].

Jacob served Laban for seven more years before he married Rachel. He entered the new covenant relationship that Christ has with Christians and his Church. Christ served both marriages but the one of the synagogue was replaced. Jacob served Laban for his speckled sheep, which symbolized the many races of people. Christ went to the cross, as a slave for all of the races of people. Justin wrote that Rachel stole the gods of Laban and hid them forever. Rachel symbolized the Church forever removing the idols from the people. Jacob had hatred for his brother, just as many have hatred for Christians. Justin warned that we should not hate one another.

Jacob symbolized Jesus in the Old Testament. Jacob had Christ's name. "Jacob was called Israel; and Israel has been demonstrated to be the Christ, who was, and is called Jesus"[42]

At the time of Jesus, the people were still under the covenant that God gave to the Jews. Jesus said in Matthew 23:2 that the religious leaders sat on the chair of Moses. However, Jesus told the religious leaders in the parable of the tenants that they would lose their position. John wrote that the chief priests declared judgment on themselves when they said, "We have no king but Caesar."[43]

Paul reminded us of the words of the prophet Jeremiah that God would establish a new covenant with the house of Israel.[44] Paul wrote that God has made the first covenant obsolete and that their time was waning (disappearing).

The Christian Church was always a Universal Church. The Spirit was given to the Church before Jesus ascended to heaven.[45] The Apostles received the Holy Spirit before there were individual house churches. Christ also prepared the Apostles for their mission while he was still with them. When there were one hundred and twenty gathered at Jerusalem, there was already a Universal Church. The twelve Apostles were the leaders and Peter (*Kephas*) was the head of the Apostles. The Church has always sent bishops out to the individual churches.

The Church was present but was hidden from the ancient Jews. When Mary said yes she was the first disciple of believers. The Church was built upon Jesus who formed a Universal Church. Individual churches belong to the Universal Church.

The Church was present when Mary said yes, the Church was present when Simeon spoke of the fulfillment of his prophesy, and the Church was made visible when Jesus built his Church on Kephas (Peter). We have an obligation to be unified.

Churches Outside the Womb of Christ's Church

Some people think that they receive special knowledge from the Holy Spirit and thus they think they can stay outside of the Church that Jesus established. Some think that human beings are the highest life in the Universe and will rule after death. Some thing that praising the Lord and waiting for the end times is sufficient. Some believe that they do not need a visible Church. Some concentrate on works to help fellow human beings. Others want a happy place of fellowship where they can be made to feel good.

These groups of people are walking along side of the faith instead of in the fullness of the faith. Their beliefs have varying degrees or hints of Gnosticism. They feel that their interpretation of scripture is correct, but they are not following the biblical and historical teachings of the Church.

Chapter 3: Overview of the Bible

The Canon: Books of the Bible
    The Church compiled twenty-seven books to be the New Testament, and forty-six books to be the Cannon of the Old Testament. During the time of Jesus the Septuagint Bible was the Cannon that the majority of Jews regarded as inspired. The Septuagint Bible was the Old Testament that had been translated into Greek. Greek was the more common language at the time of Jesus. All of the books of the Septuagint were originally written in Aramaic or Hebrew. Most of the quotes by the New Testament writers were from the Septuagint Bible. The Book of Revelation was the one book in the bible that did not rely heavily on the Septuagint.
    The Roman Catholic Church, the Eastern Orthodox Catholic Church, Ethiopian Jews, and some Protestant denominations have always accepted the Septuagint Cannon of books. Ethiopian Jews have, also, always used the Septuagint version of the Old Testament, and they still do. There were other cannons, however.
    The Sadducees only accepted the first five books of the Old Testament. The Pharisees accepted a much larger Cannon or group of books for their Cannon. The Jews of the Diaspora used the even larger Cannon that had been translated into Greek. The Church decided these books were inspired and the forty-six books of the Old Testament were to remain the official Cannon of the Old Testament.
    The non-Christian Jews decided to use another version of the Old Testament. This was because the Christians read the Septuagint and because it had been extensively quoted in the New Testament. The Catholic Church was the only authority that could act on these matters, because the Jews had lost their authority. About the year 90 A.D., the Jews adopted a collection of books at the Council of Jamnia. The Jews decided

on their present collection of books about sixty years after the death of Jesus. This Cannon of books has also been adopted by most Protestant denominations. The Jews removed seven sacred scriptures from their bible.

Table 1: Number of Books in the Bible

	Catholic	Protestant
New Testament	27 Books	27 Books
Old Testament	*46 Books*	*39 Books*
Total	73 Books	66 Books

The books of Tobit, Judith, Wisdom, Sirach, Barach, I Maccabees, II Maccabees, and sections of Esther and Daniel are the scriptural differences. These seven books were included in the Septuagint (Greek Canon) that had been compiled about two centuries before Jesus. This was the more common Cannon in use at the time of Jesus and the Apostles. From the earliest times the Church accepted the Septuagint Version. Only the Catholic Church had authority to change the Canon but it did not change the number of books in the Canon.

The books of the New Testament were written over a period of about one hundred years. In 392 A.D., the New Testament was compiled by the council of Rome under the direction of Pope Damascus I. This was four centuries after Jesus was born. Under the direction of Augustine, the Council of Hippo in 393 A.D. formally incorporated the twenty-seven books into the canon. The bishops at the Council of Carthage approved the New Testament Canon in 397 A.D. Later, the Councils of Florence and Trent tried to stop groups from removing books from the Old Testament Canon.

The Septuagint is also referred to as the LXX, which is the Roman numeral for seventy. It is thought by many that King Ptolemy of Egypt had seventy or seventy-two translators independently translate the Old Testament for the Jews. The tradition states that God had inspired them all because the scriptures were translated identically by each person.

Most modern scholars agree that the Septuagint version of the bible was compiled in Alexandria. The work began at about the year 280 BC and was finished about 200 BC. The extant LXX is more ancient than the oldest Hebrew manuscripts that have been preserved.

Tools for Understanding Scripture

The Canon is important for our salvation. The Catholic Church teaches that the books of the bible are equally and wholly inspired. Reading the bible is important and those who read it are blessed.[46] When we study the bible we first do an exegesis study which is the understanding of what the writer was saying at the time he wrote the passage. Then, hermeneutic analysis is used, and it is the understanding of what the text means to the Church and to us.

Exegesis is the method we use to find out what the scripture meant at the time it was written. The word of God means a divine communication in human words spoken and written by people who had limited knowledge and a restricted view of the world of their time. The people were facing problems that were specific to them at the point in history in which they lived, and exegesis is a means of getting to the root of a passage to fully understand it.

Hermeneutic issues can be explained by the question, "What does the scripture text mean to us today?" We must go through the first step or we will be misguided in the second step. We must first understand what was meant by a passage when it was first expressed. We study extra biblical writings, we study tradition, and we analyze the text to understand the original expression of a passage. For instance Jesus said in John 6:54 to 58, "Unless you eat my body and blood..." Catholics and some Protestants take this verse literally. Many Protestants and all Evangelical groups do not take these words literally. We must believe that the Eucharist is the body of Jesus, the Christian community has always understood this definition. We may have additional interpretations but we must believe this as a minimum.

By studying the text and studying the understanding of the text when it was written, we know that the Eucharist is the body and blood of Jesus. We know by the reaction of the Jews who were present and the actions of the disciples of Jesus that they knew he literally meant that we must eat his body. The Jews who were present murmured and argued because they understood Jesus as saying we had to eat his flesh. Many of Jesus' close disciples left because they understood Jesus to say that we had to eat his flesh. Jesus did not stop anyone from leaving and he did not add to his words or explain a different meaning to them. He just asked the Apostles if they too were going to leave him. We also know that the Greek word John used was *trogo*, which means to chew or gnaw, instead of just eating. The writer did not want to be understood to be saying that his words were symbolic. In fact, if Jesus spoke as a metaphor the language would have to imply that he wanted us to assault or to kill him. Jesus wanted us to eat his body in order to have eternal life.

Paul wrote of the tradition in the early Christian Community. He makes its clear that the Eucharist is the body and blood of Jesus.[47] The early Christian writers were also unanimous in this understanding.[48] This is an example of a hermeneutic examination of a verse. We read the wording of the text, examine the original language, and read the writings of the earliest Christian communities in the New Testament writings and extra biblical writings. Of course much more could be written on the subject of "This is my body."

Further textual study:

The Old Testament was written centuries before the New Testament, and it was written over a long period of time. When the Old Testament was written, there was little ambiguity in what was written. Later changes of customs and events in the world have made it more difficult for us to now understand the writings.

When we read scripture, we must understand what the passages meant to the writer at the time the passages were written. There are many methods or tools for us to use to come to a more complete understanding of a verse or book of the bible. The Biblical Commission outlines the following steps to follow in examining scripture.[49] The Biblical Commission's first step is to explain the text by tracing its origin and the development of the text within a diachronic perspective. The parts of the passages are analyzed.

Scholars or textual critics may first try to find or to establish a biblical text that is close to the original. They will use the oldest and the best manuscripts, as well as old papyri, certain ancient versions, and patriarch texts. These documents are used according to fixed rules to compile a biblical text as close as possible to the original.

The text is then submitted to a linguistic (morphology and syntax) and semantic analysis, using the knowledge derived from historical philology. It is the role of literary criticism to determine the beginning and the end of textual units, large and small. They also establish the internal coherence of the text. These scholars study the existence of doublets, irreconcilable differences, and other indicators as clues to the composite character of certain texts. These texts can then be divided into small units.

The next step is to attempt to assign these units to different sources. Genre criticism identifies the literary genres, the social milieu that gave rise to them, their particular features, and the history of their development. Tradition criticism tries to situate the texts into the perspective of how certain tradition developed over the course of time.

Finally, redaction criticism studies the modifications that these texts have undergone before being fixed in their final state; it also analyzes this final stage to try to identify any tendencies that are characteristic of this concluding process. The text is explained as it is written (synchronic). The diverse elements of the texts are explained by their mutual relationships. The character or understanding of the texts is read to be understood what message the author was communicating. At this point the scholar can consider the demands of the text from a pragmatic function which is the point of view of action and life that is realistic.

Historical criticism completes the literary criticism. Historical criticism attempts to determine the historical significance of a text. The literary groups or events related to history are established in the biblical writings. The various stages that lie behind the historical development of a text help us to understand the revelation of the text. We understand what the writer was expressing at the time the text was written.

The bible is the story of our salvation. We must know that God is with us, and He is for us in our journey of life. We are spiritually Jews and we must reflect on this to work out the answers of our life. This bible is not an answer book, not a history book, or a science book. The bible is for our salvation and is religious truth. We gain true knowledge when we have the eyes of a child's love.

To become a bible scholar is important to many, but we must do more than just become bible literate. Instead of just imparting information we should be renewing the face of the earth. A person of faith is one who recognizes the promise, and the fulfillment of that promise in Jesus. We know we have a promise and we know what the fulfillment is.

Brief Overview of the Bible:

The New Testament was written within the Church to record truth for the Church. The scripture writers recorded the truth to preserve sound doctrines that would increase our faith. We read scripture individually, in bible studies, and in Church services where all of the people are gathered together. The Church has always been fortunate to have great scholars who interpreted scripture for us. Justin the Martyr A.D., Origin 185 A.D., Jerome 420 A.D., and Augustine 430 A.D. are just a few of the early Church scholars. They studied the bible thoroughly so that early understanding of the texts could be recorded.

Early bibles were painstakingly copied by hand. The Church ensured the accuracy and availability of the bibles for the people. The early manuscripts were copied onto parchment made from sheepskin. A bible would have cost at least ten years salary of a professional worker because of the number of sheep required to produce the materials for each bible. Pope Damascus had St. Jerome write a version of the bible into the Latin language. This version of the bible is called the Vulgate and it was written for the Church into the common language of the time. Vulgate comes from the Latin word *vulgar*, which means common.

The Vulgate translation of the bible was the first book that was ever printed by a printing press. Bibles were posted in public places so that they could be read. The bibles were eventually copied into various languages. There were fourteen authorized translations of the Bible in German, eleven in Italian, ten in French, and two in Bohemian. Eventually, the authorized Douai Rheims version was translated into English. Later the King James Version of the bible was printed into English by the authority of King James. The Catholic Church did not authorize the King James Version of the Bible because it was a poor translation that was filled with errors. The early versions of translations by the Protestants Tynsdale and Wycliffe were also poorly translated and were corrupt. Saint Thomas Moore criticized the Tynsdale Bible and even King Henry VII condemned the translation.

The Church has always made the bible available to everyone. Pope Leo XII, a century ago said that the bible is to be made available to everyone and is to be written in that person's language. Pope Pius XII wrote *Divino Afflante Spiritu in 1943* to encourage us to use the best scientific tools available. Pius XII wrote that we should have a proper understanding of the bible. "The foremost and greatest endeavor of the interpreters should be to discern and define that sense of the biblical word which is called literal…so that the mind of the author may be made abundantly clear."

Dei verbum was written in 1965 by Vatican II and the title means the Word of God. *Dei verbum* encourages us to read scripture. Paragraph 22 states that "Access to sacred Scripture ought to be open wide to the Christian faithful." The Church not only made translations of the bible but also has been responsible to see that correct translations are made. Paragraph 25 says, "Therefore, all who are engaged in the ministry of the Word, should immerse themselves in the Scriptures by constant sacred reading and diligent study. In *Dei verbum* Pope Leo is quoted, "For it must not happen that anyone becomes 'an empty preacher of the Word of God to others, not being a hearer of the Word in his own heart.' When he ought to be sharing the boundless riches of the divine Word with the faithful committed to his care, especially in the sacred liturgy."

The American Bishops Pastoral plan for the word of God is to put scriptures the heart of the parish and at the center of our individual lives. We listen to God when we read divine writings. Prayer must always precede the reading of scriptures. We speak to God when we pray, and we listen to Him when we read the divine articles from scripture. Scripture is important in our lives, because ignorance of scripture is ignorance of Christ.

The bible is more than a body of truths, but it is God Himself who makes known His love for His people. God communicates to us through nature, mighty acts, and words. The insight of the bible is that it reveals what destroys or breaks up a people by showing the results of sin and unbelief. The bible offers us a way of life that is based on discovering and obeying a loving God.

The word bible means "little library." There are two testaments and are two statements of faith. The Canon is the officially recognized collection of books that comprise the bible. The word Canon comes from the Hebrew word *qaneh* for reed, which was used as a measuring stick. We use the reed, which is the Canon to measure everything else.

There were important guidelines for choosing the books for the Canon. First, the book, Gospel, or letter had to be inspired with the real message of God for His people. Truth must be contained in the writings for them to stand the test of time. Second, the writing had to contain a universal truth or expression of faith. It could not just be significant for a small community. Letters in the bible that were written to the churches may have been directed to individual churches, but they were written for the whole Church. Third, the writing must have been used for a long period of time. The written word can be thought of as the oral retelling of scripture in written form. In other words, the letter or book consists of the oral traditions that are in written form.

The Old Testament was written two thousand years before Christ and was written in the Hebrew, Aramaic, and Greek languages. Ancient copies of all forty-six books have been found written in Hebrew or Aramaic. The New Testament was written less than one hundred years after Christ and was written in Greek and Aramaic.

Table 2: Important Time Periods of Scripture

New Testament	Written about 46 A.D. to 110 A.D.
Old Testament	*Time Period (B.C)*
1. Abraham to Moses	1800 to 1200
2. Exodus from Egypt	1160
3. Entering & settling promised land	1160 to 1000
4. Davidic Kingdom	1000 to 580
5. Exile out of Babylon	580 to 520
6. Restoration Period	520 to the Birth of Christ

The Psalms and some of the other books of the bible were written down at an early time of history. Many of the books of the bible or at least parts of the books were written at a later time in history. There could have been centuries between the writings of the books of the Old Testament and the time of the actual historical period. The Middle Eastern culture was an oral culture. Writing was difficult and no printing presses existed. It is commonly thought that Moses did not write the five books of the Pentateuch of the bible. The Pentateuch is attributed to Moses, however.

It is speculated that many Old Testament books were written during the Babylonian exile, and then they were put into the biblical text during the Restoration period. However, the books were more likely compiled and edited during the Exile, rather than having been written during this time period.

Outline of the Books of the Bible
Old Testament

A. Pentateuch
5 books Deeds and Laws

	1. Genesis	Pre history of God's call and preparation of a people in creation, and the patriarchs.
	2. Exodus	Mighty deeds and the deliverance of Israel from Egypt are portrayed. The giving of the covenant in Ex19.
	3. Leviticus	Describes obligations of covenant
	4. Numbers	More laws and desert experience.
	5. Deuteronomy	Deepens and sums up the meaning of the covenant (Moses speech)

B. Historical Books
Deuteronomic History
(Former Prophets)

	Joshua	Conquest of Promise land
	Judges	Settlement & survival struggle
	1 & 2 Samuel	Need for Kings, Saul and David To the end of monarchy
(586 BC)	1 & 2 Kings	Religious fidelity of kings after David.

Chroniclers History

	1 & 2 Chronicles	History from priestly perspective
	Ezra, Nehemiah	History continued to 500 B.C
	Ruth, Ester, and Lamentations	

C. Deuterocanon
(Jewish Pride)

Judith
Tobit
Baruch

	1 & 2 Maccabees	Jewish revolt against the Greek government of Syria about 166 BC

D. Prophets (Stress the covenant and the Law)

Major Prophets	Isaiah, Jeremiah, Ezekiel, Daniel (Apocalyptic literature)
Minor (lesser or shorter) Prophets	Hosea, Joel, Amos, Obadiah, Jonah, Micah, Nahum, Habakkak, Zephaniah, Zechariah, Malachi

E. The Wisdom Writings Beautiful reflections on God's manifestation in nature Deuterocanon Wisdom God is a lover of souls	Job Psalms Proverbs, Ecclesiastes Ecclesiaticus Sirach Wisdom of Solomon	Suffering & God's goodness Prayers and hymns (Qoheleth) Proverbial statements & insights of wise men
New Testament		Four gospels, Acts of the Apostles, 21 Letters, Book of Revelation

Apocryphal writings were not included in the Canon. Apocryphal writings are those of dubious value that were used by only some communities, or were used by the Church for just a short period of time. Some of these writings contain heresies, and some are beautifully written and are of sound doctrine

Clement was an early Church Father who may have been the author of The Letter to the Hebrews that is in the New Testament. Clement wrote a Letter to the Corinthians about 80 A.D. This is an example of an apocryphal writing that almost that made it into the Canon of the New

Testament. The Letter is of sound doctrine, written by someone who was converted by Peter. Tertullian wrote that Clement was consecrated Peter's successor by Peter, himself. His letter was widely read in the early Church, yet it did not quite meet one or more of the critical criteria necessary for it to be made a part of the Canon

Table 3: Important Events in the New Testament and the Old Testament

Old Testament	Four Central Events	3 Central Figures
	Creation	Adam and descendants
	Exodus	Father of faith, Abraham who was a Nomadic Tribal Chieftain
	Exile	Moses lead exodus
	Davidic Kingdom	David effected Kingdom and he was a powerful king
New Testament	Three Central Events	One Central figure
	Redemption	
	Death	Jesus Christ
	Resurrection	

To a Christian, the Old Testament is a book of prophecy and prediction of the coming of the Messiah that is fulfilled in the New Testament. With the coming of Jesus, the predictive factors in the Old Testament are fulfilled with perhaps some to come later. Vatican II says, "God, the inspirer and author of the books of both Testaments, wisely arranged the New Testament to be hidden in the Old, and the Old be manifested in the New."[50]

To a Jew, the bible is divided into two halves. The first half is from the story of Creation to the story of the fall of Israel and Judah after the kingdom divided. The bible describes how they lost their land, lost their city

Jerusalem, lost their Temple, and lost everything. The first half of the bible is from creation to the destruction of Solomon's Temple in 586 BC. It is contained in the Books of the Pentateuch, Joshua, Judges, Samuel and Kings. The primary history is a story but contains legislation in it. The Torah is thought of as Laws, but it contains the Book of Genesis.

The Book of Deuteronomy and the books of the former prophets form the Deuteronomic History. Deuteronomy means, "second telling of the law". The Book of Deuteronomy is an introduction to the Deuteronomic History that continues in the books of Joshua, Judges, Samuel and Kings. The books of Joshua, Judges, Samuel and Kings form part of the primary history that ends when they lose the land and are carried into captivity. The former prophets can be considered as those before the Deuteronomic writers. The book of Deuteronomy incorporated significant changes in both beliefs and worship and well as in social and moral values.

The second part of the bible describes how the Jewish people came back from their tragic past that included their captivity in Babylon. Chronicles to Ezra, Nehemiah is known as the Writings (*Ketuvim*). The Book of Chronicles begins with Creation and echoes Genesis from the start with the first word of The Book of Chronicles being Adam. Chronicles takes us to a point in history that is continued in the books of Ezra and Nehemiah. Ezra and Nehemiah are separate but actually is one book. The Book of Chronicles, and the books of Ezra and Nehemiah are two historical narratives form an envelope around the writings. At the end of Ezra and Nehemiah, the Jews were back in the land, the Temple was rebuilt, they occupied Jerusalem and Nehemiah restored Jerusalem as a walled city again. The integrity of the Jewish Nation had been restored. They were no longer a Kingdom however and are referred to as Jews from this point on, since most of the survivors were from the Judah.

The literary prophets or Latter Prophets are the books of Isaiah, Jeremiah, Ezekiel, and the writings of the twelve Minor Prophets. The literary prophets overlap with the story of the primary history where they lose the land and are carried into captivity. They ultimately returned and there is the imminent rededication of the Temple in chapter 1 to 8 of Zechariah, as was written shortly after the return from Exile. Chapters 9 to 14 of the Book of Zechariah were written much later, during the Hellenistic period. The second part of the Book of Zechariah has a considerably different style of writing than the first part. So there is a transition of Scripture with the Book of Chronicles tying together the promise of the land, the occupation, and the loss of the land. Then the books of Ezra and Nehemiah end with them back in the land.

The whole bible was probably written by this time. Except for Daniel, Ezra & Nehemiah, the bible was probably completed during the exile. When the Book of Daniel was added to the Canon, it brought the story of a people to a date of 250 years before Christ's birth.

The Book of Nehemiah has the last word in the Hebrew Bible when he says, "Remember me, oh my God, for good." In Hebrew the wording is *"Zochrah li Elohay l tovah."* *Elohay* is a form of the word *Elohim*, and *tovah* is the feminine form of *tov*, which means good. These are the dominant words in the first chapter of Genesis where after each day, God says it is good. Elohim is repeated and tov and tovah form a totality. So, the last book ties the Canon to the first book to say that now it is done. So the books of Chronicles and Ezra with Nehemiah form an envelope around the history.

The Jews think of the bible as a legal brief for their right to be on the land. They feel that Israel was promised by divine grant, they occupied it, lost it, and got it back. They still think the messianic future needs to be fulfilled. But what the bible says is that God does not deal in real estate, instead he invites us to join in His rest in the eternal inheritance. The inheritance of the land promised by God to Abraham for his offspring (Gn 15:17, 18), is described as the entrance into the sanctuary of God (Ex 15:17, Ps 142) which is a participation in God's rest (Ps 132:7 to 8). The rest is reserved for those who truly have faith (Ps 95:8 to 11 & Heb 3:7 to 4:11). Finally, it is entrance into the heavenly sanctuary (Heb 6:12, 18 to 20), the eternal inheritance (Heb 9:15).

The Old Testament can take an appearance of an alien religion. The Letter to Galatians can make the Old Testament into law. The Old Testament predicts the coming of Christ. The Old Testament does not portray God as someone waiting for us to fail. He is loving and forgiving because He is a lover of souls.

CHAPTER 4: READING THE BIBLE

We analyze the bible and we discuss our findings with others so that we can understand scripture. We try to ascertain when the scripture was written and where it was written. We need to know to whom a scripture passage were written and who wrote it. We use the following methods of analyzing scripture so that we can fully understand what the scripture is saying to us today.

1. The Historical Critical Method of analyzing the bible is studying a passage in reference to when the writer was living and what the social, religious and economic conditions of the time were.

The books of the bible were written by limited human beings in the language and outlook of their times. The books have been gathered into the bible, which is held in faith to be God's word for all times. We cannot bypass historical criticism, which is concerned with what a passage meant to the author who wrote it. But, we need to keep in mind that the meaning of the Bible goes beyond that. The Bible ceases to be an instrument of comfortable self-affirmation for Christians and the Church when we recognize the tensions between what a scripture passage meant when it was written and what it means now.

2. Textual Critical Methods

A. Form criticism analyzes the oral tradition that is contained in the written scripture. The analyst tries to find the smallest units that are interwoven into a story. There is a supposition that many oral traditions were combined to form a book of the bible. Form criticism asks several questions. First, what kind of literature is the text, and who wrote the text? Who is the audience that the text addresses, and what was written? Where was the text written and what was the purpose of the text?

B. Rhetorical Criticism analyzes the many repetitions or seemingly unusual features that add to the dramatic force or stylistic beauty of the work. Such an artistic analysis stresses the harmony and value of the final written passage. This serves the useful function of enriching our daily scriptural reading with a deeper appreciation rather that always raising more doubts about the texts.

C. Source Criticism or literary criticism studies the specific problem of whether there are written documents behind our present text. This method studies problems of repetitions and inconsistencies in the Pentateuch. For instance, why is the Covenant Mountain called Sinai in one line and Horeb in the next? Why does the patriarch Abraham tell a foreign king that his wife is his sister? Abraham twice tells a foreign king that his wife is his sister in Genesis 12 and 20. Isaac also says his wife is his sister in Genesis 26. Source criticism is also the method of analyzing the names for God. God is called Elohim in Psalms 42 to 83, and Yahweh in almost all of the other psalms.

Source Criticism is also the technique of analyzing the stages of how the Book of Job came together. Chapters 1 & 2 and the final chapter 42:7 to 17 were written as a prose folk tale while the rest of the book was written as poetry. Elihu appeared in the Book of Job and spoke in a monologue for four chapters, 33 through 37. When Elihu finished speaking, God appeared. He spoke to Job and the three friends but does not seem to know that Elihu ever existed.

The Book of Job has four parts.
1. The Prose Tale   Chapters 1 & 2, and chapters 42:7 to 17.
2. The Poetic Dialogue   Chapters 3 to 27, 29 to 31, 38 to 42:6
3. The Elihu Speech   Chapters 33 to 37
4. The Wisdom Poem   Chapter 8

D. Historical Criticism determines the historical context of scripture at the time the book was written. Sources contemporary to a biblical passage are analyzed to determine if the contemporary sources concur with the bible passage or if they seem to contradict a biblical. For instance, when Jesus said father he used the Greek word *Abba*.

When Jesus was alive, contemporary sources used the word *Abba* for Father. After the year fifty A.D. was when the word *Abba* was used in a less formal way.

E. Redaction Editing traces a text through all levels of writing, from the most primitive oral saying up to the finished product. Redaction techniques try to determine what changes may have entered a document. For instance, scholars say that the writers of the Pentateuch consisted of four authors or schools of thought.

There are two approaches to analyzing the bible.

1. The conservative approach uses facts, figures, and structure to analyze scripture.

2. The literal approach is a process. An extreme literal approach could even try to debunk scripture.

There should be a deeper unfolding or revealing of the bible than a conservative or literal approach. Aquinas said the Truth is found in the middle. Catholics are in middle of the Protestant interpretation of books. Augustine said in the Old Testament, the New Testament lies hidden; in the New Testament, the Old Testament lies revealed. In studying the bible we should do the following:

1. Discern our experiences by asking the right question so they will last the test of time
2. Penetrate person hood
3. Express our own experience of that scripture passage.
4. Commit scripture to memory in order to make it a part of our story in our lives.

The healing of an individual is for the healing of the larger body of humanity. We should reflect on scripture and reflect on tradition as a pillar of understanding. During our lives, we should go back and forth from reflecting to understanding.

Section 2

The Old Testament

CHAPTER 1: THE PENTATEUCH: THE FIRST FIVE BOOKS OF THE BIBLE

The first five books of the bible are called the Pentateuch. The five books of the Pentateuch are thought many scholars to have been compiled during the exile of the Jews in Babylon. The books of the Pentateuch have different writing styles and different theological concerns that suggest they were written by different writers or were taken from different sources. The books were most likely compiled during their exile in Babylon while maintaining the original ways the material had been written. There are thought to be four groups of writers of the Pentateuch. A group of editors or redactors may have interwoven the texts and even wrote part of the texts.

The first four books of the Pentateuch are thought to be primarily from one source. These books are attributed to a group of writers called the Yahwist or (J) source. The Yahwist writers are thought to have written the books of Genesis, Exodus, Leviticus, and Numbers. In these four books, God is referred to as Yahweh. So, they are said to be Yahwist sources or books. The Yahwist writers of the Pentateuch present a sacred history while telling us of how God was continually intervening for our salvation.

There seems to be another source that was woven into the central writings of the Yahwist source. The other source is actually from two groups of writers called the Elohist and the priestly writers. The first is called the Elohist (E) because these writers refer to God by the name Elohim. The written material of the Elohim source is small compared to the Yahwist source. The Elohim sections are concerned about moral order. The main Elohist source had writings of historical traditions including old stories of Jacob and Moses. The other source is the Priestly (P) writings. The Prietly writers form a framework to bind all of the biblical writings together. The Priestly writings are of practices and legal traditions to emphasize continuity of Judaism. The Priestly writers wanted Judaism to continue even if there are no Kings, Temple, or Promised Land. These additions have a priestly cast of lists of genealogy, rituals, laws, and liturgical matters. The poetically written creation accounts that are found in the first chapter of Genesis are an example of a Priestly writing.

The fourth source is that of the Deuteronomist writers who deepened and summed up the meaning of the covenant. This type of writing begins in the Book of Deuteronomy, and continues through the books of Samuel, Judges and Kings. The Book of Deuteronomy has long speeches and sermons and was written by priests, Levites, and prophets who wanted to reform the practices of faith in Judah. The fourth source is abbreviated as D for the word Deuteronomist. Finally, there seems to be an editor influence to the texts. The editors added passages to the texts, and they wove together the various stories. The fifth group is abbreviated as R for Redactors or Editors. So there are the J, E, P, and D writers, and the redactors (R).

The Old Testament tells the story of salvation throughout history, and it is done in such an incredible way that we are shown that there is a supernatural design to the bible. It is hard to distinguish the J, E, and P sections from one another. There may not even be three different types of authors who separately added segments to the bible because the distinctions may only be imagined. For instance, there are two genealogies of Adam in Genesis 4:17 to 22 and in Genesis 5:1 to 32. The first list in Genesis 4:17 to 22 is called a Yahwist list but the list includes names that use Yahweh and names that use Elohim as their suffixes. The second list in Genesis 5:1 to 32 is thought to be a Priestly list that duplicates the first list. However, the lists are not duplicates. The first list is a genealogy from Adam through Cain, and the second genealogy instead of being a Priestly repetition, is actually a list from Adam through his son Seth.

There are various reasons why many scholars think that there are five different sources or schools that wrote the Pentateuch. Stories that are repeated and passages that are duplicated are two proofs that scholars offer. The duplicate passages are written in different writing styles and so it is thought that different groups added their oral or written sources to the bible. There are many examples of duplicated stories. First, there is a creation story in Genesis 1, and there is a second creation story in Genesis 2 and 3.

Then there are three different accounts of Abraham and Isaac telling a king that their wives are their sisters (Gn 12, 20, and 26). There is a story of Hagar and her son Ishmael being sent out by Abraham in Genesis 16, and there is another account in Genesis 21. There is a call of Moses to lead his people out of Egypt in Exodus 3, and again in Exodus 6. Two stories present Moses and Aaron hitting a rock to draw water (Exodus 17:1 to 7, and Numbers 20:1 to 6). The story of the Great Flood in written about in Genesis 6 through 9 and it appears to have blended a couple of sources together. First in Genesis 7:2, Noah took seven pairs of all clean animals and one pair of all unclean animals. Then, in Genesis 7:9 & 15 Noah took one pair of each species. However, the differences in numbers do not have to mean that there is more than one tradition. Two traditions are only hinted at. In fact, there is not an apparent difference in the numbers of animals taken into the ark. Seven pairs of animals could still be described as entering the ark in pairs.

There are two stories of Joseph. In Genesis 37, Reuben pleaded for Joseph's life and he was not killed. Joseph's brothers put him into a well, and then sold him to Midianite merchants. In another account of the same story, Judah pleaded for Joseph and the brothers sold Joseph to the Ishmaelites. Use of different names for the same place can also indicate different stories being combined. For instance, the covenant is sometimes given to the Israelites on Mount Horeb and sometimes on Mount Sinai. Sometimes the people living in Palestine are called Canaanites and sometimes they are called Amorites.

The following is an attempt to list the four types of writers or sources found in the Pentateuch. The Yahwist source is the main source of writings in the books of Genesis, Exodus, Leviticus, and Numbers. The Elohist and Priestly writers are said to be supplements to the Yahwist writer. The Deuteronomist is distinct from the other three sources and is found in books of Deuteronomy, Samuel, and Kings.

Table: Summary of the Four Types of Writers or Sources

Yahwist (J)	Elohist (E)	Priestly (P)	Deuteronomist
God is Yahweh	God is Elohim and is an addition to J.	God is Elohim and is an addition to J.	God is Yahweh and is separate from the J, E, and P sources.
God walks and talks with us.	Awesome sense of god who speaks in dreams and through his messengers.	Had a cultic approach to God.	Had a moralistic approach with retribution.
Blessings were stressed.	Fear of the Lord was always stressed.	Obedience of the Law was stressed.	Stress on obedience of the Mosaic Law.
Earthly speed about God.	Refined speech about God.	Majestic speech about God.	Speech recalled God's work.
The leaders were stressed.	The prophetic was stressed and they had suspicion of authorities.	Cultic was stressed.	Centralization of cult in Jerusalem and the fulfillment of prophecy.
Narratives and stories	Narratives & warnings because ethical & moral concerns important.	Dry lists and schemata (Genealogy lists)	Long homiletic speeches and a monotheistic creed.
Judah stressed with Davidic Kingdom and Jerusalem Temple	N. Israel stressed, opposed Davidic Dynasty	Judah stressed	Judah and Israel stressed with the Davidic Dynasty.
Sinai spoken have with Moses and elders giving covenant.	Horeb spoken of and people gave their assent to covenant		Covenant and the election of Israel.
Canaanite natives were present	Promise & blessing of Promised Land		Inheritance of the land through obedience and faithfulness to covenant.
	Strong stance against Baal and other idols.	Liturgy present in all of life.	Struggle against idolatry and syncretism.

The Book of Deuteronomy was written from the time of Hezekiah (715 to 688 B.C.) through the life of the prophet Josiah (640 B.C.). The Book of Deuteronomy was discovered hidden in the temple. The book of Deuteronomy was a major reason of reforms that Josiah began in 622 B.C.

During the Babylonian exile in 597 to 586, a Priestly school is thought to have gathered the Jewish Cultic practices and legal traditions together. They included lists of ancestors that were probably kept in the Temple. The Priestly writings were developed out of the literary sources that had been in existence for long time periods. Writings that describe the presence of things in the Tabernacle date the Priestly writings to before the Babylonian Exile. These things were not written about for the second temple. An early date for the Priestly writings is indicated by the way that the ephod was made as described in Exodus 39. However, the late language indicates the Priestly literature was written at a date after the exile. Dating of the Priestly writings is difficult and it seems contradictory unless it was written during the historical times that were written about. Editors may have redacted material at a later date. The writings of the Priests helped the people to live without Kings, a Temple, or the Promised land. Priestly (P) writers emphasized the continuity of our relationship to God. The Priestly writings supplemented the writings of others, and their format is present in the following list.

1. The use of genealogies were used to trace the human history up to Abraham (Gn 5 & 11) and then away from him (Ishmael's family in Gn 25, Esau's family in Gn 36, and Jacob's family in Gn 46). Then the Priestly source recorded the stories of Abraham's descendants.

2. The Priestly writers used names of places where the Jews camped in the exodus desert experience. Six places were listed to lead up to Mount Sinai (Ex 12:37, 13:20, 14:1, 15:22, 16: 17:1, 19:2) and six places were listed to describe them returning from Mount Sinai (Nm 10:12, 20:1, 20:22, 21:10, and 22:1). The taking of a census of the Israelites and the order of encamping and marching were described in a priestly manner. Liturgy is described in detail in these writings.

3. They established laws for future generations by relating past traditions to the people in present. In Genesis 2:3, observance of the Sabbath was described. It is written (Genesis 9:4) not to eat fat, or drink blood or eat bloody meat. Circumcision was discussed in Gn 17:9 to 11. The Sinai covenants and regulations were discussed in Leviticus 1 through Numbers 10. The Priestly laws were interwoven into descriptions of the laws of purity and regulations concerning sacrifices that were discussed in the building of the Tabernacle.[51]

4. The Priestly writers emphasized the Divine presence (YHWH's kavod) in the Ark of the Lord and in the dwelling tent was described in Ex 25 through 40. The Priestly writers considered the tabernacle to be the most important event in history. The plan of the temple of Solomon was described in 1 Kings 6 through 7. The role of sacrifices and the importance of feast were described in the regulations of Moses. The cult was discussed, including how to appoint priests, Levites and other priests. The Priestly writers wrote that God was close to his people and His glory filled the tent and went with them through the desert (Ex 40).

5. The Priestly writers wrote that God's word (Heb. *Rema*) created the important moments in the history of Israelites. The creation of the world in Gn 1, the Great flood in Gn 6:13 to 21, Abraham's covenant in Gn 17, the promise of the land in Ex 6, and instructions for the building of a sanctuary with the ark of the covenant for Yahweh in Ex 25.

6. The Priestly writers wrote of God having an enduring promise of blessing upon the world. Chapter one of Genesis records how God blessed the first humans, and chapter nine of Genesis tells how God blessed the people after the flood. God creates and blesses humanity and God is our symbol of Hope.

The writers referred to as Priestly writers were concerned about liturgy, and things for the liturgy, especially the Ark of the Covenant and the detailed encampment of the tribes. Numbers 31 is a good example of Priestly writings where distribution and purity of booty was emphasized but the writing, which was about the war with the Midianites barely, mentioned the fighting.

CHAPTER 2: GENESIS 1 THROUGH GENESIS 11

The creation account in the book of Genesis is a short poem about God's wisdom in building or carving out the Universe. Genesis 1:1 through Genesis 2:3 is beautifully written in a way to stir us up so that we can feel the power of God. The first part of the Gospel of John is also patterned after the creation account to emphasize the seventh day. John wanted us to know that we are living in God's rest. The book of Hosea also takes us back to the creation so that we can become reborn. This pattern is used throughout the bible including the Book of Chronicles, Exodus 39 and 40, and in the writing of the falling of the walls of the City of Jerico when the Jews entered the Promised Land.

A background of creation is important to understanding scripture. The following table lists Genesis 1:1 through Genesis 2:3 in the first column. In the second column are the possible scientific explanations correlating to the sequences in Genesis.

Table: Comparison of the Creation Story with Scientific discovery.

| Gn 1:1, 2, In the beginning, God created the heavens and the earth, the earth was without form and void (*tohu*); and darkness was upon the abyss, while a mighty wind swept over the waters. The earth and solar system comprised a shapeless nebula in a dark space.
Day 1: God said let there be light, and there was light. And God saw the light and saw how good the light was. God divided the light from the darkness.
The earth cooled, no atmosphere was yet present.
Day 2: Genesis 1:7, God said, "Let there be a firmament in the midst of the waters, and let it divide one from the other." And God made firmament and divided the waters which were under the firmament from the waters were above the firmament: and it was so.
Day 3: Genesis 1:9 & 10, God said, "Let the water under the sky be called "the sea." God saw how good it was.
Genesis 1:11 to 13, then God said, "Let the earth bring forth vegetation: the herb yielding seed, the fruit tree yielding fruit after his kind, whose seed is in itself. God | Matter space and time were created fifteen to twenty billion years ago. About 4.6 billion years ago the matter from which God formed the earth and the solar system was comprised of a shapeless nebula in a dark space. About four and a half billion years ago the sun began burning and exploding. The solar system was saturated with radiation, and it was filled with heavy dust. Nebular dust cleared, the earth cooled, but no atmosphere was yet present. About four billion years ago, the earth cooled and the volcanic steam surrounding it condensed and covered the earth's surface. Eventually an air space formed between the clouds and water.
About two and a half to three billion years ago the earth's crust began to form. Later, continents pushed up through the ocean. By this time, the single celled aquatic life began to appear. About two billion years ago, great amounts of oxygen appeared in the atmosphere, yet hydrogen gas was quickly escaping from the earth's atmosphere. |

saw how good it was.

Day 4: Genesis 1:14 to 19, God said, "Let there be lights in the firmament of heaven to divide day from night. Let them be the signs for the season. They were made visible to divide day from night. Let them be for signs, for seasons, days, and years, and let them be lights for the firmament of the heavens (sky) where they could be two great lights, the greater one to govern the day, and the lesser one to govern the night, and he made the stars. God set them in the firmament of the heaven to give light upon the earth, to govern the day and night God saw how good it was.

Day 5: Genesis 1:20, 23, God said, Let the water bring forth abundantly the moving creatures that have life, let birds fly above the firmament of the sky. God saw how good it was. God blessed them saying, "Be fertile and multiply, and fill the waters. Then the seas and let the birds multiply on the earth. (The Hebrew word 'OWPH means flying insects, fowl, and birds.)

Day 6: In Genesis 1:24 & 25, God said, Let the earth bring forth the living creatures; cattle, creeping

The sun, the moon and stars were made visible when the thick cloud layer cleared around the earth. They were presented in the sky where they could be used for determining the seasons.

There was an explosion of aquatic life forms about five hundred to six hundred million years ago. True fish began emerging about three hundred and seventy million years ago. Insects, the first creatures with true wings, appeared about three hundred million years ago. Then, fossil records suggest the emergence of the first amphibians began appearing three hundred to three hundred thirty million years ago. Then, about one hundred seventy million years ago the first known birds appeared with true feathers. Possibly two hundred thirty million years ago the reptiles emerged, followed by the dinosaurs about one hundred twenty million years ago. Most mammals were present on earth by about seventy million years ago. The tool-using man appeared in fossil records about five hundred thousand years ago. Possibly forty thousand years ago God created the

things, and wild creatures that crawl on the ground. Then God said, Let us make in our image, after our likeness. Let them have dominion over the fish of the sea, birds of the air, and the cattle, and over all the wild animals and all the creatures that crawl on the ground.	first fully modern human beings. But, it could have been one hundred thousand years ago that the first fully modern humans appeared. We are to live with nature and we are responsible for the care of nature.
Day 7: Genesis 2:1 to 3, Thus the heavens and the earth were finished and all the hosts of them. On the seventh day God ended the work he had made. He rested on the seventh day from all the work he had undertaken. So God blessed the seventh day and sanctified it, because that in it he had rested from all the work he had created and made The Creation story emphasized the seventh day where we enter into God's rest.	

Most people do not get involved with debates on creation and evolution. Our faith does not rely on winning arguments. Scientific facts cannot be denied, but that does not mean that scientists can attack Christianity. Recognizing scientific facts is not a reason to be an atheist. In fact, many scientists are Christians. The creation story in Genesis is written for our salvation, but science is also God's work. There is a correlation of the bible and scientific findings. The correlation of creation as described in the Book of Genesis with scientific observations are not always exact, because the Genesis creation account is short and the scientific fossil evidence is not abundant, especially pertaining to plants, birds, and humans. We know that the chance of DNA being formed by random chance is not statistically possible. Scientists can selectively argue for a digestive system of human beings developing through evolution or they can argue that the energy producing mitochondria of the cell came about by evolutionary symbiosis. But scientists cannot convincingly argue that all of the miraculous functions of human beings came about by chance or by evolution. It is impossible to think that humans developed through evolution when you consider our complexity. We have incredible thinking capabilities, coupled with our sight with color, our smell, our hearing, our sense of touch and our nervous systems. Our immunological systems protects us from diseases, and our reasoning functions, our reproductive system, and all of our other miraculous, biochemical, electrical, and symbiotic biological functions that we possess are all brilliantly designed. It is even more impossible to think that the miracle of human life came about twice, once for males and once for females. God had his hand in creating everything in the world. This fact can not be adequately disputed by science.

We thank God for creating us, for creating all life, and for creating the Universe, and for calling us his children. The first story of creation is a table of contents to the remainder of the bible. Just as the prologue of John is an outline to the Gospel of John.

An Allegorical Interpretation of the First Chapter of Genesis

The wind, which came on the first day, was God's spirit, and it still comes with a rushing excitement to fill the voids. There are moments when we sense danger and the exhilaration inside of us quickly goes away when a butterfly flutters by, we hear a familiar voice, or we see the safety of our home. On day one, God filled the darkness of the *tohu* with His light. The wasteland is called *tohu* in Hebrew and it was the void at the beginning of time and it is void where sin still abides. God's Spirit is still hovering over the waters of baptism through which He works to bring us His light.

On day 2, God separated the waters from the water. Just as the sound of His voice calls out to us through all of the noise and the other sounds that surround us. Or like the bread that feeds our soul is separate from the bread that nourishes our body and like being born from above is different from being born in our mother's womb. God lets us know that the rising Light of morning always brightens all other light. He is the firmament, which offers protection of a safe shelter.

The third day God blessed twice. A double blessing to signify a marriage feast between God and His creations. The first fruits were created. The most advanced type of vegetation is that which produces fruit and these were brought forth. Jesus is the first fruit who brings us into heaven. Jesus at the wedding feast in Cana changed water into wine to show us that we would be nourished not only by him but also with him. The waters of earth He gathered together as if in a bowl and He called the water, sea. The sea represents the human race. The pitchers of the seas were in the Temple of Solomon. They were made of bronze to signify our sins and the sea was supported by the strength of twelve oxen. A pitcher of water was carried to the Passover Sacrifice of Jesus' Last Supper.

The dry land represents humanity with the Spirit of God upon them. God sent the wind over the chaos before time, He sent the wind again after the Great Flood of Noah, and He sent the Wind on Pentecost to those who were gathered there.

On the fourth day, God cleared away the clouds that surrounded the earth. The sun shone forth and gave pattern to our time. Not only would there always be the rising light in the east, but the lesser light would light the night sky. He wanted us to know that no matter how dark our light is that God would always see us. He can see us in our mother's womb; He can see us if we lie down in Purgatory because the darkness of Sheol cannot hide us.[52] Jesus calls us to come to him. If our light is darkness, how deep will that darkness be? We can only serve God and we must always seek first our heavenly Father and His way of righteousness.[53]

Water always represents God who brings forth light abundantly in a supernatural way. God uses nature as a sign so we will know that He exists. We have sacraments to give us nourishment for our perseverance to the end. On the fifth day, God filled the air with winged insects and birds, and the seas with creatures of all kinds. The sea teamed with fish, mammals, and a myriad of sea life.

On the sixth day, God brought forth-wild animals and animals to be used by man, and He brought forth-creeping creepies upon the earth. The earth was filled with life so that it became a living organism, balanced ever so delicately. Then he sent forth from Himself a soul for each of us, filled with life because we are faithful to God. He wanted us to have life from Him and we remember that from two become one but life is entirely in God's time.

On the seventh day God finished His work and He calls us into His rest. Life is a wedding feast where we live in happiness. We must celebrate with great joy, and bring Christ to all that do not share in him. He provides the wine that we drink to bring us joy. We must rejoice with strength in him because we must be strong. There is great abundance in the Kingdom of God and we must rest our souls in our Lord and Savior.

Fig Trees: An Overview of Israel

Fig trees produce a fruit that is not only delicious but also the fruit is refreshing. A ripe fig is moist and the fig is cool on even the hottest of days. The leaves of the tree are wide and hang in such a way that they effectively hide the figs so that they cannot be seen. Even after a diligent search, the fig leaves will manage to hide a few ripened figs from view. It is frustrating to overlook ripe figs because they split open and attract beetles, ants and the birds of the air.

Cultures tend to describe the world in terms of being male or being female. For instance, the sun is commonly referred to as male and the moon and nature are commonly referred to as female. A fig tree is one of the best examples of a plant that can be used to represent a female. Botanist describe fruit as more advanced in development than vegetables and other plants because the fleshy fruit is actually an ovary with the fruit surrounding the seed. Consequently, a fruit tree is a good choice to describe a female. White milk like liquid is produced when you pick a fig or pull a leaf from the fig tree. The milk adds to the fig tree being an allegory of a mother.

Man and Woman (Husband and Wife)

Eve is commonly referred to as representing nature and her name signifies that she is the mother of all the living. The Genesis account of Adam and Eve is a story about a couple whom was in a unique relationship with God and then they fall out of favor with Him. God established a relationship between men and women, which is what we call marriage. Genesis 2:24 says, "That is why a man leaves his father and mother and clings to his wife, and the two of them become one in body." These words need to be taken seriously because, If a person joins himself to a prostitute, he becomes one body with her.[54] So in joining with someone else, a person becomes one with that person and with every person that had relations with that person. God wants us to be one in body with our spouse, and one in spirit with Him. When we are joined to God, our marriages are blessed because we are in a covenant relationship.

A man and a woman are one, yet their existence is dependent on each other, both psychologically and in social order. A woman is dependent on a man.[55] However, a man is also dependent on his spouse. When God put Adam to sleep He was actually making a new creation of man. The word used in this passage for man means both male and female.[56] The smallest unit of life consists of two human beings, a man and a woman together. Only together can they become one. That is why God brought forth the woman and the man. When Adam did not take his responsibility to be the spiritual head of the family, they sinned[57] and both used fig leaves to try to hide their nakedness from God. The sin was doing what they thought was right rather than doing what they knew God wanted them to do. "Then the eyes of both of them were opened and they realized they were naked so they sewed fig leaves together and made coverings for themselves."

The mother like qualities of a fig tree may be why Israel was often represented as a fig tree. The prophets Jeremiah, Ezekiel and Hosea often warned of punishment to Israel by calling Israel a fig or a fig tree. Following are a few examples of Israel being referred to as a fig tree. First, Jeremiah wrote of threats of punishment to Israel in the Book of Jeremiah 8:13.

> I will gather them in, says the Lord:
> there will be no grapes on the vine,
> Nor figs on the fig tree,
> foliage withered.

Later, Jeremiah referred to Jerusalem as a fig.

> I will make them like rotten figs,
> too bad to be eaten.[58]

Hosea also referred to barren Israel as a fig tree when he warns that the Lord "will lay waste her vine and fig tree."[59]

So the story of Adam and Eve hiding behind fig leaves is much more than it may first seem. The fig tree is representative of Israel and Judah. So it can be said that they hid behind what was to become the Jewish nation. They had walked with God and did not notice their nakedness because their thoughts were focused on Him. When they stopped focusing fully on God, they became aware of their nakedness and became afraid. They were sent out of the garden, and this represents the first time that God was to deprive people of their homeland. The bible describes many more times that the Jews were unfaithful and lost their homeland. God always loves his people so he covered Adam and Eve with animal skins.[60] Animals were killed so that God's children could be kept warm.

We are saved through faith by the grace of God and our works show witness to our faithful unity with God. Jesus destroyed a fig tree as a sign to show that judgment would come upon Israel because of her apparent holiness or closeness to God (piety) lacked the fruit of good deeds. In other words, Israel's faith was not being demonstrated by goodness. They were not faithful, they were giving lip service to God instead of bearing good fruit. Jesus cursed a fig tree and it was a warning that Israel would soon bear the punishment of her fruitlessness.[61]

The prophecies of Ezekiel and Jeremiah were fulfilled by Jesus as was the prophecy God made when Adam and Eve were expelled from the Garden of Eden. When God found Adam and Eve hiding behind fig leaves, He disciplined them while announcing a savior. God announced that Jesus would be born of a woman and would come to crush Satan (sin). God told the following to Satan,

> I will put enmity between you and the woman,
> and between your seed and her seed;
> He shall bruise your head
> while you shall bruise his heel. [62]

God always speaks of forgiveness and deliverance. The word woman (gunë) was used eight times in Genesis 3. Eve was referred to as "woman" seven of the times. Seven times represented completeness, the eighth time represents being prophetic. The eighth time the word woman was used, it is recognized as being in reference to Mary. It is unusual for scripture to speak of the seed of a woman rather than of a man. The woman's offspring in Genesis 3 hints as being Jesus Christ and this is the first promise in the bible of a redeemer. Jesus was the fulfillment of the first prophecy of God in the bible. Also, this prefiguration of Jesus and Mary foretold that justification and life would come through Jesus. Jesus overcame death and sin so that we can have life eternal. Sin entered the world through Adam and Jesus is now the new Adam. All of God's people are descendants of Jesus. Mary did bear Jesus in her body, so we can consider ourselves as having come forth from Mary's womb. Mary listened to the Holy Spirit and her obedience changed the world forever. Jesus is infinitely more than Adam, of course, the Holy Spirit is infinitely more than Adam and Eve's tempter, and Mary now replaces Eve as a symbol for our mother and as symbol for the church because she is infinitely more than Eve. Jesus is the head of the church that is symbolized by the purity and obedience of Mary. The Holy Spirit leads us to Jesus.

God spoke of enmity of Satan, a hatred that was so great that he would try to destroy the Church. Joseph took Jesus and Mary and fled to Egypt to escape the slaughter ordered by Herod. Had Jesus been killed as an infant, Satan would have succeeded. Jesus called Mary "woman" in the Gospel of John to remind us of the promise in Genesis 3:15. Eve was mother of all the living. Mary is the new Eve who became mother of all disciples of Jesus who have eternal life in Jesus. Eve said, "God has given me a son to replace Abel whom Cain killed" (Genesis 4:1).

The word used for God in Genesis 4:1 is Yahweh. It is from this point in the bible that the world began referring to God as Yahweh. Today, Yahweh is more commonly translated as "Lord."

A son is given to Mary.[63] Revelation 12:2 describes a woman in her birth pangs who is pregnant with the Messiah. The woman is struggling with a dragon like the serpent in Genesis 3. She is the mother of the

Messiah,[64] but she has other offspring who are described as those who keep the commandments of God. We are her offspring and we stand with her in the war raged against her by Satan. Mary in Luke's infancy narrative and Mary in the Johannine Gospels is the mother of Jesus who is Lady Zion who brings forth a new people with joy.

Adam and Eve tried to hide behind leaves from a fig tree. "Can a man hide in secret without my seeing him? says the Lord. Do I not fill both heaven and earth?" God can not be contained in an ark, God can not be contained in a temple, and a person cannot hide from God even traveling to the ends of the earth.[65]

Genealogies Used as Messages

The Book of Genesis has two lists of Genealogies that began with Adam. One list continued through Adam's son Cain and ended with the descendant named Tubalcain. The second list continued through Adam's son Seth and ended with Noah. The first list is called a Yahwist list and followed the genealogy from Adam through Cain and Lamech to Tubalcain and his sister Naamah (Genesis 4:17 to 22). It branched through Lamech, which is a name derived from the root of lament meaning despairing. Cain's line of descendants cried a terrible cry of vengeance.

The first list ended with the descendant Tubalcain that signified that the line of Cain creates, cities, music, tools, weapons, and it acquires property, wives, fruits, and vengeance. Isaiah 14:11 described Satan as being brought down to the nether world by the music of his instruments. This first list is confusing because it did not flow smoothly. This was not the list that led to Noah. God was present but so was evil, and vengeance seemed to dominate. The list was broken because Lamech had two wives. Lamech's wife Adah bore Jabal and Jubal, and the prophecy goes in a second direction because Lamech's second wife Zillah, bore Tubalcain. So the genealogy come full circle. It started with Cain whose name meant acquiring possessions, and ended with Tubalcain whose name meant creates or brought forth (Tubal) and acquiring (cain).

The names in the lists impart information that summarizes the Book of Genesis.

Genesis 4:17 to 22 (Yahwist list)   Meaning of names.

Adam[66]   Man
Cain[67]   acquired possessions
Enoch   but, dedicated to
Irad[68]   fleeting things
Mehujael   was smitten by God.
Metusael   Who is of God
Lamech[69]   is despairing.
Married to two wives.
Adah   One wife is an ornament
Jabal[70]   and God brings streams of running water (to tent dwelling people) with
Jubal[71]   announcement of a Jubilee (Year acceptable to the Lord).

Zillah   The other wife is in shadows and
Tubalcain[72]   from God he will bring from Cain music tools and weapons and will acquire property, wives, fruits, and vengeance.

Naamah   yet he has a sister of loveliness.

The flood came when the world was in danger.[73]

Read the meaning of the names from top to bottom and a mini gospel is present, which shows evidence of design.

Genesis 5:1 to 32 (Priestly list)	Meaning of Names
Adam	man
Seth[74]	appointed
Enosh[75]	mortal
Kenyan	sorrow
Mahalalel	the blessed God
Jared[76]	shall come down
Enoch	dedicating
Methuselah	His death, shall bring[77]
Lamech[78]	the despairing
Noah	rest.

Every seventh year was a time when the ground was rested, people celebrated, debts were forgiven and captives were freed. The fiftieth year was a jubilee and was even more important. The bible says that Noah was 500 years of age, and 500 years is a year of a great Jubilee, and Luke 4 talks about a Jubilee in the coming of Jesus in his announcing a year acceptable to the Lord. Enoch was seven generations from Adam, and Jesus ass seventy generations from Enoch, which signifies completeness.

Wickedness of Man, the Flood and the New Covenant

The bible began with the creation of Adam and Eve. Later, a Great Flood is descried when their descendants did not follow God. "When the Lord saw how great was man's wickedness on earth and how no desire that his heart conceived with ever anything but evil, he regretted that he had made man on the earth, and his heart was grieved. The story of a family riding on the safety of the Ark now comes about.79 The story described a family riding on the safety of an ark The family rode on an ark, symbolizing the Church riding through the troubled waters of history.

Was the flood a flood of the whole world or a flood of the Mediterranean region? The bible refers to the flood as a worldwide flood. At the end of the last Ice Age, the Mediterranean was an area that had a couple of land locked sea basins. These basins were not connected. There may have been a river that overflowed from one basin to the other when there were heavy rains. What could have happened is described in the Outline of History, by H. G. Wells, Garden City Publishing, Garden City, NY, 1931. The Adriatic sea and the Red sea could be thought of as having been massive rivers. The Nile River, the Adriatic sea, and the Red Sea fed into this basin. It is even thought that there may have been a river that poured down the mountains of the Greek Archipelago. So, a lot of fresh water flowed into this basin and flooding was bad.

Today, the Mediterranean has more water evaporating from it than there is fresh water flowing into it. The Mediterranean Sea has a current of water that flows into it from the Atlantic Sea, and another current from the Bosphorus and Black seas. The Black Sea is continually overflowing from the waters it gets from the big rivers that flow into it. The Mediterranean Sea would have sunk to a level much lower than those of the outside oceans would, at a time in history when it was not connected to the Atlantic Ocean and the Black Sea. For instance, the Caspian Sea is presently sinking and the Dead Sea has sunk even more than the Caspian Sea. So, at one time there could have been great areas of land located where parts of the Mediterranean Sea is now located.

The area of land could have been present during the last Glacial Age when early humans lived on the areas that are now submerged. There could have been two lakes in the Mediterranean depression. One fresh water lake in the eastern depression drained into a lake that was in the western depression. At the end of the ice age when the ice began to melt, the ocean levels began to rise. The melting would have gradually caused the oceans to pour into the Mediterranean areas. The increasing inflow of water would have caused the erosion of the channel while the ocean level was steadily rising. Eventually, there could have been an enormous torrent of water that flooded into the basin and developed the present day Mediterranean Sea.

The Straits of Gibraltar has an enormous valley running up from the depths of the Mediterranean, right through the Straits, and continuing out onto the shelf of the floor of the Atlantic Ocean. This valley or gorge could be the result of the untiring waters of the ocean at the end of the period of interior drainage. This event could have happened between 15000 and 10000 B.C.. Of course, this could have been one of the greatest events of the early history of our race.

The first civilizations would have chosen to live in the area because of the abundance of water. This area was near the eastern lake that flowed into it from the Nile, and two great "rivers" that are now the Red Sea and the Adriatic Sea. When the water began to break through the westward hills, the people living there could not have found refuge. The flooding would have been unbelievable quick. Their lower settlements would have been submerged, and then the waters would have filled the upper valleys driving races of people out of the area. The water would have filled the area faster and faster, covering the tree tops on the hills as it filled the Mediterranean basin until it reached the cliffs of Africa and Arabia.

There are written records of a great flood that occurred in ancient times. Long before there was written history, this unprecedented catastrophe would have occurred. It was such a great natural event that it would have been transmitted by word of mouth for many centuries. Babylonians and other civilizations have records of a great flood. The flood occurred so long ago that even the earliest written records cannot adequately describe it.

What happened worldwide is hard to reconstruct. After the flood, the bible tells us that God made another covenant with man. God said all animals are eatable, as are all plants. Flesh was not to be eaten with blood still in it.[80] God made us accountable for our own lives and for the lives of every animal. Murder of others is not allowed and God makes us accountable for lives we take.

> Who so ever sheds man's blood,
> Shall man shed his blood;
> For in the image of God
> made He-man. [81]

We are responsible for ourselves, for nature and most importantly we are responsible for the lives of others. There is one thing that is worse than being killed. It is living with the fact that you have killed someone else.

Chapter 3: The Bible Account of the Great Flood

There are a lot of questions people ask about Noah's Ark. These questions and many others are important, but this section will discuss the salvation message of the story of the Great Flood and relate it to what it should mean to each one of us. We shall see that this story was preserved as an allegorical message of cleansing of our hearts, to have a new heart. We need to create a new heart for the Jesus to have a place to dwell. This section is an example of combining the analytical methods and then making the story a part of tradition.

There are numbers that are important when reading the bible. For instance, the number seven represents completeness because in ancient Hebrew the number seven meant covenant. Sometimes it was used to mean Holy or Heavenly. The number seven can be thought of as Heavens time or when God is ready. The earth was created in seven days is an example of its usage.

The number six refers to nature, the earth, or sin. Six is the number that was used for not being complete. Seven is the number that represents being complete. Three and a half are half of seven and are the number that represents evil or severe trauma. For instance, a draught is described in scripture as being a span of three and a half years with no rain on the land.

Forty represents time of judgment and it also represents a generation. In the Old Testament, a generation is forty years in length. When God took the Israelites out of Egypt to bring them to Him, they wandered for forty years. Moses went to pray for forty days. Jesus went into the desert for forty days to overcome the shortcomings of the Jews when they wandered in the desert for forty years. Jesus is the new Israel, so it was important that he went into the desert and overcame the temptations that the old Israel did not resist.

Why did the flood occur? Scripture says, the flood put an end to the people because their hearts had become so bad that every inclination of thought was evil.[82] Sexual immorality and violence were so bad that God could no longer stand to look at it. God is purity and even though he created all of us, God cannot stand to look at sin. More important the story is a story of Faith, Hope, and Love. The flood showed the power of water that is part of our baptism.

The story starts out in Genesis 7:4 with the Lord saying, "Seven days from now I will bring rain down on the earth for 40 days and 40 nights. Genesis 7:6 says that Noah was 600 years old when the flood waters came upon the earth. His age with a number six symbolized Noah was at an age when the earth had given itself completely to sin. In the New Testament, Elizabeth was in her sixth month when Mary went to visit her. As soon as seven days were over, the flood covered the land (Gn 7:10). As soon as God was ready the flood came, and the second biblical creation was about to begin. God had directed Noah to build an Ark of wood, to make rooms in it and to coat it with pitch inside and out (Gn 6:14). The Greek word for the coat is kopher, and it has a stronger meaning than coating it with pitch. The Ark was coated with the spirit of God for the price of life.

The exact age of Noah was recorded as 600 years, 2 months and 17 days. Attention was drawn to his age for a reason that is later explained. On that day all the springs of the great deep burst forth, and the floodgates of the heavens were opened, and rain fell on the earth forty days and forty nights. The waters flooded the earth for a total of a hundred and fifty days (Gn 7:11,12).

The spirit of God is described in the bible as the sound of wind. On Pentecost the spirit descended with the sound of a wind. The spirit also descended on Jesus with the sound of the wind and with the brightness of lightening. Genesis 8:1 says, "He sent a wind over the earth and the water receded." One interpretation of this passage is that God sent his spirit over the earth to bring His life.

Genesis 8:6 says that Noah released a raven and it flew until the water dried. Ravens are usually associated with death. The raven flew around and only death was present.

Later, Noah sent a dove out on three separate times. The first time a Dove left the Ark, the Dove returned. A dove represents the peace of the spirit of God and the story can be discussed as an allegory with a hidden meaning. The world had been dead in sin and the spirit of God tried to find a place to land. The dove found no place to land so it returned. Noah waited seven days and sent another dove and it returned with an olive branch. Finally, a third dove was sent out and it stayed away. The spirit found a place in the heart of mankind to stay. In God's time, in heaven's time, the spirit hovered above the waters and found that peace was present in the hearts of man.

The world had been dead in sin and God sent his spirit to bring back life. God waited for a renewal of the heart of His people. Forty days represented a time of judgment. the doves represented God searching for a place to dwell.

The writer of this passage with the inspiration of the Holy Spirit draws our attention to the date when the Ark came to rest upon the mountains of Ararat. In Genesis 8:3 we are told, "At the end of 150 days the water had gone down, and on the seventeenth day of the seventh month the ark came to rest on the mountains of Ararat." Nissan is the seventh month of the civil calendar of the Jews. The civil calendar was the original calendar of the Israelites, and because the flood occurred before a religious calendar came into effect. The religious calendar changed the month of Nissan to the first month of the year.

Much attention placed on this date by the writer of Genesis. The day that the ark came to rest is the very date that Jesus rose from his tomb. Passover is the fourteenth day of the month of Nissan in the Jewish calendar. The third day after crucifixion of Jesus was the seventeenth day of the seventh month. The two dates are not coincidental. The flood marked a new beginning, as Jesus is the new beginning.

God established a covenant for all ages to come, "Never again shall all bodily creatures be destroyed by the waters of a flood to devastate the earth." God set his bow in the clouds to serve as a sign of the covenant between Him and the earth.[83] The effect of the rainbow lasted for quite awhile, but history shows that eventually we allowed our lives to spiral downward. There was no place for the first dove to land, similarly Mary was carrying Jesus in her womb and there was no room for them in the inn. So Jesus came to again break the sin that was dwelling in the hearts of everyone.

This is summarized in the bible with a poem.

As long as the earth remains,

seed time and harvest,

cold and heat

Summer and winter

and day and night

shall not cease.[84]

Jeremiah 33:20 to 21 also speaks of this covenant. "If you can break my covenant with night, so that day and night no longer alternate in sequence, then can my covenant with my servant David also be broken. So that he will not have a son to be king upon his throne, and my covenant with the priest of Levi who ministers to me."

Day a night follow a twenty-four hour pattern of light and darkness that is associated with the time of year. Day light can be shorter than night in the winter and longer in the summer, but day and night follow a set sequence. Jeremiah wrote that if the normal sequence of days and nights were interrupted, it would be a sign that God was breaking the covenant.

Mark 15:33, describes this type of occurrence, "At noon darkness came over the whole land until three in the afternoon."

There have been winters where it rained a lot. Sometimes, it seemed like it was never going to stop raining, but it always does. It is hard to do things like mowing the lawn, driving, and doing other out of door activities. During Noah's time, the people thought that it would stop raining, but it rained and rained, until all the springs of the great deep burst forth, and the floodgates of heavens were opened.

Sometimes our lives can be described like this. We have problems that seem to rain down upon us. We see rain in our lives and we think that eventually the rain will stop. But it keeps raining, until the problems get so big that floodgates open up and it is too late to stop the flood.

We have lots of storms in our lives and if we are with Jesus, he will calm them for us. Sometimes instead of calling out to Jesus for help, we hold onto the storm. Rain can enter our lives in many ways, but usually they are subtle. There are many examples of problems we have each experienced or that we have seen in other people's lives.

Articles are sometimes written about women who cannot control their spending. Some women need to buy clothes or other material goods to satisfy some undefined need that they have. These women can be very imaginative. For instance, they will come home and say to their husbands, "I bought this $200 dress for only $20. It was originally marked down thirty three percent, then there was an additional fifteen- percent mark down in the price. and then with my special discount it was reduced more. They practically paid me to walk out of the store with the dress."

Or a man may comment on his wife carrying a new purse, or wearing a new dress and she wife will say, "Oh, I bought this dress a long time ago, don't you remember it?" And that type of answer works, because most men are not sure of what clothes their wives have. Another example was of a woman who cut up her credit cards so that her husband would think she was changing her shopping habits. Then the woman borrowed a credit card from her mother and continued her compulsive shopping.

Something like this can just spiral, and it will not spiral upwards, it spirals downward until it is out of control.

One day a woman can walk into the house after having deceived her spouse for a long time. This could be after ten years or maybe after just a few years, when a light turns on in his head. The rain had been falling for years and it was just ignored. Thinking this problem was not noticed by anyone else, suddenly you realize why your spouse was quiet all of these years. Or you realize why your child has been acting the way he did. All of this time Jesus was there to help you. Jesus wanted to be a part of these lives, but there was no room for him. Just talking to Jesus would have helped, but sometimes we wait too long. We sometimes wait for the flood to come, and sometimes it is may be too late to correct.

Men don't go buy clothes like women do. Can you imagine most man coming home from shopping and saying, "Look dear, I bought a new shirt, isn't it beautiful." Men often have much worse spending habits. We men don't come home with just a new shirt, they come home with expensive items like a new pickup truck. Then men cannot understand why their wives are not happy.

This recently happened to a friend of mine. He had a truck that was only two and a half years old. He came home one day and was really excited. He called for his wife to come look at the truck, and he was he surprised when she was not excited, too.

His wife did not yell. Instead she asked, "Honey, isn't your pickup fairly new?" "Well, yes", he said, "but this new truck was such a good deal." She then asked him, "Did you pray about this, before you purchased this truck?" He answered, "Well, I thought about praying." He could not understand why she was upset, and why she didn't want to go out to dinner to celebrate. She understood the finances, of the family so she was worried. Fortunately, their problems did not spiral completely out of control because he was willing to listen to his wife and he began to allow God into his decision making. He made room in his heart so that God could have a place.

Jesus carried all of our sufferings on the cross and he will still calm the storms in each of our lives. In Matthew 8:23 to 27, Jesus and the apostles were on a Lake and a terrible storm came up. Jesus was in the stern sleeping on the cushions. "Lord Save Us," the disciples cried in fear, "We're going to drown." Jesus replied, "You of little faith, why are you so afraid? Then He got up and rebuked the winds and the waves. Who is this they asked? Even the wind and waves obey him.

This story reminds us that Jesus can calm the storms in our lives. He rebuked the apostles, not for asking Him for help, but for being afraid because they did not have faith that He was with them. Yes, Jesus is with us when we are in storms. We can talk to him, and he can get us out of the storms. More importantly, if we speak to him when it starts to rain, Jesus will calm our lives so that the storm will never come. If Jesus is in your heart, it is easy to communicate with him. If He is not in you, it is easy to ask him in. We must make room for Jesus in our hearts and we must ask him into our hearts before the floods of our lives come and overwhelm us. Everything we do will affect our children. When we pray before meals, when we show affection to one another, when we learn about Jesus together: all of these will be observed by and remembered by our children.

Jesus was with us a generation to teach us that we needed to renew our hearts. He said unless we are like one of the children that we cannot enter the Kingdom of God. He was saying in this passage that we needed to cleanse our hearts and start anew. God gave Noah an ark that he wanted people to gravitate toward. The ark symbolizes the church. The Church went forward in time, traveling on an ark into history. The story of the Apostles with Jesus on the boat is also an example of the Church continuing forward in time. We are in an Apostolic Church with Jesus as our head. Today we have Jesus and he lives in our presence through the visible church he left behind.

Peter said, "…while God patiently waited in the days of Noah during the building of the ark, in which a few persons, eight in all, were saved through water. This prefigured baptism, which saves you now. It is not a removal of dirt from the body but an appeal to God for a clear conscience, through the resurrection of Jesus Christ, who has gone into heaven and is at the right hand of God, with angels, authorities and powers subject to him."[85]

Peter wrote that baptism now saves us. Now that Jesus has come, we live in God's time. The flood of Noah is fused into the saving power of baptism. God sees the flood and the baptism of Jesus as being one event because He is outside of time. We do not fear the flood. We should not think of the water as a cleansing of the human race, but as a means of saving the human race.

Chapter 4: The Books of Genesis, and Exodus with Judges, and Kings

The Old Testament (the Hebrew Bible) we read is a translation of an earlier Hebrew work. The Christian faith community shares the Hebrew Bible with another faith community. Reading and studying scripture helps us grow in our faith. Asking difficult questions is important because finding the answers is what helps build our faith. Two main events in Jewish history are the Exodus from Egypt and the Exile into Babylon. Moses is considered the central figure in the Old Testament.

The Exodus from Egypt and the entry into the Promised Land is the story of a nation emerging. The background of Egypt is important to understanding the Book of Exodus because it is also the background of the Jewish Nation. The first Passover and the Exodus began in Egypt. The Israelites emerged as a new nation called forth by God. They came with dreams of a bright future, and with a strong belief in Yahweh. They also brought with them Egyptian beliefs and traditions that remained part of their thinking. At times, many of the Jews wished they had not left, but they grew and God led them through the desert.

Moses was the central figure who influenced the entire bible.

1. Moses has a direct relationship to the tradition of Law because Moses was the one who was the lawgiver. Studying the law is important to a proper understanding of the bible. Other chapters of this book discuss how Moses not only influenced the style of the Old Testament, but also the New Testament.

2. The time of wandering in the wilderness is important because the people were formed through the desert experience.

3. Moses influenced what happened to each of the twelve tribes. He not only helped to shape their traditions but he shaped how they would act on

entry into the Promised Land under Joshua. They were a people who had a radical new way of living their lives. The story of Exodus is a story of the formation of a Nation, the formation of the ancient Israelite people.

4. After the Israelites entered the Promised Land they struggled with the concepts of judges and kings. The period that spanned the time from the Judges to King Saul was influenced directly by Moses. Moses also influences the reaction of the people to David and the future kings who ruled the nation.

II. The exile of the Jewish people to Babylon is the end of the nationhood for the people. They were still a nation but they did a not have Davidic Kingdom. The end meant that the people had to ask a difficult question. They asked, "How are we the people of God?" They had to examine who they were and had to establish himself or herself as a people of God.

First, it is important to examine the region developed by the Nation of Israel. Israel is located in a region called the Sinai and was a main thoroughfare between Egypt and Mesopotamia. Egypt was developed along the fertile valleys of the Nile River. Mesopotamia was developed along the Euphrates River.

Sinai

The beginning of history for the ancient Near East is centered on the Nile region and Mesopotamia. The diagram below allows us to visualize the geography of the ancient Near East.

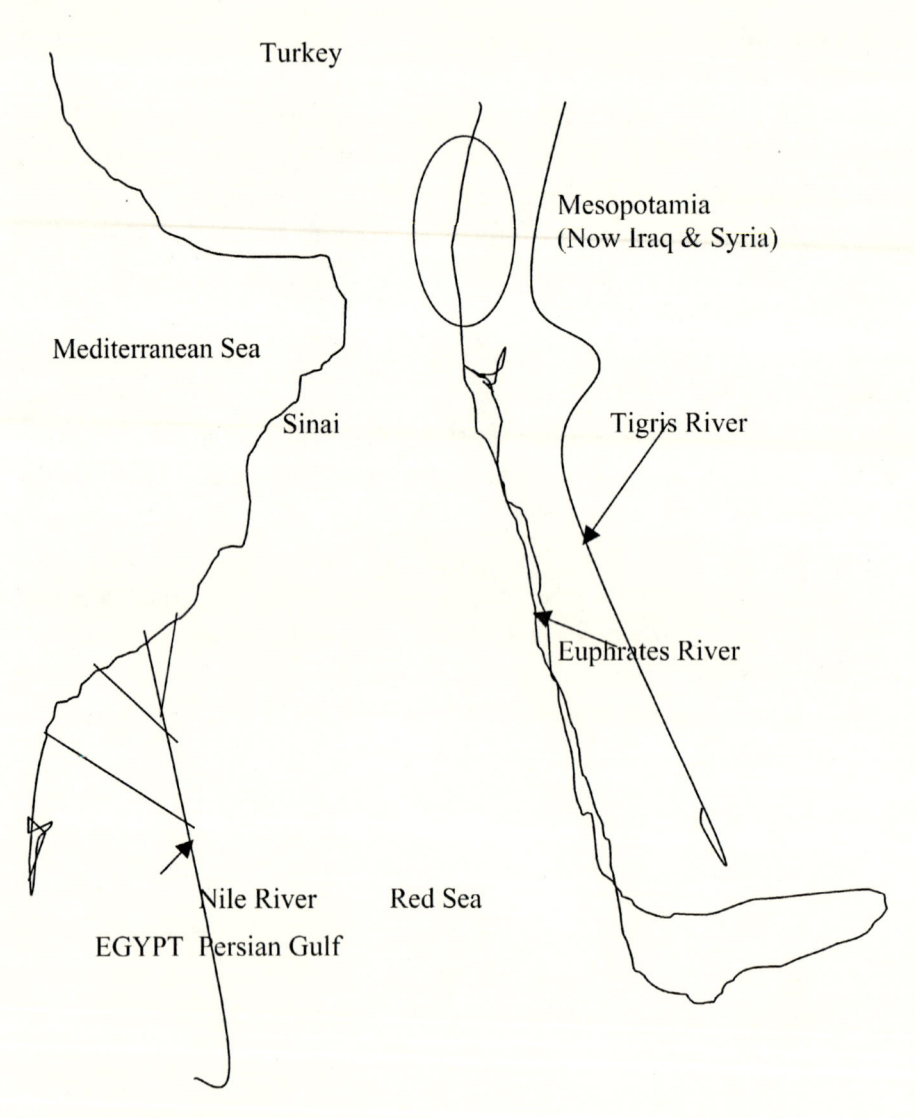

84 • An Overview of the Old Testament and How it Relates to the New Testament

The Ancient Near East (Not drawn to scale)

The country of Egypt developed along the Nile River. The presence of fresh water from the Nile River was the reason for the settlement of Egypt. The banks of the Nile River provided rich fertile soil for farming. There was also access to the Mediterranean Sea, which influenced the climate, and the food of Egypt and the surrounding areas. At this time in history, the Egyptians were strong. They had a presence from Northern Africa to India.

We do not know much about the civilizations of the Sinai region until about 3300 to 3000 B.C. This is the time that civilizations began to record history through writing, and so it is the beginning of our knowledge of history. During the time before things were written down, we have to guess at what happened. History is based on what is written, but we do not have all written records. For instance, the Books of Kings is thought to have been compiled beginning in the middle part of the sixth century B.C.; and the combined narratives of the Pentateuch is thought to have been compiled about the late sixth century. Yet, the contents of the books are much older, but we do not have copies of these writings.

There is much proof that the contents of the Pentateuch are much older than the sixth century. If books were written many years after the history that was written about, then many errors would occur in the writings. For instance, the Book of Kings preserves a lot of accurate historical information that can be confirmed with extra biblical sources. There would be inaccurate historical knowledge if the Book of Kings had been entirely written in the sixth century. This would be expected because doctrines, oaths, and stories of their time would influence the writers. For instance, a modern day historian will write about World War I, but during the war it was not called World War I. There are many other examples like this, and a writer would not be concerned about the historical accuracy of the time if the information being transmitted was correct. Proof of accurately transmitted historical biblical writings will be discussed later in this chapter.

About the year 3000 B.C. is also the time the pyramids started being built. A centralized, hierarchical leadership began to develop in Egypt and this occurred quickly. Egypt left the Stone Age and quickly changed into an advanced country. First, Egyptians started to travel and then they wanted to control and conquer other people. The building of the pyramids would require the presence of a centralized hierarchical power. Some scholars think that religious functions occurred at the pyramids, and the famous leaders (Pharaohs) were entombed inside. The advance in culture resulted in a hierarchy of leadership to amass labor to construct the pyramids. Scholars say that this hierarchy of labor required the existence of an advanced civilization. So, from the pyramids we infer that the nation of Egypt was advanced, and that it had a centralized leadership.

There are three ancient Egyptian kingdoms spoken of in the written records.

Old Kingdom	3000 to 2200 B.C.	Rise of a hierarchical leadership
Middle Kingdom	2000 to 1750 B.C.	Hacksaws invasion of Egypt
New Kingdom	1500 to 1100 B.C.	Hacksaws conquered and driven out and the Egyptian power resumed

Written records were made in about 3000 B.C., and the thousand years that followed was called the Old Kingdom which was the time of the emergence of Egypt into a modern civilization. A line of rulers from Canaan conquered and controlled Egypt during the first part of the second century B.C. This period was called the Hacksaws Dynasty. The Hacksaws Dynasty was from about 1648 to about 1540 B.C.

The third kingdom was called the New Kingdom, and it is important to bible study because the Exodus events are dated during that kingdom. Exodus events are recorded to about 1280 B.C., which was probably during the reign of Ramesses II because there are two biblical references to Ramesses. First, there is a reference to Israelite slavery, "Accordingly, taskmasters were set over the Israelites to oppress them with forced labor. Thus they had to build for Pharaoh the supply cities of Pithom and Ramesses." Ramesses is also mentioned when the Israelites leave Egypt.

"The Israelites set out from Ramesses for Succoth, about six hundred thousand men on foot, not counting the children." This was a time of the rise of a centralized society and slavery was present to provide for labor.

Slaves allowed nations to have a power. The Jews were slaves in Egypt. However, there may have been three types of slaves in Egypt during this time period.

A. Conquerors may have brought conquered people into Egypt and the defeated people were forced into labor.

B. Many people may have come to Egypt for a better life and became slaves because the life was better than living in the bad economic times that existed in their own countries. They may have thought it was better to live as a laborer than die of starvation at home.

C. Perhaps the labor was done willingly. This is hinted at in Isaiah 19:19 to 20 when an altar near the Egyptian and Israel boundary is mentioned (this is in Gaza

"On that day shall there be an altar to the LORD in the midst of Egypt, and a sacred pillar at the border thereof to the LORD. It shall be for a sign and for a witness unto the LORD of hosts in the land of Egypt, for they shall cry out unto the LORD because of the oppressors, and he shall send them a savior, and a great one, and he shall defend them." Perhaps the passages from Isaiah are referring to the Great Pyramids of Egypt.

When the Old Kingdom era ended, a break in the written history occurred. Scholars can only guess why the Old Kingdom ended. Perhaps the Old Kingdom ended because there was famine in the region; perhaps the rich did not pay taxes; or perhaps as Egypt expanded into Sudan and Sinai, it got too big and had economic or government problems. Historical writings have not been found to explain what happened, and so we can only speculate as to what happened.

There was first an intermediate period before the beginning of the Middle Kingdom era. Texts that were written of Palestine explain what was happening in Canaan. There were letters from messengers who were sent to Canaan. Messages were brought back to Egypt that wrote about life in

Canaan. During the Middle Kingdom, there is no sign of centralized leadership in Canaan. The occupants of Canaan seem to be a fighting, hunting, and semi nomadic tribe that traveled back and forth between wells of water.

By the end of the Middle Kingdom period, there were changes that were marked with growth of villages and agriculture of the Canaanite inhabitants. Information was obtained because Egypt was taxing these regions. Silver from Canaan was important to Egypt because Egypt had no natural resources. There was intricate silver work in Canaan, as well as wines and spices, and these were of interest to Egypt. Perhaps the people were also of interest to Egypt as a work force since labor was important.

The work force of the nation can be diagrammed as follows

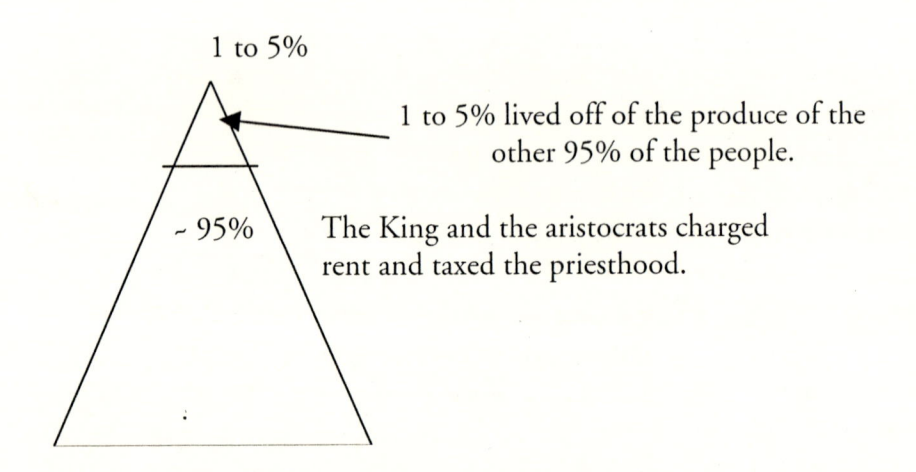

1 to 5%

1 to 5% lived off of the produce of the other 95% of the people.

~ 95%

The King and the aristocrats charged rent and taxed the priesthood.

The Canaanite religion was based on priests and temples.

The Middle Kingdom came to an end when the Hyksos invaded Egypt. The Greek name Hyksos probably comes from the ancient Egyptian word that means foreigners. Written records tell us that the culture and foreign rule made the Egyptians bitter. The Egyptians were overtaken by the foreign people who were living in Egypt and by invaders who crossed into Egypt through the weakly fortified borders. The Egyptians had imported too many people and were simultaneously overthrown from within and from a foreign power.

The New Kingdom began when Hyksos was conquered. The Amarna age is what it was called. The Information about Canaan was learned from texts sent to Egypt. Settlements and walled cities in Sinai were mentioned in these texts. Walled cities imply that there was a hierarchy and urbanization was present. One to five percent of the people is thought to have lived off of the other ninety five percent of the population.

There was a phenomenon that is recorded. There is information from Canaan that discusses rebels or bandits called `apiru. The Egyptians provided protection from the 'apiru who were a real threat to security of adjoining lands. Egypt wanted no threats that might affect its empire. The records say that these bandits roamed the countryside, were organized and conducted guerrilla activity.

Some scholars suggest this was the beginning of a term that would become the word for Hebrew. It is thought that these bandits eventually became a nation. Not enough information is available to prove it, but these bands could have been the beginning of what was to be formed into Hebrew people

There are two ancient records that seem to describe Israel as a nation.

There is a carving that has been dated 1300 to 1100 that gives reference3 to Pharaoh Nierneptah (Merneptah) who ruled Egypt about 1213 to 1203 B.C. He invaded northward and defeated a people called Israel in the central highlands. So, a people named Israel existed and the people were significant enough for the Pharaoh to boast about the conquest. His conquest is written on a seven and a half-foot tall monolith and it recounts Merneptah's campaigns in Canaan. This carving is evidence that 200 years before David, the people of Israel were significantly present in history.

1. The Pharaoh left a sign with reference to "Israel". He wrote, "Israel is laid waste: his seed is not"

A sign of unity may have emerged from these troublemakers. The second record describes a group of people as trouble makers and the word used was Shasu.

2. Shasu probably means "bandits" or "troublemakers". There is a reference in the writing to the Shasu calling God by the word Yhw that means Yahweh or God in English. This may mean that the wandering group was the predecessors to the Israel Nation.

Scholars wonder if eventually this was the group that became unified under the leadership of David and developed into the nation of Israel. This is an interesting hypothesis but there are only a few references to Shasu, so not a lot is known about them. There may be two reasons why little is written about Israelites.

1. Perhaps the writers did not want to acknowledge the Shasu because they were a visible failure of Egypt's power. So not much was written about this group.

2. Palestine was not important to Egypt, except that it was part of the route to Sinai. You had to travel through Palestine to fight wars; it was part of a land route to the Beirut seaports, and a route to Lebanon to buy wood. Egypt did not care enough about the people or what was happening to them in Palestine. But, the Lebanese would pass through Palestine.

During the life of Moses, only a few people may have known him. Moses was important to the surrounding nations, but perhaps he was not important enough to be noticed by the leaders in Egypt. Egypt was only concerned about what power might affect its security.

The Egyptians were only concerned about what prevented them from taking what they wanted from Palestine. There are only two reasons why Egypt might be concerned about people. A group of people causing trouble to Egypt would be a concern to Egypt. Also, people were an important source of labor to Egypt, both by choice, and perhaps by force, because labor was necessary for the building of the Egyptian pyramids.

Manuscripts that were written during the time of Moses describe Canaan as not being important to Egypt. One manuscript sent to Egypt described an Egyptian serving in the Army on the Gaza Strip. This passage shows that there is not a lot interest in Palestine.

"I am living in hell with no supplies. No people to bake bricks, nor any bricks or straw in the district. Those supplies I brought are gone and there are no donkeys since they have all been stolen. I spend the day watching the birds and doing some fishing. All of the while, eyeing the road that goes to my home with homesick longing. Under the trees with no edible foliage, I take my siesta because their fruit, whatever was there is perished. The gnats attack in sunlight, and the mosquitoes in the heat of noon, and the sand flies sting, they suck at every vessel. Whenever I open a jar of coda wine, whenever it is open the people come to get a cup but there are also two hundred dogs and three hundred jackals waiting at the door. The heat never lets up."

The Iron Age

The Bronze Age ended at about 1200 B.C. and the iron age began. The nations that had iron had an advantage over those who still had bronze. Copper is a soft metal that can be hammered and molded as it is mined. Bronze was an important invention because it is a harder metal than copper that had many uses. Bronze is copper with a small amount of zinc. Bronze was mentioned in the book of Exodus when Moses is asked to collect contribution of gold, silver and bronze.[86] A bronze scepter as made to protect the Israelites who were dying in the desert after being bitten by snakes.[87] The Israelites had much skill with bronze, and bronze is one of the means of dating the exodus to the end of the Bronze Age.

Later, iron was made and the Iron Age was introduced. Iron was much harder and durable than bronze, so the nations that could manufacture iron were in a better economic and military position than those who could not were. For instance, the Hyksos military in Egypt had superior arms made of brass, but the Philistines had better military arms because they were made of iron. Consequently, the Philistines were a major threat to Egypt during this period. The Philistines came from Turkey and Greece. Since they were "outsiders", they were considered mysterious to the people in the area. They were a sea faring people who had landed in southern Palestine near the Gaza strip. They were a real threat to both Israel and to Egypt.

God was trying to mold a people of God. Deuteronomy 4:20 says, but you he has taken and led out of that iron foundry, Egypt, that you might be his very own people, as you are today. In other words, the Israelites were able to live in foreign land under foreign rule and still emerge as a people. Iron foundries are extremely hot, and only certain metal could survive. This is a metaphor for the Israelites that they would survive. They were to go to Canaan, which was a land that contained deposits of copper, and iron.[88] If this were a nation that was emerging at the end of the Bronze Age, and the beginning of the Iron Age, then having silver, and both copper and iron on the land would be important.

The Hyksos were very organized and Israel (Canaan) had no organization in comparison. Israel was not organized as a military power until David became King of Israel. David probably learned military and governmental organization from the Philistines, because he lived with them.[89] Canaan settlements started expanding in the tenth century B.C., and there is evidence of the culture of the Israelites being characterized by a centralized work force and of having a hierarchy. The central Negev also had organized settlements that changed from a pastoral way of living. Archeologists think that only about 5000 people may have lived in Jerusalem at the beginning of the Iron Age. Size was not as important as was David's desire to have the capital in Jerusalem.

After Hyksos, there was Pharaoh Akhenaton who was called a heretical Pharaoh, because he brought up a concept of One God. He said that the sun god was the only god. The monotheism view has similarities to the Jewish religion, but there are too many differences for the idea to have come from Akhenaton. Egypt had a concept of the afterlife was well defined, and they wrote about lands that the deceased Pharaohs would travel to. They would go in boats provided to them when they were buried. They were also provided food and drinks for travel. It must be emphasized that this is very different from the Jewish concept of afterlife.

There are signs of the Egyptians influence in the Book of Proverbs. Two or three chapters were probably copied from the Egyptian wisdom of Hosimatu. But we must remember that wisdom is wisdom, Wisdom is secular and tells us how to face life the best we can. Egypt provided a lot of this type of thought. These scholarly finds may not pass the test of time. They are still theories and are still being argued about. They may not stand up to serious investigations.

Much work is still needed in archeology to understand the written material. Some archeological evidence seems to be contradictory, and some things are becoming clearer that were once thought to be contradictory. For instance, the first reference to the house of David was found just a couple of years ago. Only two references to David are known outside of the bible, but for awhile there were no archeological records. All historical events are not completely understood, but they develop and become more complete every year. For instance, even the reference to David is not completely accepted, because the six letters "bytdwd" could spell the name of a yet unknown village.[90] Logically the six letters mean, "house of David", but more records would be more conclusive. History is proved with archeological data and every year more evidence is uncovered, so an open mind is necessary until evidence supports or disproves a theory.

Archeological records of King David 1003 to 971 B.C.

	Source	Text
1	Tel Dan (Nineteenth century)	1. "house of David" byt (house of) dwd (David)
2.	Stella of the Moabite king Mesha 849 to 820 B. C.	2. "house of David"

Many scholars feel that they know more about the bible now than we have at any other time in Christian history. For instance, the Dead Sea Scrolls discovered in 1948 changed a lot of our biblical understanding and they clarified problematic texts. There is reference in hieroglyphics in the Merneptah Stella from Egypt in the late 1300 BC and is the earliest known reference to Israel. The population of Israelites started to increase shortly after this time.

Moses

Moses in many ways is the central figure in the bible. The following is a basic outline of the influence of Moses in the Exodus.
1. All tradition about the release of the people from Egypt is centered on Moses. His birth: bringing up of Moses; he is the key figure in the ten plagues, and he is involved in the events leading up to the Exodus.
2. Moses is the central figure in the stay near Sinai, and the traditions centered on the coming of the Law.
3. Moses is the mediator of the Law received by the people.
4. The Exodus ends with Moses as the central figure in the approach to the Promised Land. Then the book ends with the death of Moses and the continuation of the story with Joshua.

It is a consensus of the scholars that there was a historical Moses despite the fact that there are legends in the story. The legends do not subtract from Moses being a historical figure. Many scholars are bothered because there are no Egyptian writings of slaves leaving Egypt. Scholars think the Exodus would have been a recognizable event and would have been written about in secular history.

We know that Moses was born into Israelite slavery, the bible says that he was amongst those Hebrews who migrated into Egypt. This would have been at about the time of the Hyksos invasion. We know that it is a historical fact that there were many slaves in Egypt during this time period.

Moses is a historical figure who has his life described in the bible. However, it bothers many scholars who point out that the tradition of

Moses' birth and being put in a basket is similar to the theme of an ancient Sumerian story of a King called Sargon I. The Story of Sargon I was written centuries before Moses lived. The story says, "Sargon, the powerful king, the king of Akkadia am I; my mother was poor, my father I knew not; the brother of my father lived in the mountains. My mother, who was poor, secretly gave birth to me. She placed me in a basket of reeds, she shut the mouth up with bitumen, she abandoned me to the river, which did not overwhelm me…"

Sargon was rescued by an irrigator, and he became a gardener and eventually Sargon became a king.[91]

Some scholars think that perhaps the Israelites borrowed from the story of Sargon because they had no record of their own. This hypothesis is unfounded, however. The theme of the story of Sargon I says that he was put into a basket. But the story of Sargon is much different from the story about Moses. Scholars often try to find one story in the bible that is similar to secular writings and then they write that the bible writers copied the story from the secular writing. This is an example of poor historical criticism.

The story of Moses' birth and then being placed in a wooden basket is connected to the episodes of the Ark of the Covenant, and the cross of Jesus.[92] All three episodes are about new beginnings Mount.

The following two page shows the parallel of Matthew's Gospel with, and how wood is used in God's plan of salvation. The story of Moses is a great event in salvation history, and the story enriches our faith. The source of our faith is Jesus.

Some scholars speculate that Moses might have been an Egyptian who was sympathetic to Hebrew slaves. He became angry when he saw a slave being beaten; he killed a man, and then he wandered in the desert with dwellers that may be predecessors of the Jewish people. Scholars think that Moses may not have been Jewish because his name is not Jewish, and he married into a semi nomadic family of Midianites. The name Moses means, "to draw up" as to take out of water. *Thutnosis* is an Egyptian name meaning "son of". Scholars wonder if Moses name may have once been changed from the word nosis.

But scholars can find little historical data to support that Moses may not have been Jewish. Moses had a religious experience with God, and he found out that he should help by doing things "God's way". The bible describes Moses as being a Hebrew.

Moses was engaged in an unsuccessful attempt at liberation and had to quickly get out of Egypt. When we take matters into our own hands, we often fall on our faces. We must remember that God's ways are not our ways. So Moses had to spend time in the desert. The desert is usually a place for refuge and for meeting God. Matthew parallels Moses in his Gospel, and the Gospel of Matthew is written as the new Torah. Moses had the Law, and Jesus gives Christians the new Law of the Sermon on the Torah.

Table: Comparison of Matthew's Gospel and the Torah
Table: OLD AND NEW ISRAEL

OLD ISRAEL		JESUS AS THE NEW ISRAEL	
To Egypt under Joseph Gn 46		To Egypt under Joseph	Mt 2:13
Sojourn in Egypt Gn 47		Sojourn in Egypt	Mt 2:14
Israel (Jacob) tended sheep for a bride Gn 29:16 to 30		Jesus tended His sheep & the church is his bride	Mt 25: 1 to 13
MOSES		JESUS AS NEW MOSES	
Slaughter of male children by Pharaoh	Ex 11	Slaughter of male children by Herod	Mt 2:16
Moses Saved	Ex 2	Jesus Saved	Mt 2:13 to 15
Exodus under Moses		Christian exodus with Jesus	Mt 2:20 to 23
Water	Ex 14	Water	3:13
Sonship	Ex 4:22	Sonship	3:17
Desert	Ex 15 ff	Desert	4:1
Temptation	Ex 24:18, 34:28 Ex 16 to 17	Temptation	4:1 to 11
Mt. Sinai	Ex 24:16 to 17	Mt of Beatitudes	5:1 ff
10 Plagues	Ex 7 to 12	10 Miracles (Jesus)	8 to 9

Moses fasts 40 days Ex 24:18, 34:28	Jesus fasts 40 days Mt 4:2
Moses as mediator who Ex 32:31 associates himself with the people and can no longer see God face to face. Moses offered himself as a substitute for sins.	Jesus as mediator who offered himself on the cross for us.
Forms a church 12 chiefs & 70 elders	Forms a church 12 apostles & 40 disciples Lk 10:1
Go back…for all the men who were seeking your life are dead	Ex 4:19
Go…for all those who sought the child's life are dead	Mt 2:20

OUTLINE OF MATTHEW'S GOSPEL

I. THE FORMAL BEGINNING Chapters 1 & 2 have genealogies and then five beginnings in 1:18, 2:1, 2:13, 2:16 & 2:19 and each section has a prophesy.

Mt 1:23	Call him Emmanuel, God is with us, Is 7:14 (Jesus).
Mt 2:6	Born in Bethlehem, Micah 5:2 (Beth El Hem or House God Bread) Jesus is the bread of life.
Mt 2:15	Out of Egypt I called my son, Jer 31:15
Mt 2:18	Rachel weeping for her children, Jeremiah 31:15. Slaughter of boys.
Mt 2:23	He will be called a Nazarene (Is 11:1 (The Hebrew word is neser).

II. FIVE BOOKS OF NEW TORAH given by Jesus who the new Moses.

Book I	Chapters 3 to 7	Narrative 3 through 4	Deeds
		Sermon 5 through 7	Teachings
Book II	Chapters 8 to10	Narrative 8 through 9	Deeds

		Mission of 12 to go out and heal	
		Sermon 10 through 11.1	Teachings
Book III	Chapters 11 to 13	Narrative 11 through 12	Deeds
		Sermon 13:1 through 13.53	Teachings
Book IV	Chapters 14 to 18	Narrative 14 through 17 Church	Deeds
		Sermon 18 through 19.1	Teachings
		Forgiving (What the church is about)	
Book V	Chapters 19 to 25 End times	Narrative 19 through 23 Seven woes	Deeds
		Sermon 24 through 26:1	Teachings
		Goats & Sheep at End Times	

Mt 25: 35 to 37 Feed, clothe, visit (How did you take care of your brother?) When you see Jesus hungry, naked, or imprisoned, do you help him?

III. The Solemn Conclusion   Chapter 28:28 Jesus is with us, Emmanuel.
    Chapters 26 to 28   Passion, death, resurrection, commission.

There are 5 endings beginning with each starting with the Greek word *de*, which means but 27:57 to 61, 27:62 to 66, 28:1 to 10, 28:11 to 15 and 28:1 to 20.

The beginning with five books (new Torah) and the conclusion equals seven, which is the number for completion or covenant. Matthew liked groups of seven to identify perfection. In each of the five books, Jesus is seen doing something (deeds), and concluding with a collection of teachings. This implies that for us Christians we are to have both faith and action, they go hand in hand.

The wilderness experience is discussed in Chapter three of the Book of Exodus. From a burning bush God calls Moses. "I am the God of your father," he continued, "the God of Abraham, the God of Isaac, the God of Jacob." Moses hid his face, for he was afraid to look at God. But the LORD said, "I have witnessed the affliction of my people in Egypt and have heard their cry of complaint against their slave drivers, so I know well what they are suffering." But Moses said to God, "Who am I that I should go to Pharaoh and lead the Israelites out of Egypt?" He answered, "I will be with you; and this shall be your proof that it is I who have sent you: when you bring my people out of Egypt, you will worship God on this very mountain."

After God identified himself, Moses still had to ask God to explain who He is. Some scholars say this would make sense only if he was not a Jew, otherwise why does he ask God who He is? However, this cannot be supported. Ancient people thought there was power in knowing a name and they especially wanted to define God. But God the Father cannot be understood.

Ex 3:13, But, Moses said to God, Behold, when I come unto the Israelites and say to them, 'The God of your fathers has sent me to you,' and if they say to me, 'What is his name?' what shall I say to them?" And God said to Moses, "I AM WHO AM." Then he added, this you shall to the Israelites: I AM sent me to you." God spoke further to Moses say, and God said to Moses, you shall say unto the children of Israel I Am has sent me unto you. And God also said to Moses, you shall also say to the children of Israel, the Lord God of your fathers, the God of Abraham, the God of Isaac, the God of Jacob, has sent me to you. This is my name forever; this is my memorial for all generations.

This call of Moses influenced the rest of the text of the bible with the following structure:
1. God initiates the call.
2. There is a setting of mystery/Holiness
3. Resistance of Moses (Moses thought he was not sufficient).
4. Reassurance of God
5. Commission: Now Go is the command.

This is a common theme in the bible including the Book of Jeremiah, Isaiah chapter 6, Matthew chapter 28, and other books of the bible. The first chapter of the Book of Jeremiah is constructed just like Exodus 3:
1. God initiates the call: Jer 1:4 The word of the LORD came to me thus:
2. Setting of mystery / Holiness: Jer 1:5, Before I formed you in the womb I knew you, before you were born I dedicated you, a prophet to the nations I appointed you.
3. Resistance of Jeremiah:
Jer 1:6 "Ha, Lord GOD!" I said, "I know not how to speak; I am too young."
4. Reassurance of God: Jer 1:7, But the LORD answered me, Say not, "I am too young." To whomever I send you, you shall go; whatever I command you, you shall speak.
Jer 1:8 Have no fear before them, because I am with you to deliver you, says the LORD.
5. Commission: Jer 1:9, Then the LORD extended his hand and touched my mouth, saying, See, I place my words in your mouth! Jer 1:10 This day I set you over nations and over kingdoms, To root up and to tear down, to destroy and to demolish, to build and to plant.

The pattern is also found in the New Testament. Of course, Matthew used this pattern since his gospel is patterned after the Pentateuch.
1. God initiates the call: Mt 28:16, Jesus ordered the disciples to a mountain in Galilee.
2. Setting of mystery / Holiness: Mt 28:17, When they saw him they worshipped.
3. Resistance of disciples:
Mt 28:17 b, but they doubted.
4. Reassurance of God: Mt 28:18, Then Jesus approached and said to them, "All power in heaven and one earth has been given to me."
5. Great Commission: Mat 28:19, Go, therefore, and make disciples of all nations, baptizing them in the name of the Father, and of the Son, and of the holy Spirit,

Mat 28:20, teaching them to observe all that I have commanded you. And behold, I am with you always, until the end of the age."

This same structure can be recognized in Isaiah chapter 6:
Is 6:2 Seraphim were stationed above; each of them had six wings: with two they veiled their faces, with two they veiled their feet, and with two they hovered aloft.
Is 6:3 "Holy, holy, holy is the LORD of hosts!" they cried one to the other. "All the earth is filled with his glory!"
Is 6:4 at the sound of that cry, the frame of the door shook and the house was filled with smoke.
Is 6:5 Then I said, "Woe is me, I am doomed! For I am a man of unclean lips, living among a people of unclean lips; yet my eyes have seen the King, the LORD of hosts!"
Is 6:6 Then one of the seraphim flew to me, holding an ember that he had taken with tongs from the altar.
Is 6:7 He touched my mouth with it. "See," he said, "now that this has touched your lips, your wickedness is removed, your sin purged."
Is 6:8 Then I heard the voice of the Lord saying, "Whom shall I send? Who will go for us?" "Here I am," I said; "send me!"
Is 6:9 And he replied: Go and say to this people: Listen carefully, but you shall not understand! Look intently, but you shall know nothing!
Is 6:10, You are to make the heart of this people sluggish, to dull their ears and close their eyes; else their eyes will see, their ears hear, their heart understand, and they will turn and be healed.

The prophets saw the defense of the Law as the measuring stick for all of our lives. The measuring stick of the law is the rule. There was usually a period of time in the wilderness before a prophet becomes a major spokesman for tradition.
Moses returned from wilderness to be a leader of the people.

There were things that influenced how Moses would lead the people. Moses was raised in Egypt and was thus influenced by Egyptians and he perhaps picked up their philosophies, culture, and theology.

Exodus 21:32 says when a ox gores someone, "But if it is a male or a female slave that it gores, he must pay the owner of the slave thirty shekels of silver, and the ox must be stoned." This was the cost of a slave in the fourteenth to thirteenth century B.C., and is a means of dating the biblical story of Moses and the Exodus from Egypt.

1. God (Yahweh) is central in their tradition. At this point in history, the Israelites were not yet speaking about monotheism, only one God. You shall not have any other gods before me, does not say that there are no other gods. Monolatry says that we have our god and others have their god. Perhaps this is why Moses asked God who He was. Moses probably thought other people had their own gods. Moses was the first to hear the name, Yahweh.

2. The Israelites worshipped in a tent, which was a similar tent dwelling, used by the Midianites. The Midianites were nomadic people who worshipped in a tent. Tents are not married to a piece of real estate; God goes where you go when you worship in a tent. David wanted a permanent place, and a permanent place brings nationalism, prejudice, etc. Nationalism makes us think that God is married to a land, but God does not deal in real estate.

3. The basis for our religion is Covenant.

Covenants are deals between God and man. One example is, "You will be my people, and I'll be your God." A deal is made with God, and the deal has stipulations for us. Like "Ill get you out of Egyptian slavery and you will obey my commands (laws). There were two stipulations, "I'll be your God and bring you out of slavery, and you will obey me."

Many Christians have little understanding of the significance of laws. Martin Luther who turned people into thinking that Paul was anti Law influenced us. The Law gives us ethics, and without ethics we have perfume only. With proper ethics and doctrine, we have real meaning in our lives. Law is not an oppressing thing but a liberating aspect of religion. Law tells us how we should live and how we are to relate to each other.

The Law at the time of Moses was a new social presence, and is a root of our faith. Moses showed us a new way to live. The Law is a social reality and not just an experimental idea. Matthew, also, wanted us to see the sense of Jesus reinforcing the Law. We do not get involved in legalism, but we must acknowledge that the teachings of Jesus do matter. Human issues in the world are important because ethics are part of our faith. The Law is central to the beginning of this faith with a God who goes where we go and a religion that tells us how we live our lives. Our tradition has ethics that are rooted in the Law.

There were ten plagues that were brought about by God. Moses went to Pharaoh and in the name of Yahweh said, "Let my people go." God was the source of the plagues. The concept of Satan was not developed yet. Some scholars say that Satan was not fully developed in the entire Old Testament. The Book of Enoch was written in 280 to 250 B.C., and there is fallen angel figure in this book. Job called the angel Satan, but this was not the later concept of the Prince of Darkness. This was a person debating with God and was not the later concept of Satan. The fully developed Satan figure comes with Enoch.

Historically and textually, the ancient Hebrews thought that all things came from God. This Satan in the Book of Job held counsel with God. The ancient Hebrews seem to have been able to live with both the good and the bad coming from God. They did not compromise their unified view of God by introducing a second figure. Some scholars say we could live with a secondary figure because it helped with the source of evil, and so Satan came about. This implies that Satan was invented. However, the verses in the Old Testament that deal with Satan seem to imply that there is an archenemy of good, called Satan. The Book of Enoch was written in 280 to 250 B.C., so it is not very old. There are other verses that describe Satan and are as follows:

Gn 3:14 Then the LORD God said to the serpent: "Because you have done this, you shall be banned from all the animals and from all the wild creatures; On your belly shall you crawl, and dirt shall you eat all the days of your life.

Gn 3:15, I will put enmity between you and the woman, and between your offspring and hers; He will strike at your head, while you strike at his heel."

1 Chr 21:1 As Satan rose up against Israel, and he enticed David into taking a census of Israel.

Continuing in Job 1:6 to 12,

One day, when the sons of God came to present themselves before the LORD, Satan also came among them. And the LORD said to Satan, "Whence do you come?" Then Satan answered the LORD and said, "From roaming the earth and patrolling it." And the LORD said to Satan, "Have you noticed my servant Job, and that there is no one on earth like him, blameless and upright, fearing God and avoiding evil?"

But Satan answered the LORD and said, "Is it for nothing that Job is God fearing? Have you not surrounded him and his family and all that he has with your protection? You have blessed the work of his hands, and his livestock are spread over the land. But now put forth your hand and touch anything that he has, and surely he will blaspheme you to your face." And the LORD said to Satan, "Behold, all that he has is in your power; only do not lay a hand upon his person." So Satan went forth from the presence of the LORD.

Zech 3:1 to 2 also spoke of Satan.

> Then he showed me Joshua the high priest standing before the angel of the LORD, while Satan stood at his right hand to accuse him.

> And the angel of the LORD said to Satan, "May the LORD rebuke you, Satan; may the LORD who has chosen Jerusalem rebuke you! Is not this man a brand snatched from the fire?"

The Ten Plagues

The story of Moses' dealings with the Pharaoh continues in Ex 7:3, "I will harden Pharaoh heart and multiply my signs and wonders in the land of Egypt,"

This verse sounds like God did not want to help Pharaoh, but God's plan was just the opposite. God made Pharaoh obstinate (hardened his heart) so that He could help him and the Egyptians. The Book of Exodus tells us that when, eventually, the Egyptians found out that they were the reason for God having to interfere, they were bothered by it. When the Egyptians recognized the bad they had done, they turned to God.

Isaiah 19:21 says that God shall make himself known to the Egyptians and they shall offer sacrifices and will carry out the vows they make to the Lord. God was not only to punish Egypt but he would turn them to Himself and then heal them. The book of Wisdom also talks about this.

Wisdom 11:13 to 16, For when they heard that the cause of their own torments was a benefit to these others, they recognized the Lord.

Him who of old had been cast out in exposure they indeed mockingly rejected; but in the end of events, they marveled at him, since their thirst proved unlike that of the just.

And in return for their senseless, wicked thoughts, which misled them into worshipping dumb serpents and worthless insects, You sent upon them swarms of dumb creatures for vengeance;

That they might recognize that the very things through which he sins might punish them.

The stories of the ten plagues are a set pattern made up of three groups of sayings. Each one follows a pattern. First they begin with the words, "early tomorrow morning. Second, God tells Moses to "Go to Pharaoh. Then there is "the request of an act." The three sets of three ends with a tenth plague and

Pharaoh finally saying, "Get out of here." So, there were nine plagues, and an order of expulsion in the tenth plague as described in Exodus 10:24.

Sometimes, we approach the world with things that we think are very impressive. The world has a lot that impresses many of us, so faith does not come about through healings, miracles of nature, and other things. Too many people think that the world has wonders of its own, or we are immune to things and so we cannot recognize the greatness of God. Pharaoh was not impressed with snakes. Ex 7:10 Then Moses and Aaron went to Pharaoh and did as the LORD had commanded. Aaron threw his staff down before Pharaoh and his servants, and it was changed into a snake.

Ex 7:11 Pharaoh, in turn, summoned wise men and sorcerers, and they also, the magicians of Egypt, did likewise by their magic arts.

1. The first plague took place in the morning, and describes water turning into blood). Ex 7:15, Tomorrow morning, when he sets out for the water, go and present yourself by the river bank, holding in your hand the staff that turned into a serpent.
2. Ex 8:1, The second plague has God saying to go to Pharaoh (via Aaron) and the plague is of frogs that over run the land.
3. Ex 8:12, The third plague, Tell Aaron tomorrow morning Request an Act.
4. Ex 8:16, The fourth plague is "early tomorrow morning."
5. Ex 9:1, The fifth plague says, "Go to Pharaoh."
6. Ex 9:8, The sixth plague requests an act.
7. Ex 9:13, The seventh plague, "Early tomorrow morning.
8. Ex 10:1, The eighth plague, "Go to "Pharaoh."
9. Ex 10:21, Requests an Act

There is a set pattern of nine plagues that are grouped in three as outlined above. Pharaoh was still obstinate so the tenth plague was required (Ex 11:1). The Passover tradition takes root in the final plague. Unleavened bread is used because it symbolizes quickness, before Pharaoh changes his mind.

The pattern of the way the plagues were written, suggest to some scholars think that there are two traditions of the ten plagues that are interwoven with each other. The first tradition is the three groupings of the first nine plagues. The nine plagues are a pattern with a conclusion. Then one more plague was added. The tenth plague is considered the second tradition. Throughout the bible there are groupings of three because they are easier to remember and the plagues seem to be written in three groups of three.

However, there are also groups of ten. There are Ten Commandments, ten camels, ten plagues, etc. Perhaps, scholars think that they had more than one tradition, so they did not want to lose one or the other, so they combined them. It is easier to memorize groups of three, so it could have been a pattern developed to make it easier to remember the first nine. Then the tenth plague begins a story, a story of the Exodus of God's people from Egypt.

The effect of the tenth plague is bad and should not be minimized. Pharaoh had abandoned what he knew was the truth. The killing of the first born was bad, but human suffering is not to be tolerated, and the covenant had to be enforced. Two aspects of the tenth plague are the death of first born of all non-believers, and the death of the Egyptian army

Today, a Passover dinner remembers the suffering of the Egyptian people who were involved in the Exodus. Isaiah 19:21 says, "The LORD shall make himself known to Egypt, and the Egyptians shall know the LORD in that day; they shall offer sacrifices and oblations, and fulfill the vows they make to the LORD. Is 19:22, says "Although the LORD shall smite Egypt severely, he shall heal them; they shall turn to the LORD and he shall be won over and heal them."

God does not make death; killing is a result of the effects of sin in the world. This is mentioned in the Book of Wisdom 1:12 to 13. "Court not death by your erring way of life, nor draw to yourselves destruction by the works of your hands. Because God did not make death, nor does he rejoice in the destruction of the living."

Today, during the Passover meal, participants dip their fingers into some wine and then they dash out drops onto a napkin to mourn the suffering of the Egyptians.

Moses is central to the Hebrew Bible and he is has influence over into the New Testament. He is very significant in salvation history.
1. The legal tradition was rooted in Moses
2. The prophetic tradition was rooted in Moses (The end of the Book of Deuteronomy referred to Moses as a prophet.)
3. The priesthood through Aaron was rooted in Moses.
4. The leadership of the elders was rooted through Moses. The elders were selected to help Moses do various tasks (even though it was an ancient tradition).
5. The stories of Moses and the exodus were reused in later biblical traditions. God will take us back to the wilderness and there we will be married to Him. Exodus is the root story of the bible and of our lives.

The wilderness story was used in Isaiah who used the wilderness language from Exodus. Hosea used imagery of marriage as a loving relationship. Hosea used beautiful imagery of God who will take us back to the wilderness and there we will be married.

Covenants and Laws

The Law is written in two forms, Causative Law (Case Law) and Apodictic Law.

1. Causative Law is Case Law written in the form, If this is done, then this result will happen. This is the form of law used in the ancient Mid East. Mesopotamia and Babylon had this type of law as seen in written form on documents dated to about 1900 B.C.

2. Apodictic Law is written as if God is speaking the law directly to you. Apodictic Law uses the form: You shall not do the following.

The Book of Exodus 21: 12 to 17 contains lists of what are considered four of the oldest laws in the bible. The laws are short and easy to remember. Legal material of the time was written in the same Casuist style. Older lists like this are recognized and dated because the lists are usually in-groups of ten and five. They were grouped like this because they had to be memorized.

> Ex 21:12, Whoever strikes a man a mortal blow must be put to death.
>
> Ex 21:13 He, however, who did not hunt a man down, but caused his death by an act of God, may flee to a place which I will set apart for this purpose.
>
> Ex 21:14 But when a man kills another after maliciously scheming to do so, you must take him even from my altar and put him to death.
>
> Ex 21:15 Whoever strikes his father or mother shall be put to death.
>
> Ex 21:16 A kidnaper, whether he sells his victim or still has him when caught, shall be put to death.
>
> Ex 21:17 Whoever curses his father or mother shall be put to death.

These laws were not meant to be absolute, they were guidelines. In reality, the laws are not as exact as is written above, because extenuating circumstances are also part of the law. The law must evolve; it must be developed and played out over time. For instance, we need to develop the laws about boundary stones, and oxen to meet our present times of computers, cars, and fences.

Joseph, the son of Jacob, is a good example of how we are to use the laws. His own brothers kidnapped Joseph and they sold him into slavery. Later, he became the "prime minister" or right hand man of the Pharaoh of Egypt and he had the power to put them to death when they appeared before him. But he forgave them, reconciled them into the family and to God.

Law was written during different time periods, and there are many ways that a law can be dated. The dating of Law Codes takes into account the following:

1. What the law is about can help date it. For instance, moving boundary stones would date the law to a time where stones were used to mark boundaries.

2. Does the law say nothing about Kings, and where the worship of Yahweh was centralized? Does it presume everyone is building altars?

3. The written form of the covenant also tells us the time period in which it was written, because the form of a covenant can be dated by comparing it to non biblical contracts that were present in different time periods.

There are three major collections of Laws, the Covenant Code laws, the Deuteronomic Code, and the Holiness Codes.

1. The Covenant Code is the largest collection of laws, and is also the oldest collection. They were written about 1400 B.C.

An example is fidelity to God and fidelity to marriage. A law that is found in Proverbs on fidelity to marriage is in Proverbs 2:17 to 24,

> Who forsakes the companion of her youth and forgets the pact with her God.
>
> For her path sinks down to death, and her footsteps lead to the shades;
>
> None who enter thereon come back again, or gain the paths of life.
>
> Thus you may walk in the way of good men, and keep to the paths of the just.
>
> For the upright will dwell in the land, the honest will remain in it.
>
> But the wicked will be cut off from the land; the faithless will be rooted out of it.

2. The Deuteronomic Code was written about 640 to 609 B.C., and is a copy and revision of the Exodus Code. The Exodus Code which was compiled about 1900 B.C., but was in existence before this time since it was part of the oral tradition. The Deuteronomic Code updated many elements of the Covenant Codes.

The Deuteronomic Code has major advances in thinking in ancient Israel. For instance there was laws for kings (There are no such laws in the Covenant Code). There were advances in the legal code because there was worship in a centralized place due to King Josiah's great reforms that banned altars.

Laws were a living part of the people of Israel. They had varying circumstances that required the meaning of the law to be developed.

3. There were the Laws of slavery. Code 1 from the Covenant Code is found in Exodus 21:1 to 11 and it says, "When you purchase a Hebrew slave, he is to serve you for six years, but in the seventh year he shall be given his freedom and his debt is paid in full." In the Covenant Code, men and women were treated differently from one another. This difference disappeared as the law was more fully developed.

The Covenant Codes and the Deuteronomic Codes also dealt with civil issues. Other codes are as follows:

Code 3: The Holiness Codes or the Priestly Codes were the laws of the Jewish cult that describe how to offer sacrifices, when to offer sacrifices, what to eat, and what to touch. The Jubilee is also described in these codes.

Slavery:

It is important to note that slavery described in the bible is different from our concept of slavery. In ancient Israel there were ways to pull you out of poverty. To raise money, you could lease the tribal land that had been allotted to you. You could not sell the land but you could lease it to someone else. To raise money, you could also sell yourself or sell members of your family. A person could keep slaves for no more than seven years. This is not really slavery; it is similar to indentured servitude and is definitely different from slavery that we know from our country's history.

African American slaves and Indian slaves were treated brutally. For African slaves, there was an international marketplace for these human beings. Slavery and racism were mixed which made it especially bad. This type of slavery was not common in ancient times, even ancient Roman and Greek slaves were from their own house. Roman slaves were usually Roman, and Greek slaves were usually Greek. In other words slaves were indentured servants. This type of slavery is not good, but it is much different from our concept of slavery.

In the Deuteronomic Code, men and women were treated the same. Prior to this, the men were treated more favorably. The rules changed and were applied equally to men and women. This was the beginning of the development of an understanding in of faith. The slave was thought of as a brother who was to be helped once he had paid his debt by being in the service of someone. Code two from Deuteronomy said, "He is to serve for six years, but in the seventh year you shall dismiss him from your service a free man. You shall not send him away empty because the slave has worked hard for you"[93]

The Deuteronomic Code stated that an abused slave could not be given back to his master. The law was more humanitarian than earlier laws. A person had to properly care for slaves and could mistreat them. The bible does not justify slavery. The bible does not support slavery, because there is development away from that institution.

> Dt 23:16 "You shall not hand over to his master a slave who has taken refuge from him with you.
>
> Dt 23:17 Let him live with you wherever he chooses, in any one of your communities that pleases him. Do not molest him."

In the New Testament, Paul, writing about Onaissis and Phelemon says to treat a slave like a brother in Christ. Doing this is pulling all of the teeth out of slavery. This is also what 1 Pet 2:18 to 20 says, "Slaves, be subject to your masters with all reverence, not only to those who are good and equitable but also to those who are perverse. For whenever anyone bears the pain of unjust suffering because of consciousness of God, that is a grace. But what credit is there if you are patient when beaten for doing wrong? But if you are patient when you suffer for doing what is good, this is a grace before God."

There is a kind of institution called slavery in the bible, but there was a development in a direction away from the institution of slavery. There was also a development of how we are to view capital punishment. The covenant codes stated the seriousness of obeying a law, but they needed to be developed to their full meaning. We understand God and as our faith grows, so does our understanding of how we are to act. First the grave nature of the offense was described, and a strict punishment was prescribed in the bible. Then the nation had to put the Covenant Code into perspective. An example is the development of the ancient law of talion, or "eye for an eye".[94]

Capital Punishment (An Eye for an Eye)

Just cursing your parents is reason for you to be put to death according to the covenant code described in the Book of Exodus. This law was written in a strict form because the purposes of the covenant laws were to outline the serious nature of the sins. Murder is a serious crime that affects the community and the covenant code said that a murderer had to be killed. The covenant code also said that acts against the family were to be punished by death. You are not to strike your mother or your father because the family is important. Killing is a serious crime but we cannot interpret the bible to say that the state can kill someone. In the bible there is a development of the laws concerning capital punishment until it becomes harder to carry out the punishment.

The Book of Deuteronomy was written after the Exodus writings. The Book of Deuteronomy developed the law of capital punishment to a fuller understanding. In Deuteronomy 19:15 to 17 it says that a trial was required, and adequate proof by at least two witnesses was necessary to put someone to death. Then, the Book of Numbers reminds us that blood shed is not allowed because it desecrates the land, and God lives in the land, and does not want to be in a land that is desecrated. In the story of the woman caught in adultery, Jesus did not contradict the law of capital punishment but developed it forward to make it impossible to carry out

Laws on capital punishment were first outlined in the more ancient books of Exodus and Leviticus.

Ex 21:12 whoever strikes a man a mortal blow must be put to death.

Ex 21:13 He, however, who did not hunt a man down, but caused his death by an act of God, may flee to a place which I will set apart for this purpose.

Ex 21:14 But when a man kills another after maliciously scheming to do so, you must take him even from my altar and put him to death.

Ex 21:15 Whoever strikes his father or mother shall be put to death.

Ex 21:16 A kidnaper, whether he sells his victim or still has him when caught, shall be put to death.

Ex 21:23 to 25 But if injury ensues, you shall give life for life, eye for eye, tooth for tooth, hand for hand, foot for foot, burn for burn, wound for wound, stripe for stripe.

In Leviticus the code is described as follows:

Lv 24:17 "Whoever takes the life of any human being shall be put to death;

Lv 24:18 whoever takes the life of an animal shall make restitution of another animal. A life for a life!

Lv 24:19 Anyone who inflicts an injury on his neighbor shall receive the same in return.

Lv 24:20 Limb for limb, eye for eye, tooth for tooth! The same injury that a man gives another shall be inflicted on him in return.

Lv 24:21 Whoever slays an animal shall make restitution, but whoever slays a man shall be put to death.

Lv 24:22 You shall have but one rule, for alien and native alike. I, the LORD, am your God."

In Leviticus 24:18 to 19 it says that anyone who injures an animal must make restitution for it and anyone who injures another that the same shall be done to him. The term "takes the life of" is not present in verse 19 because the law was still speaking about the result of striking a man or an animal, and the law does not separate the two types of punishment.

In other words, if you killed an animal, you were to make monetary restitution as did killing a human being requires monetary restitution. An eye for an eye can not be the possible punishment enacted by a civilized person, because the result cannot be duplicated. If a person blinds a woman, her husband may develop ulcers, and even mental illness because of the stress. How do you extract this type of punishment from the original offender? You do not cut off another man's arm, you instead require him to make restitution to the person he injured. It is obvious that these laws showed the seriousness of the crime and then they had to be developed further. Verse 17 does not really imply capital punishment because it is immediately followed by restitution to be given to the injury of an animal. "So shall it be done" means a monetary type compensation.

Exact punishment was unjust and would make the enforcer of the law barbaric. If you were to rip out someone's eye to punish a person, you would be as bad as the offender of the original crime. Compensation was practiced in the ancient Near East and the courts of Israel probably practiced it, also.

Milgrom[95] writes that, "The biblical formulation of talion law (eye for an eye) was theory in the bible but was not practiced." The legal text could not be altered, but the centralized government of Israel interpreted the law to mean compensation, as implied in verse 18. The original message was to instill in the hearts of the people appreciation of the great evil of harming or killing another person. The government was to determine how to punish an offender. And as the people grew spiritually, so did their interpretation of the laws. Number 35:33 said, "Bloodshed desecrates the land, and it is atoned by the land." This verse does not distinguish between blood taken by a person from the blood taken by a government that uses capital punishment. God does not want bloodshed.

Numbers 35:30 to 34 stated that payment was to be mad for principal limbs and body parts, but payment was not allowed for a murderer. This seems conclusive except that it says there must be two eyewitnesses for a capital offense. Not even one eyewitness was sufficient to put a person to death for committing a murder. Circumstantial evidence was not enough. Yet, we go beyond this in the United States. In Orange County, we had a guilty verdict at a trial where there was not even physical evidence to link the defendant to the crime.

Every year, the Orange County Court system spends all of its money that is budgeted to ensure guilty verdicts. Then they threaten to lay off all workers unless more money is allocated. The Book of Numbers teaches us how critical it is for the state to be certain of what it is doing. A hung jury used to indicate that there was reasonable doubt, now it means that the prosecution can use the court system to limit the defense tactics to help it get a verdict of guilty.

The Book of Numbers then carried the concept of the death penalty forward to say that only God can take a life of a person. God wants everyone to realize the serious nature of murdering another person, but at the same time God does not want any kind of blood shed on the land.

"Whenever someone kills another, the evidence of witnesses is required for the execution of the murderer. The evidence of a single witness is not sufficient for putting a person to death. You shall not accept indemnity in place of the life of a murderer who deserves the death penalty; he must be put to death. Nor shall you accept indemnity to allow a refugee to leave his city of asylum and again dwell elsewhere in the land before the death of the high priest. You shall not desecrate the land where you live. Since bloodshed desecrates the land, the land can have no atonement for the bloodshed on it except through the blood of him who shed it. Do not defile the land in which you live and in the midst of which I dwell; for I am the LORD who dwells in the midst of the Israelites."

The final word seems to be that all bloodshed is wrong and we have to recognize it as being wrong. This passage first says that two witnesses are required for an execution of a defendant. Circumstantial evidence is not good enough. Two or more people have to stand up and give testimony of their eyewitness to the crime. Then this passage reaffirms that you can seek refuge in certain cities for some murders. You cannot leave until the death of the high priest, but the high priest was not a high priest all of his life. This opens up another window of getting around the exile of the person. How can executing someone atone for the death of another? The murdered person does not get satisfaction, so the usefulness of this punishment is diminished. The dead person's life cannot be atoned, so capital punishment is not justice, but is actually revenge by others. Finally, this passage tells us that bloodshed has to be left in the hands of God.

Jesus carried the concept of justice further to include forgiveness, rather than extracting talion. Tallon means "an eye for an eye."

> You have heard that it was said, 'An eye for an eye and a tooth for a tooth.' But I say to you, offer no resistance to one who is evil. When someone strikes you on (your) right cheek, turn the other one to him as well. If anyone wants to go to law with you over your tunic, hand him your cloak as well. Should anyone press you into service for one mile, go with him for two miles.
>
> Give to the one who asks of you, and do not turn your back on one who wants to borrow. "You have heard that it was said, 'You shall love your neighbor and hate your enemy.' But I say to you, love your enemies, and pray for those who persecute you, that you may be children of your heavenly Father, for he makes his sun rise on the bad and the good, and causes rain to fall on the just and the unjust.[96]

Jesus spoke about forgiveness, and acting in a godly manner to the people who are on the margins of society, because all people have souls. We need to be a light to people who are not followers of God. Jesus gives us another way of looking at capital punishment. We need to recognize every person as having a soul, and since every person is a temple of God we cannot destroy what belongs to God. Murder is very wrong, but neither does society have the right to destroy what God has anointed.

I have written to one person who was accused of murdering his baby. Nevada had just passed a law that said a person would be executed if a child died as a result of child abuse. The press and the people were hungry and wanted someone to convict. The man could not fight for his life because of the political climate. His wife is not in jail and she was also accused of the crime. He was sentenced to about ten years in prison. If he had pled not guilty he would have received the death penalty. So, if he had exercised his rights in court, then the just penalty would have been to execute him. By pleading guilty, society got a just punishment. I cannot comprehend the logic of this thinking.

The bible tells us not to interfere with or to harm the anointed of God. In the Old Testament, the "anointed" referred to priests, prophets and kings who were anointed by God. The concept was so important that David killed the person who mercifully finished killing King Saul who was dying. Saul had pleaded for death so his enemies, the Philistines[5], would save him from torture and humiliation. David said to the Amelkite in 2 Sm 1:14 and 16, "How is it that you were not afraid to put forth your hand to desecrate the Lord's anointed? You testified against yourself when you said, 'I dispatched God's anointed.'"

Judgment comes upon those who go against God's anointed. Saul was an earthly king but even more importantly, he was anointed from above. Being anointed is not just a function of an office, but also the heavenly connection to the office. Saul was not just a king; he was a king who was anointed by God, through the prophet Samuel. David was pursued by Saul, yet he did not lay a hand on Saul when he had the opportunity to do so. He knew God anointed Saul.

As people mature in their understanding, God expects more from them.

The New Testament gives greater meaning to the concept of being anointed. 1 John 2: 20 says, "But you have the anointing that comes from the holy one, and you all have knowledge." He then tells us that we have eternal life from God's anointing. Peter also speaks about our anointing and how to live our lives accordingly:

> But the one who gives us security with you in Christ and who anointed us is God; he has also put his seal upon us and given the Spirit in our hearts as a first installment.

This passage continues, saying that we should let ourselves be built into have tasted that the Lord is good. Come to him, a living stone, rejected by human beings but chosen and precious in the sight of God, and, like living stones, let yourselves be built spiritual houses and to be a holy priesthood. We are a holy priesthood through Jesus Christ.[97]

> Rid yourselves of all malice and all deceit, insincerity, envy, and all slander. Like newborn infants, long for pure spiritual milk so that through it you may grow into salvation. For you into a spiritual house to be a holy priesthood to offer spiritual sacrifices acceptable to God through Jesus Christ.[98]

> But you are "a chosen race, a royal priesthood, a holy nation, a people of his own, so that you may announce the praises" of him who called you out of darkness into his wonderful light. Once you were "no people" but now you are God's people; you "had not received mercy" but now you have received mercy. Beloved, I urge you as aliens and sojourners to keep away from worldly desires that wage war against the soul.[99]

Finally, we are told, "Do you not know that you are the temple of God, and that the Spirit of God dwells in you? If anyone destroys God's temple, God will destroy that person; for the temple of God, which you are, is holy."[100]

God anoints us, so we are all important in the eyes of God. "For however many are the promises of God, their Yes is in him; therefore, the Amen from us also goes through him to God for glory. But the one who gives us security with you in Christ and who anointed us is God; he has also put his seal upon us and given the Spirit in our hearts as a first installment."[101]

In conclusion, the concept of capital punishment is developed in the bible as part of our faith through Jesus. We can not justify killing another person, and we cannot give the wisdom of that decision to the state. Only God can take another life. The United States is the only modern western country that allows capital punishment. Russia is saying that they too will end the practice of having the state kill a person. Israel has capital punishment but they do not use the power.[102] The last person executed in Israel was a war criminal and that was decades ago.

God tells us in the first book of the bible that we are made in His image. But he also says that when a man and woman marry that they are to remain married in conjugal union, forever. "What God has joined together, let no man interfere with." Yet Moses allowed divorce.

They said to him, "Then why did Moses command that the man give the woman a bill of divorce and dismiss (her)?" He said to them, "Because of the hardness of your hearts Moses allowed you to divorce your wives, but from the beginning it was not so.[103]

Moses allowed people to divorce each other, even though the Book of Genesis made it clear that marriage was a permanent sacrament. Paul says in 1 Corinthians 7:11 that a woman may separate but not remarry, and that a man may not divorce. After all, God does not divorce Himself from us. Divorce was allowed because people were not mature enough. We mature through history, and now thousands of years later we more mature, and we live by the wonderful sacrament of marriage.

We must remember that God did not kill Cain after he murdered his brother Abel, instead He protected Cain.[104] Moses killed a man, and yet God forgave him, formed him, and then made him the leader of his people.[105] God does not sanctioned bloodshed. This was demonstrated when

King David told his son Solomon that he had wanted to build a house to honor the Lord. David said, "But this word of the LORD came to me: 'You have shed much blood, and you have waged great wars. You may not build a house in my honor, because you have shed too much blood upon the earth in my sight.'"[106]

Jubilee or Kinsman Redemption

Lv 25:1 to 28 speaks of a Jubilee. A Jubilee was to occur every fiftieth year. It is a time of kinsman redemption. A Jubilee is a time of justice where all debts are canceled and are considered paid in full. A Jubilee is also called a time of rest, the day of the Lord, and a true fast. In the Book of Isaiah a Jubilee is described as a true fast where external worship must done only when it is sincerely part of us.[16] It is internal worship that God wants, but it must be expressed externally. The two cannot be separated. God says we must release those who are unjustly imprisoned, we must remove the yoke from those in hardship, and we must set free those who are oppressed, and break every yoke. We must share our food with the hungry, shelter the oppressed and the homeless, clothe the naked, and not turn our back on other Christians. God says that he will answer us, only if we take care of the marginalized, who are the weak people among us. Isaiah says that we must follow God's ways and call the Sabbath a delight, and we must fully honor the Lord's holy day.

Leviticus chapter 25 describes a Jubilee year. First, we must let the land rest. Every seven years we had to let the land rest. Planting crops and pruning of vines was not allowed.

In ancient Israel, when you fell into poverty, you could lease your land to someone until you could afford to buy it back. But your debt was canceled and you automatically got your land back during the year of Jubilee. This tradition prevented poverty from being inherited, because the land eventually went back to the family. Today, we inherit wealth, but poverty seems to continue.

During the eighth year, all foods must be shared with everyone in your household, all of your hired help, and all of the indentured servants.

Then Lv 25:8 to 9 mentions a great Sabbath after seven times seven years, so that the fiftieth year is described as a Jubilee year. This great year was to be announced with blasts of trumpets throughout the land on the tenth day of the seventh month of the year.

A Jubilee year is described in Lv 25:10.

This fiftieth year you shall make sacred by proclaiming liberty in the land for all its inhabitants. It shall be a jubilee for you, when every one of you shall return to his own property, every one to his own family estate.

The land was redeemed when it was returned to the original owner. Misfortune or blunder of parents would have caused poverty to be inherited by their children. This prevented poverty from being inherited. A provision is also stated that says the closest relative may redeem the property.

Lv 25:13 "In this year of the jubilee, then, every man shall return to his own possession.

Lv 25:23 "The land shall not be sold in for ever; for the land is mine, and you are sojourners and strangers with me.

Lv 25:24 Therefore, in every land of your possession, you must permit the land to be redeemed.

Lv 25:25 When one of your countrymen is in such poverty and that he has to sell some of his property, his closest relative can come to redeem it, he may redeem the property that was sold. Lv 25:26 If, however, the man has no relative to redeem his land, but later on is able to redeem it; 25:27 he shall make a deduction from the price in proportion to the number of years since the sale. Then pay the amount to the man to whom he sold it, so that he may return to his possession.

Lv 25:28 But if he is not able to restore it, then that which is sold shall remain in the hand of him that has bought it until the year of jubilee and in the jubilee it shall go out, and he may return unto his possession.

If a house were sold in a walled city, the seller would have only one year to redeem the house. If the house was not redeemed within a year, it would remain the property of the buyer and would not be redeemed even in a jubilee

C. The proper treatment and the eventual redemption of those who sold themselves into slavery were required. They were not to be treated as bondservants but as a hired servant.

Lv 25:39 to 42, "And if thy brother that dwells with you be waxen poor, and be sold unto thee; thou shalt not compel him to serve as a bond servant; but as an hired servant, as a sojourner, he shall be with thee. He shall serve thee unto the year of jubilee and shall he depart from you, he and his children with him. They shall return unto his family and unto the possession of his fathers. For they are my servants, which I brought forth out of the land of Egypt: they shall not be sold as bondsmen.

D. The Israelites were expected to be humble because they were servants of God because He brought them out of slavery. Lv 25:55 says, "For unto me the children of Israel are servants; they are my servants whom I brought forth out of the land of Egypt, I, the LORD, your God."

The concept of the Jubilee came to its full realization when Jesus announced a year of Jubilee for the whole world.[107] He declared a Jubilee, "a year acceptable to the Lord."

"...And there was delivered unto him the scroll of the prophet Esaias. And when he had opened the book, he found the place where it was written, the Spirit of the Lord is upon me, because he has anointed me to preach the gospel to the poor; he has sent me to heal the brokenhearted, to preach deliverance to the captives, and recovering of sight to the blind, to set at liberty them that are bruised, to preach the acceptable year of the Lord." ..."And he began to say unto them, This day is this scripture fulfilled in your ears."

Ezekiel said that was how a shepherd of the people should act. Ezekiel wrote that God's people were scattered because there was no shepherd to watch over them. God said that he Himself would bring His people out of foreign lands and will care for them and give them rest. As shepherd he will seek the lost, he will bring back those who strayed, he will bind up the injured, and heal the sick. This is the right way to shepherd or lead the people.[108]

Ezekiel was prophesying about the Son of man, which is a title or name for the Messiah. Ezekiel 34:23, "I will set up one shepherd over them." Jesus also said, "And other sheep I have, which are not of this fold: them also I must bring, and they shall hear my voice, and there shall be one fold and one shepherd." Jesus expected to have a succession of the leader of his Church. Peter is an office that was designed to last forever so that there would be one shepherd over His people.

A Summary of the Law and the Kinsman Redeemer

The Ten Commandments are outlined in Ex 20:1 to 17 and in Deuteronomy 5:6 to 21. The laws are not all worded in the same style in the books of Exodus and Deuteronomy. There is fluidity between Covenant and Deuteronomy laws: we do not use one law to privilege one law over another. We cannot say that Jesus delivered us from the law and then use the laws to speak against other laws. It seems like Christians often go to the Laws of Moses when they want to take a hard line on an issue. Otherwise they speak with love and compassion about the graces from God. We cannot use the law to suit our personal agendas. We must look at the Covenant Law, then read about it's parallel in Deuteronomy, and then study the law's further development in the bible. We cannot have bumper sticker answers to complicated questions. The Law of Moses is thought to be the easiest place to go for short answers, but we cannot use one law over another law, and we must study its development.

Legal tradition may seem archaic but it is only because the law needs to be understood after it has been developed. The laws in Ex 21:28 to Ex 22:9 are the foundations of justice, but they need to be fully developed to account for various circumstances, changes in the world, and to ensure we live in the justice of God. For instance, Ex 21:28 says, "When an ox gores a man or a woman to death, the ox must be stoned; its flesh may not be eaten. The owner of the ox, however, shall go unpunished." We do not have oxen in most of the world, but we do have automobiles, and consequently laws need to be updated.

    A case is not decided until the elders have made a decision. The elders would meet at the gates of towns to discuss the laws and to determine justice. In the Book of Ruth a case is made to the elders at the gate of the city. The nearest living relative would redeem a woman if she was childless and she asked to be redeemed. In the Book of Ruth, Boaz presented the case and the nearest kin decided not to redeem Ruth. When he passed his sandal, Boaz became the kinsman redeemer and was able to redeem Ruth. Justice was accomplished when the sandal was passed. Through the act of redemption, Boaz returned Naomi to her land and also took the gentile Ruth as his wife. The story of Ruth is a process of legal tradition that is wedded to Moses. From the marriage of Ruth who was a Moabite, and Boaz who was a Jew, came the house of David

    Deuteronomy 23:4 says no Ammonite or Moabite may ever be admitted into the community of the Lord. Ezra and Nehemiah ousted foreigners as part of their reform. The Book of Ruth says that God says the opposite is true.

    The Book of Ruth is a story of a gentile woman who is welcomed through marriage into God's community. Isaiah 56:6 to 8, also says that foreigners who join themselves to the Lord are welcome. And, Numbers 15:1 to 15 says there is one law for both the sojourner and the native born persons. The Book of Ruth tells us that God wants all nations to be part of His community. The Church is the Gentile Bride and the Groom or Kinsman Redeemer is Jesus. We must always remember that faith is what matters, not bloodlines.

Chapter 5: Entering the Promised Land

The Exodus story began in Egypt as a first step in the creation of a people of God. Moses saw the Promised Land but he died before entering Canaan. The entire generation that left Egypt did not enter the Promised Land, because they were not worthy of receiving the gift of the land. Joshua became the leader of the people when Moses died. Joshua took the people into the Promised Land, and the people of God continued forward in history (time). When Joshua came into the land, the Canaanite religion was atrocious. Much had to be done to bring about religious and social change in the region.

The Book of Joshua is often thought of as a story of a lightening strike conquest of Israel. Modern day investigations of ruins has provided a lot of information on ancient Israeli cities. At first, the archeologists who uncovered buried cities found there was a layer of ash. The ash seemed to prove a hostile type of conquest of the cities by the Israelites. The archeological record eventually got more ambiguous, since some cities seem to not have been burnt. These cities do not have an appearance of being destroyed. These findings somewhat agree with Joshua 11:13, "However, Israel did not destroy by fire any of the cities built on raised sites, except Hazor, which Joshua burned." These finding disagree with other texts if the cities were conquered by military means. There were no burn levels even on the cities that Joshua said were conquered.

Since 1950, archeology is not completely agreeing with our concept of what happened in the conquest of the Israelites. However, study of sites thousands of years ago is a difficult endeavor. We deduce from the bible that the Israelites conquered Israel by military force. The archaeology of Jerico is especially troubling to biblical scholars. The Exodus is thought to have occurred during the time of Ramesses II (The Pharaoh). The wilderness wandering was for about forty years. The number forty represents a time of judgment or the time of a generation, and so is not an exact number of years. Entry into the land is thought to have occurred at about 1240 to 1200 B.C. The well-known British archeologist Kathleen Kenyon and others have shown that Jericho was already in ruins by the time of Joshua. The town of Ai was not even in existence yet. So, dating of the event is still being worked out.

There is a record of Jericho, Ai Gibeon (East of Gezer) where the Gibeonites tricked themselves into the city to conquer it. Scholars think that perhaps more of this type of conquest (subterfuge) occurred in history. Joshua 9:17 says that the inhabitants of Gibeon, Chephirah, Beeroth, and Kiriath jearim tricked the Israelites into an oath to spare themselves and be aligned with the Israelites.

There are three major theories on how the Israelites occupied Israel. One theory of the Jewish occupation of Israel and Judah is that they occupied the cities by using military force. This is the most accepted explanation of how the Jews took over the lands. The Old Testament first describes the occupation of three cities, Jericho, Ai, and Gibbeon. This is described in the first seven chapters of Joshua. The conquest of the remaining cities is only briefly described. The bible often gives the reader the impression that a lot is happening, but it does not describe every detail. An example is in the translation of the Gospel of John 18:17 where John wants us to visualize a lot of people inquiring about Jesus, but he does it by describing only a couple of people. There is a lot of visual imagery or the conquest of Canaan. However, the description of the conquest brief.

I. Military Conquest of the Land of Canaan

The first theory is that the land was swiftly conquered by military force. This is the view that is most widely accepted. The Book of Joshua mentions the defeat of the Kings of Jerusalem, Hebron, Jarmuth, Lachish, and

Eglon.[109] The Kings were defeated by the Israelites in order to protect the city of Gibeon after the Israelites had entered into an alliance with the people of Gibeon. Chapter ten describes the defeat of the kings in what is called the Southern Campaign and then it describes the conquests of Makkedah, Libnah, Lachish, Eglon, Hebron, and Debir. The king of Gezer was also defeated at Lachish. No other conquests are described but we are told Joshua conquered the entire country with all of its Kings.

The text does not describe how the total conquest of Israel was accomplished. We assume that the conquest was quick. Chapter twelve of Judges speaks of the giving of regions of land to various tribes, and Judges 12:10 indicates that the city of Jerusalem was given to Hebron.

Chapter eleven of Joshua describes what was referred to as Joshua's Northern Campaign. First the Israelites defeated Jabin, king of Hazor, Jobab, the king of Madon, and the kings of Shimron Achshaph, and the northern kings. The northern kings reigned in the mountain regions; in Arabah near Chinneroth; in the foothills, and in Naphath Dor to the west. The kings of Hazor, Achshaph, Shimzor, and Dor, Meron were also defeated. These were cities and regions in and around Galilee. These were the Canaanites to the east and west, Amorites, Hittites, Perizzites and Jebusites in the mountain regions and Hivites at the foot of Hermon in the land of Mizpah.[110] The numerous kings came out with all their troops, and are described as an army numerous as the sands on the seashore, and with a multitude of horses and chariots.

After the defeat of all of these people, Joshua captured Hazor and burned it. The conquest is summarized in Joshua 11:16 to 17.

> So Joshua captured all this land: the mountain regions, the entire Negev, all the land of Goshen, the foothills, the Arabah, as well as the mountain regions and foothills of Israel, from Mount Halak that rises toward Seir as far as Baal gad in the Lebanon valley at the foot of Mount Hermon. All their kings he captured and put to death.

Later the Israelites are described as having captured Hebron, Debir, Anab, and the entire mountain regions of Judah, and of Israel. Joshua 11:23 says, "Thus Joshua captured the whole country, just as the LORD had foretold to Moses. Joshua gave it to Israel as their heritage, apportioning it among the tribes. And the land enjoyed peace."

However, the bible does not detail the capture of all of the cities where most of the Israelite tribes settled. The conquest of the important cities are assumed to be taken by military action. However, the bible does not describe how these cities were occupied.

Some scholars say that the cities may not have really been taken by force. Scholars, point out that Jerusalem was given to Hebron in Judges 12:10. However, Jerusalem was not conquered by military force during this time period. Later, the bible describes the conquest of Jerusalem by David, and not Joshua.

II. Theory of Israel Emerging From Within the Land of Canaan

A second theory described the conquest of the land as being more gradual. There was immigration into the land by Israelite families from the time of Genesis. There is a theory that says that this may be how the settlement of Israel took place, instead of by the invasion described in the Book of Exodus. The settlement of Canaan (or Israel) may have been as described in the Book of Genesis. The story of Abraham takes place after the story of Babel, and the people were scattered all over the earth.[111] The Israelite people may have entered the land of Canaan during this time when people were scattered after the destruction of the tower of Babel. This theory infers that the Israelites were actually Canaanites, so no large-scale migration was necessary.

Genesis describes Abraham's Father being called out of his homeland, but he did not go far enough. Terah took his son Abram, his grandson

Lot, son of Haran, and his daughter in law Sarai, the wife of his son Abram, and brought them out of Ur of the Chaldeans, to go to the land of Canaan. But when they reached Haran, they settled there.

So, God skipped a generation before he told Abraham to go to the land. But, by the time Abraham reached the Promised Land, it was already occupied by the Canaanites. It seems like others migrated directly to Canaan after the fall of the Tower of Babel. The bible text does not say that the Israelites migrated to Canaan after the fall of the Tower of Babel. So this is just a theory, and it is need of a lot evidence.

The scholars say that the Genesis type conquest of Israel does not agree with some of the archeological records.[112] The genealogy lists imply the making of nations through Adam's son Cain, and through Adam's son Seth. The people who migrated were semi nomadic. The scholars have no explanation of what would have brought the nomads together as a nation. What could have unified these semi nomadic people? This theory is possible, but there is not enough biblical or archeological evidence to support the theory of the Israelites occupying Canaan at this time.

III. Theory of a Social Revolution with the Word of God

The third model is a social revolution model proposed by Norman Gothwold and others. Egypt had an aristocracy, and a central government, and these scholars say that there are records of a small aristocracy or unstable people in the countryside of Canaan that were called Shasu. These people called Shasu may have called their God Yhw, which is the Hebrew word for God. So just possibly, the Israelites were in Canaan at the time of Pharaoh Nierneptah. The archeological record is not abundant, so it is only possible that the Shasu people could have been the seed of what became Israel.

The social revolution model teaches that Joshua came into the land with a sword that was powerful. They may not have engaged in physical combat, instead they may have used a sword that was the Word of God. Joshua had the word of Yahweh and this third theory proposes that it caused a great social revolution to take place. Masses of Canaanites rose up and began to follow Yahweh after hearing about how great God is. These scholars say that there were some military battles but most of the settlements accepted Yahweh and were liberated by His Word. This theory explains the unevenness in the archeological records.

This idea for this theory is taken from focusing on the Great Commission where Jesus tells his disciples to go forth and baptize all of the Nations in the Name of the Father, and of the Son, and of the Holy Spirit. Jesus is with the Church and it has spread throughout the world. Similarly, this was how the Israelites may have originally conquered Israel and Judah (Canaan). With God anything is possible.

This model says that the twelve tribes of Israelites did not come from Egypt. Only Joshua and his small group came from Egypt. The scholars point out that the word for thousand in Hebrew can also mean "tent groups". So, the number 500,000 can also mean 500 tent groups. Plus, no records in Egypt have yet been found that describe masses of tens of thousands, or two million people leaving Egypt. There would not be any records of a massive migration if there was only a small group that left with Moses. According to archeological estimates, there may have been only three to four million people in all of Egypt at the time of the Exodus. A migration of millions would have been recorded elsewhere, because it would have quite significant. Especially since the Jews were the work force of Egypt.

Some scholars think what happened is that the Israelites migrated to Israel and told a story that explained everything in a better way, because it was the only way. The truth about God caused a social revolution to take place. They would have said to the people, we once were slaves in Egypt and this is what God did for us. The scholars say that God was with them, and so conversion was easy.

This theory seems to explain the question that is asked of everyone, throughout time. The words expressed in Joshua 24:13 make better sense if the conquest is described as a love story, instead of Israel's occupation as a conquest story. Joshua was addressing everybody throughout time when he asks whom will we serve. He said, "I gave you a land which you had not tilled and cities which you had not built, to dwell in; you have eaten of vineyards and olive groves which you did not plant. Joshua continues with words that seem to be addressed to peoples of mixed gods instead of believers of the One God. And you must decide,

If it does not please you to serve the LORD, decide today whom you will serve, the gods your fathers served beyond the River (Mesopotamia) or the gods of the Amorites in whose country you are dwelling. As for my household, and me we will serve the LORD.[113]

This speech does not seem to completely make sense if Joshua was addressing Jews who came out of the wilderness with him. It makes more sense if Joshua was addressing a mixed crowd of Jews and Canaanites.

At our approach the Lord drove out (all the peoples, including) the Amorites who dwelt in the land. Therefore we also will serve the Lord, for he is our God. Joshua in turn said to the people, "You may not be able to serve the Lord, for his is a holy God; he is a jealous God who will not forgive your transgressions or your sins. If, after the good he has done for you, you forsake the Lord and serve strange gods, he will do evil to you and destroy you." But the people answered Joshua; "We will still serve the Lord."[114]

This model is a theory that is not proven. The assumption has disquieting undertones associated with it. This model could imply that there was no Exodus. Then it would follow that the Old Testament was fiction. In essence, since these scholars have not yet found evidence of the early migration, they invented their own story. The scholars even ignore the archeological finding that support the Old Testament. Evidence must be available for scientists to come to conclusions, so it is wrong to accept this model in an extreme fashion, unless further evidence can support it.

The model is still a possibility but it is presently not valid. It is possible that there was a combination of all three models of the conquest. The Ark of the Covenant was important to the Israelites. When they crossed the Jordan River, it was the priests carrying the ark that led the way. The River halted, backed up, and became a solid mass when the ark was brought into the water.[115] God led the Israelites directly to Jerico, which was the most important city because of the fertile soil, and the abundance of water. It was also the strongest fortress in all of the land of Canaan.

The writer used Genesis creation poetry to describe the victory over Jerico, which was the strongest city in the area. The conquest is described as a liturgy. For six days the Israelites circled the city and each day they marched once around it. They were led by the weakest of the Israelites; the priests to show that victory belonged to the Lord. They carried the ark before them, with the priests blowing seven rams horns. On the seventh day, they marched around the city seven times and when the priests blew their horns, all of the Israelites shouted and the walls of Jerico tumbled down. The power of the ark was astonishing. Hebrew's 9:4 described the ark as containing items that God had touched; the pot of manna, the rod of Aaron, and the table of the word (10 commandments).

The men went up into the city after the wall had fallen, and took the city. God was working with the Israelites, so there was more than military might involved. In fact they lost the next battle because men had not obeyed God. The victories with the liturgy centered on the ark showed that there was more involved than just military might. In fact fear of the Israelites spread fast because the people knew God was on their side.

The biblical account is the major source of the record we have. The bible was written to give the reader a feeling of what was going on, but it does not detail every event. For instance, in the Gospel of John it is stated that Jesus was bound and taken to the High Priest, and then was lead from the High Priest to the Praetorium. We feel like Jesus was questioned by the High Priest. Actually, John did not describe Jesus before the High Priest. This is a brilliant tactic that the writers of the bible used throughout the bible. This is history, when we become part of it, even when it is inferred to us. The Holy Spirit inspired the bible and it must be viewed as such.

The Jews created a new direction for mankind. The Jewish Nation changed history by living life in a progressive fashion. We continue forward in time by not only living today, but by being connected to our past, and to our future. Our God is a God of the past, present, and future, and our lives cannot be confined to living only for the present. It is too easy to go astray when we think that we are only living for the present. Our standards, our morals, and our fidelity to God can only be great if we realize that we are a nomadic people who travel through time. We respect our past, and we recognize that our future as Christian people is influenced by what we do today. Cahill says in his book that the bible teaches that each of us are unique, and we each affect the future.[116] The Jews taught that God was unchanging and was part of every aspect of ever life. They had a code to live by, a code that was Divine in origin. The Ten Commandments would shape every life in history.

Chapter 6: The Book of Kings

Kings until about 1030 B.C did not rule Israel. For two hundred years there was no king in the land of Israel. When the Israelites entered the land of Canaan at about 1200 B.C. they did not set up a central government with a king. When they did set it up, the attitude of the people toward a king was mixed. Perhaps it was because they had just come from this type of hierarchical leadership in Egypt. Many were not in favor of kings because the kings in Egypt had mistreated them. Many were in favor of kings because they were a people who continually failed and they need a consistent leader. In the past they would almost become extinct before a capable ruler stepped forward to lead them.

The Canaanite religion was based on myths. The Canaanite religion was a nature religion, centered on agriculture, because the cycle needed to be maintained for their survival. A god named Baal was their god of storms and rains. It was a religion of status quo, a religion of keeping things as they are. The economy of the Canaanites required them to have a king, but the Israelites had never depended on a king. God had always been the "King" for the Israelites.

Tribal Israel existed without a king, and God sometimes gave Israel a leader for a required task. The Israelites had no kings, no military, and no centralized hierarchy. The kings, of course, preferred the Canaanite way of doing things because it allowed them to reign as kings. The prophets did not want a king because they wanted to protect the Mosaic way of doing things. Circumcision marked them as belonging to a socioeconomic system and the prophets did not think that the Israelites needed to take another step forward of having a kingdom.

Two social economic systems were present in the area as well as two religions. The religion of Yahweh is a religion of open change. Things can be different, and so the people of Yahweh are sojourners who do not have set places in life because everything changes. Canaanites were in a system of closed things. The Canaanite way could not exist with the Israelite way. The prophets understood that the true way was for the individuals to be liberated, and not to have assigned roles. Thomas Cahill[117] says the cyclical events in the world implies that no event is unique, just as spring comes around every year, every event will continue to be enacted again and again. People would not change their position in life, because change cannot take place if this culture is to survive.

The Exodus desert experience is a story that was written for the world. We liberate ourselves by allowing God to lead us to His rest in his heavenly throne. American slave owners did not want blacks to read the bible, because they knew the blacks would read the Exodus story. The Exodus story of Moses is the center of Afro American tradition, because blacks can directly relate to this biblical story.

Twenty black African captives arrived in Jamestown in 1619, and a faith was born. This faith has wound itself through history. Samuel DeWitt Proctor says that faith strengthened their spines so they could endure the long hard days of labor. Faith put zeal in the souls of the slaves and put light in their minds to keep the vision on God in the forefront of their lives as they hoped for a better day.[118] They wrote songs to express their pain and their hope. The songs were simple but complete. One song was simply a repetition of the words, "Fix me, Jesus fix me." Their songs reminded the blacks of the miracles that God performed through Abraham, Moses, Joshua, Elijah, Daniel and others.

Liberation theology in Latin America says we can be different instead of continuing in a cycle of poverty. Moses talked about openness and unlimited possibilities. Liberation theology tries to upset the inheritance of poverty in a system that says the rich are to remain rich; where kings are kings, and peasants are always peasants. Unfortunately, liberation theology talks too much about now instead of about eternity, so in the long run it fails.

The Israelites were individuals who were part of the community. The bible can only be understood in the context of the family. The individual was not the entity that God had chosen to be the unit of His people. The family was the basic unit that was needed to carry God's people through time. Tribal Israel had a family structure that consisted of three groupings. An individual belonged to each of these three groups. The Israelite community was organized in the following fashion.

1. Bet 'Av "House of the Father" which was the extended family. It consisted of all of the living descendants who were directly under the oldest living male relative. The Bet 'Av was the smallest unit in Israel.

2. Mishpaha is the Hebrew word for clan. The Bet 'Av were grouped in these clans.

3. The tribe was the largest grouping for the Israelites. The people were divided into thirteen tribes.

The Book of Judges has a good example of these groups in the call of Gideon. Judges 6:15 says, But he answered him, "Please, my lord, how can I save Israel? My family is the meanest (weakest) in Manasseh, and I am the most insignificant in my father's house."

Gideon was an individual who was part of a clan that was connected to, the Tribe of Manasseh. He said, "I am the most insignificant in my Bet 'Av." The elders were the living heads of what are called the House of the Fathers. The Bet 'Av shifted when an elder dies, but the clans remain the same.

Also, the verse on the sin of Achan in Joshua 7:1 mentioned Joshua being a member of the household of Carmi, a member of his father's house, and a member of the tribe of Judah. Jericho was conquered by the Israelites when they crossed the Jordan River. Achan took things from Jericho that was dedicated after the Israelites were told to take nothing. The concept of grouping is made more clean when Joshua was told to wait until morning to bring each tribe forward, then to bring the clans of the guilty tribe, then each household of the guilty clan was to be questioned until the individual could be discovered. So to find the one who took articles from the city of Jericho, they first had to find the tribe that was responsible, then which clan in the tribe, then which Bet `Av. Finally, they found which individual did wrong.

The Book of Judges is a story of the downward spiral of the failing of the Israelites, and of God saving them. The Jews failed continually, and God keeps saving them. The biblical history explained how sins got them into bad situations. The greatest sin seems to be because of their involvement in the Canaanite religion and culture. This was why the prophets condemned the kings. Josiah had to clean out the Canaanites from the Temple itself. Josiah had to remove a Baal image of Asherah, Canaanite priests, and Canaanite prostitutes.

There was mixing of idolatry of Baal with the Canaanites. Farmers related to Baal because the idol was an idol of nature. The Israelite people would worship Yahweh but it seemed like they never turned completely away from their old worship of Baal. They attempted to undo the social revolution of Moses, and they almost succeeded in completely messing things up. Today, we still have examples of this. For instance, reading horoscopes seems harmless, but the cumulative effect of similar things can harm a person and a nation. God is dynamic and He lives with his people. The Canaanites knew what was going to happen because they kept the status quo. Their survival depended on everything staying the same. With Moses you did not know what was going to happen, because God lives in a tent. You do not know what God is going to call you to do, so it can be upsetting because we are always unstable. We are pilgrims traveling through history.

A King was chosen for Judah and Israel.

Priests and Judges ruled Israel and they failed continuously. Samuel was a great Judge who succeeded Eli. When Samuel was called by God, he said, "Here I am Lord, your servant hears you."

When Samuel got old, the people saw there were no Judges worthy enough to lead them. Saul was chosen as the first king and he is described as being head and shoulders above everyone else. Later, David was anointed by Samuel as the king of the Israelites was. David would not go against Saul but worked with him, and eventually fled to live with the Philistines because Saul wanted to kill him. When Saul died, his son Ishbaal was made king and he ruled for two years over all of Israel except for Judah. Only the tribes of Judah and Benjamin followed David during the rule of Ishbaal.

The King of Tyre was an ally to King David and he offered great protection for Israel and the trade route through Israel was kept open for the King of Tyre. David brought an empire to the Israelites that are called the Davidic Kingdom. David ruled a mini empire after he defeated Aram Zobah of Damascus and the Arameans became subject to him. He defeated Damascus, Moab, and Ammon, which was east of the Jordan as recorded in 2 Samuel 8 to 10.

David's son Solomon was anointed king by David to succeed him. King Solomon was one of the most splendid and wisest of men. He helped Hirem, and Hirem helped him. He needed Hirem's help because Israel was caught between the powers of adjoining countries. Solomon kept the mini empire intact and ruled the Davidic Kingdom, which extended to the important Euphrates River. Solomon built a Temple to God, which was about one hundred feet in length by about thirty-five feet wide. The warnings of the prophets about the expenses of a king were visualized when Solomon was king. The taxes must have been oppressive to develop all of the projects of King Solomon.

God wanted a king who would follow Him. David would sin but would immediately turn completely from his sin and would focus his whole being back to God. He kept away from idols and led his people in unity. God promised Solomon that He would confer His name upon the temple forever and His heart and eyes would be there always. God said that there would always be someone on the throne from the line of David if he lived in God's presence and followed His commands, ordinances, and statutes and the people must be kept from idols.

The temple provided a central place to worship God in prayer and sacrifice, especially for the annual Passover sacrifice. God was everywhere but He chose one central place of worship. He wanted to ensure unity of His people, to mold the people into realizing the Messiah would die in Jerusalem, and to set apart the people for the world to see, and He wanted to keep the Israelites from not conforming to the ways of the surrounding peoples. God's name was in the temple.

The Davidic Kingdom was established with David and was completed when Solomon finished the Temple. The temple provided a resting-place for the Ark of the Covenant and the temple was fashioned to represent a model of heaven and earth. Solomon represented Wisdom that Jesus is the fulfillment of.

The writer of Kings (including the two books of Samuel) was a brilliant writer. He set two accounts that were like moving screens that ran simultaneously. The writer followed the kings of Israel, and the kings of Judah. The two histories were interjected with stories of prophets sent to help both Israel and Judah. Jerusalem was God's holy city and was separate from both countries just as Washington DC is not part of any individual sate of the union. The writer spoke of prophets who urged unity and the central sacrifice in Jerusalem, which prefigured the Passover of Christ and the institution of the new covenant of the body and blood of Jesus in communion.

The writer also interjected accounts of kings, and people of other countries who interacted with the Israelites and influenced them. The Queen of Sheba even said that she could see that God had blessed Israel. Also, Elijah anointed Hazael as king of Aram at the time of Ahab of Israel.

The writer wrote of the kings of Judah by comparing them to the first king Jeroboam I who failed with God. Jeroboam I did not want unity with Judah, and he set up new places of worship. The kings of Judah were listed with the Queen Mothers who helped them rule. The Queen Mother was exemplified by Bathsheba who the Queen Mother of Solomon. Everyone kneeled before the king and the Queen Mother. Even Solomon is described as having prostrated himself before Bathsheba and setting up a throne at his right hand, which symbolized power.

The United Monarch lasted one hundred years from 1030 B.C. with King Saul to about 930 with the death of Solomon and the rejection of the hardships of King Rehoboam. The divided monarchy lasted from about 930 B.C. with King Rehoboam to 586 B.C. with King Zedekiah of Judah. Babylon defeated the people of Judah. The Kingdom of Israel lasted from about 930 B.C. with King Jeroboam I to about 722 with King Hoshea. Samaria defeated Israel. The Southern Kingdom of Israel lasted about 208 years and there were about nineteen kings during that span of history. There were twelve kings in Judah during the same time period. The Northern Kingdom of Judah lasted about 344 years and there were about nineteen or twenty kings during that longer span of history.

The Book of Numbers (The 12 Tribes)

The Book of Genesis ends with Jacob blessing his sons and telling them what is going to happen to each of them.[119] He speaks to each one individually and talks about each son and sometimes he makes a prophetic statement. The meanings of the names of the twelve Patriarchs tell a story. When the names are listed as Jacob mentions them, the meanings of the names on the list when read from top to bottom tells an interesting story.

Jacob foretells what will happen to each of the Tribes from his twelve descendants. Jacob foretells the supremacy of the tribe of Judah from which comes the Davidic family and ultimately Jesus. Joseph too will be blessed by the "Shepherd, the Rock of Israel ('ebhen yisra'el)." The Messiah was to come through the line of David and some say through the line of Jacob's son Joseph, too. Jesus' stepfather was named Joseph and this was not by coincidence. The genealogy listed below, also tells a story that echoes Isaiah 53, "By his hand he will justify many." Read the meaning of the names from top to bottom and the list becomes a mini gospel of the New Testament.

Table I.

Genesis 49:1 to 27	Meaning of Name
Jacob	Israel
Reuben[120]	Behold a son who has substitutionary seen my misery,
Simeon[121]	one who hears,
Levi[122]	joined
Judah[123]	in thanks and praise
Zebulon[124]	to Yahweh who has brought me a precious gift (dwell)
Issachar[125]	as my payment.
Dan[126]	But I judged to
Gad[127]	cut off the (cut off means capital punishment)
Asher[128]	righteous one
Naphtali[129]	to wrestle
Joseph[130]	the one set apart (blessed) for
Jacob	Israel.
Joseph	Yet, he adds, and
Benjamin[131]	by his hand, he
Joseph	justifies many.

The book of Genesis has lists of genealogies especially for the descendants of Adam, and Jacob. The Book of Numbers begins with genealogies of Jacob's descendants and these lists are also in the book of Deuteronomy. Jacob left the home he lived in with Laban and he took his wives Leah and Rachel. When Jacob pursued Jacob he demanded the return of his idols that had been stolen from him. Jacob unknowingly cursed Rachel when he said to Laban, "But as for your gods, the one you find them with shall not remain alive!"[132] Rachel had stolen the idols and was pregnant with Benjamin. Rachel died giving birth to Benjamin. Jacob may have been scared that he was responsible for Rachel's death. He thought that Benjamin would also die from his curse. Benjamin's name recalls the sad oath of Jacob because the name Benjamin means "oath with uplifted right hand". Rachel wanted to name him *Benoni* which means "son of affliction", which brings to mind the concern of Rachel and Jacob. When Joseph disappeared and Jacob thought he was dead, it was very disconcerting to Jacob. Jacob showed his relief by leaving a double portion of his inheritance to Joseph. The lists mentions the coming of a Messiah interwoven with the oath of Jacob in regard to Laban's idols.

Table: Comparison of Names in the Book of Numbers and the Book of Deuteronomy.

Numbers 1:5 to 15	Meaning of Names	Dt 33:1 to 29	Meaning of Names
Reuben	Behold a son	Reuben	Behold a son
Simeon	An upright & devout man	Judah	in thanks and praise
Judah	thanks and praise	Levi	joined
Issachar	as my compensation	Benjamin	an oath of
Zebulon	A dwelling, God has	Ephraim	double portion given me
Ephraim	double portions	Manasseh	causing to forget.
Manasseh	causing me to forget given me	Zebulon	A dwelling, God has

Benjamin	the oath to	Issachar	as my compensation,
Dan	achieve justice.	Gad	was cut off
Asher	Asher god (idol)	Dan	to achieve justice
Gad	cut off	Naphtali	from the wrestling of
Naphtali	from the one I fought.	Asher	idols.

The names in the genealogy lists tell stories. A good illustration is the comparison of the meanings of the names. Both lists are in the two lists in the Book of Numbers. Numbers 1:5 to 15 has a list of names that is immediately followed by a list of names in Numbers 1:20 to 42. By just changing the position of the name Gad to follow Simeon, the census tells another story. So, instead of reading, "Behold a son, an upright and devout man, thanks and praise for my compensation of a dwelling...." The story in Nm 1:20 to 42 described what happened to the Tribe of Simeon. The genealogy names reads, "Behold a son, an upright and devout man cut off...." The Tribe of Simeon had 59,300 men in the previous census, but many were cut off (killed) from the Tribe of Levi so that the second census counted 22,200 men. The men were killed because they worshipped an idol.[133]

The lists of genealogies could have been one of the ways of how the bible stories were remembered by the Hebrews. They memorized the names of the tribes and they could recall stories by the order of the names. By changing the sequence of one name, the story would change and the events would be recalled. So, the lists of names correspond to the history of the twelve tribes.

The list of names in Numbers 1:5 to 15 includes sons of the patriarchs, and their names also tell stories (See definitions below that are taken from Strong's Concordance). The meaning of the names can be added to the meaning of the patriarch's name. For instance, From Reuben: Behold a son, rock of God and spreader of light.

Table: Meaning of Names in Number 1:5 to 1:15.

Numbers 1:5 to 15	Meaning of Names
From Reuben (Behold a son) Elizur & Shedeur	Rock of God & Spreader of Light
From Simeon Shelumiel, son of Zurishaddai	Peace of God from rock of Almighty
From Judah Nahshon, son of Amminadab	Enchanter from free people
From Issachar Nethanel, son of Zuar	God is given from small
From Zebulun: Eliab, son of Helon	God of his Father is strong
From Ephraim: Elishama, son of Ammihud	God hears people of splendor
From Manasseh: Gamaliel, son of Pedahzur, for the descendants of Joseph;	Reward of God, the Rock has ransomed and will add (justify many).
from Benjamin: Abidan, son of Gideoni;	Father of Judgment from warlike
from Dan: Ahiezer, son of Ammishaddai;	Brother of help from liberal people.
from Asher: Pagiel, son of Ochran;	Accident of God from?
from Gad: Eliasaph, son of Reuel;	God is gatherer of friends of God
from Naphtali: Ahira, son of Enan.	Brother of Wrong from having eyes

The Levites were put under the direction of Aaron and Aaron's sons. The Levites were responsible for the custody of the furnishings of the meeting tent and were put in charge of the duties in the service of the Dwelling. Only Aaron and his descendants were appointed to have charge of the priestly functions. Laymen were not allowed to do duties of the appointed priests.[134] The Levites were given to service to the Lord in place of the first born of each couple.[135] The people of Israel were considered a holy priesthood in the eye of God, but they did not understand their priestly functions. There were certain things that had to be done only by consecrated priests. Two hundred and fifty respected leaders of the community met "and held an assembly against Moses and Aaron, to whom they said, "Enough from you! The whole community, all of them, are holy; the LORD is in their midst. Why then should you set yourselves over the LORD'S congregation?" When Moses heard this, he fell prostrate."[136] Eventually fire consumed the two hundred and fifty leaders and the ground swallowed Dathan, Abiram, Korah and their families and the men of Korah because they had been rebellious in not coming to Moses when he summoned them to answer why they thought they were equivalent to ordained priests. Christians are all priests, prophets and kings.[137] There is also an ordained priesthood with special ministerial functions. The two types of priesthood are not in opposition but in a dynamic role of announcing Jesus to the world.

Chapter eight of the Book of Numbers says the Levites were consecrated to the Lord by being sprinkled with water for remission of their sins, and then by having the whole community lay their hands upon them. The Levites then had to lay their hands on an offering to the Lord. God was beginning to show the people that there is a bridge to Him through the priesthood. The chapter begins with a discussion of setting up the seven lamps made of gold so that their light shines forward. Gold symbolizes divinity, and the seven lamps symbolize God shining His light to lead His people forward. The priests were to be the visible light of the people to lead them forward. We should remember that Jesus is the light of the world, and he told us that we are now the light of the world. "You are the light of the world. A city set on a mountain cannot be hidden. Nor do they light a lamp and then put it under a bushel basket; it is set on a lamp stand, where it gives light to all in the house. Just so, your light must shine before others, that they may see your good deeds and glorify your heavenly Father."[138]

The Book of Numbers describes functions that were foundations to the life of these pilgrims or wayfarers in the desert. These foundations are important for understanding what happens in the remainder of the bible. They are also important for understanding Jesus. Chapter five speaks of recognizing unclean diseases, making restitution for ill-gotten goods, and for dealing with women accused for adultery. Scripture is beginning to describe adultery as a breaking of trust with God. Adultery and Idolatry eventually become synonymous. Chapter six talks about Nazirites

(Nazier) who set themselves apart for the Lord. One thing is that they cannot drink wine, grape juice, or anything that comes from grapevines. Then God teaches Moses how to have Aaron and his sons bless the Israelites, so that God will bless the Israelites when they invoke His name.

> The Lord bless you and keep you!
> May the Lord's face shine upon you, and
> be gracious to you.
> The Lord look kindly upon you and give you peace.[139]

Offerings were then discussed in chapter seven. The leaders of the tribes provided the material means of supporting the service of meeting tent. They honored God by making these offerings. The importance of offerings is emphasized by the fact that an offering to the Lord can be refused by the Church. Moses became very angry with Dathan and Abiram who would not listen to authority of Moses who was a direct representative to God. Moses told the Lord, "Pay no heed to their offering."[140]

Numbers chapter nine reminds the Israelites that Passover is the evening of the fourteenth day of the first religious month that they are to celebrate the Passover. The first religious month corresponds to the seventh month of the non-religious Jewish calendar that was in effect before the Exodus. Those who miss Passover can celebrate it during the fourteenth day of the second month. Passover is the central event of the people and later it was to be when Jesus would die. The Israelites traveled with the Lord. A cloud covered the Dwelling and the Israelites moved camp only when the cloud rose. The cloud had the appearance of a flame at night. The light represents Jesus. "Rising light from High" or Greek "Anatole ex hypsous" is a name for Jesus. Matthew and Luke both speak of 'Anatole' or rising light.[141]

In chapter ten, the Israelites are told to blow a trumpet for moving camp and for religious celebrations, festivals, and feasts. An earthy trumpet horn is used to connect the thoughts of the people to God. Then the Jews depart from Sinai (the mountain of the Lord) until they come to an area near Shittim, which is in the lowlands, northeast of the Dead Sea. They remained there until they crossed the Jordan River to capture Jericho. A lot happened to the Israelites before they camped near Shittim.

After leaving Sinai, the community started to become discontent, and consequently Moses needed help. The spirit of the Lord was on Moses. God took some of the spirit that was on Moses and bestowed it on seventy authoritative elders of the people. The seventy elders immediately spoke with great passion when the spirit entered them. God then showed he was mighty by providing enough quail to feed the entire camp. A wind arose and the camp was filled with quail. However, instead of seeing the power and the goodness of the Lord, many people were filled with greed. The greedy were killed, and the place in the desert was named Kibroth hattaavah, which means "graves of greed".

They then went to Hazeroth where Miriam and Aaron challenged Moses' office. Earlier, the priestly authority was questioned, now Miriam and Aaron question the hierarchy type leadership. They felt that God speaks through others, so that a central office was not necessary. But God distinguishes between prophets whom He speaks to, and to Moses the leader of His community. God wanted one leader who was in charge. As a result of her action, Miriam became a snow-white leper and was cleaned outside of the camp, and then brought back into the community.[142]

The Israelites then went to Paran where Moses sends twelve scouts to reconnoiter the land of Canaan.[143] They returned forty days later with a branch containing a single cluster of grapes. These grapes signify "plenty" in the Promised Land and are a prefiguration of the wine of Jesus' new covenant. The scouts saw fierce people living in the land and most of them became scared. They wanted to walk into a land filled with milk and honey but wanted it to be unpopulated. They lacked faith and seemed to forget that God was with them. Only Caleb wanted to go in and seize the land. The other scouts discouraged the people, saying the land was bad and giant people (Nephlim) were in the land.[144] Joshua and Caleb were found to be righteous, the other scouts were killed

In chapter fifteen of the Book of Numbers, the Jews are told to offer sweet smelling oblations to the Lord and a cake from the first batch of dough. The cake is like the show bread. The sweet smell is symbolic of taking something earthly and to think of it as a bridge between man and God. The Israelites were to put tassels on the corners of their garments to remind them to keep all of the commandments. The hem of their garments is what became important for the Israelites to decorate. When Jesus passed through a crowd, the hem of his garment healed a woman through her faith.[145] The hems of the garments of the Israelites were to be reminders of their faith. The Israelites were then taught to ask forgiveness for sins they unknowingly commit as individuals and as a nation (Gn 15:22). A young bull was offered for these sins. Jesus while hanging on the cross became a sin offering and he uttered the words, "Father forgive them, they know not what they do."[146]

Numbers chapter nineteen says that a red heifer was sacrificed to purify an unclean person. The red heifer was to be free from every blemish and defect and never to have had a yoke on it. The bull was led outside of the camp and was offered east of the camp, and later east of Jerusalem. This offering prefigured Jesus whom was sacrificed east of the city walls. The ashes of the heifer were used to purify water. An unclean person was sprinkled with this water on the third day and on the seventh day. He became clean again on the seventh day. The story of the ashes of the red heifer is needed to understand the wedding of Cana in Chapter two of the Gospel of John. John 2:6, "Now there were six stone water jars there for Jewish ceremonial washings, each holding twenty to thirty gallons." These stone jars were the jars used to hold the purified water spoken of in the Book of Numbers. The Wedding at Cana takes place on the third day of the week. The third day is Tuesday, which was given a double blessing in the creation story in Genesis. John was relating the story to creation so that we will have a proper understanding of the seventh day of rest. Jesus birthed forth a new creation in the Eucharist celebration, which is a marriage. We celebrate our marriage to Jesus the groom and share in the abundance of the Kingdom or God.

They went to the desert of Zin in the first month and they settled at Kadesh. This encampment was filled with events. Miriam, the sister of Moses died and was buried there.[147] In Kadesh they ran out of water and things did not go well for them. They did not go to the Church, instead they grumbled against the Church.

He and Aaron assembled the community in front of the rock, where he said to them, "Listen to me, you rebels! Are we to bring water for you out of this rock?"

Then, raising his hand, Moses struck the rock twice with his staff, and water gushed out in abundance for the community and their livestock to drink.

But the LORD said to Moses and Aaron, "Because you were not faithful to me in showing forth my sanctity before the Israelites, you shall not lead this community into the land I will give them." These are the waters of Meribah, where the Israelites contended against the LORD, and where he revealed his sanctity among them.

Moses struck the rock twice and water of life poured out from the rock. When Moses hit the rock, he did not show the Lords sanctity and this was so serious that Moses was barred from entering the Promised Land.[148] Moses was allowed to see the Promised Land but he died before they entered into it. The act caused a punishment, yet, the text is not real clear as to what brought about the severe pronouncement upon Moses. But, Moses was once told that he would be killed unless he followed the precepts of God. He was to lead the Israelites in a holy way, as a leader that represented God.

Moses was supposed to show the sanctity of God, because he was the head of the Old Testament Church. God expects us to be holy, "Since I, the LORD, brought you up from the land of Egypt that I might be your God, you shall be holy, because I am holy."[149] Not only was he to show the people that God was watching over them, but 1 COR 10:4 to 8 explains that the rock was Jesus, and all drank the same spiritual drink, for they drank from a spiritual rock that followed them, and the rock was the Christ. Yet God was not pleased with most of them, for they were struck down in the desert. These things happened as examples for us, so that we might not desire evil things, as they did. And do not become idolaters, as some of them did, as it is written, "The people sat down to eat and drink, and rose up to revel." Let us not indulge in immorality as some of them did, and twenty three thousand fell within a single day.

As leader of the Old Testament Church, Moses was to show the sanctity to God. But he was also supposed to show sanctity to the living water, which was Jesus.

The Israelites then went to Mount Ho where Aaron died. Aaron's garments were given to his son Ulcer whose names means "helper of God". The office was to continue on, just as Moses' office was to continue on after his death. Joshua entered the Promised Land as the leader, after Moses died.

They then traveled toward the Red Sea bypassing Idiom. The people grew tired of the manna, even complained about it. They were complaining about manna which is food sent from heaven, so venomous snakes bit many of them and they died. Moses made a bronze serpent idol and mounted it on a pole.[150] A person bitten by a snake would look up at the pole and recover. Bronze represents sin, and this prefigures the death of Jesus on a cross.[151] The Gospel of John says, "And just as Moses lifted up the serpent in the desert, so must the Son of Man be lifted up, so that everyone who believes in him may have eternal life."

They then traveled to Both, and then to Abram, and then to the Wad Zeroed, and then camped on the other side of Arson. From Arnon they went to Beer where the Lord said, "Bring the people together and I will give them water."[152] It was at Beer (the name means well) that the tone of the scripture suddenly changes and Israel sings, "spring up, O well! so sing to it...". From Beer they went to Mattanah, to Nahaliel, to Bamoth and onto a cleft in the plateau of Moab overlooking Jeshimon that is on the west side of the Dead Sea. The Israelites defeated the Amorites and settled in their cities. Then they defeated King Og of Bashan at Edrei. They took possession of his land. Chapter twenty-two says that they encamped in the plains of Moab that are on the lowlands northeast of the Dead Sea, and is near Shittim. This was the last place in their desert wanderings. Here they prepared for the crossing of the Jordan River from the East Bank to the West Bank and into the Promised Land.

The lists of names in genealogies are poetic. The numbering of the people in the tribes of Israel is also incredibly enlightening. The Book of Numbers begins with a census and then in Numbers 26:5 to 31 another census was taken. The two census figures are listed below according to the arrangement of the tribes. The Tribe of Reuben that camped south of the central camp became noticeably less populated. Comparison of the two census figures shows that about fifty thousand men reduced Reuben's camp. While the Israelites were camped at Shittim, the men had relations with Moabite women. Worse yet, they participated in their sacrifices to Baal, and they ate of the sacrifices and worshipped this idol. Here, scripture is starting to show the parallel of adultery with idolatry. They are similar transgressions. Twenty four thousand Israelites were killed because of the idolatry, including Zimri, son of Salu who was a prince in the house of the Simeonites.[153] This explains why the Tribe of Simeon decreased so much between the first census and the second census. All three tribes in the camp of Reuben decreased in population, but Simeon had the notable decrease.

Table of Census:

	First Census Nm 2:19	Second census Nm 26:2	Arrangement of the tribes	Meaning of the Names
			Lord	
			Moses	Drawing out (rescued)
			Levi	joined
			Aaron	By the bringer of light
1. East side	74,600	76,500	Judah	in thanks and praise
Towards the sunrise	54,400	64,300	Issachar	as my compensation
	57,400	60,500	Zebulon	A dwelling, God has given me
Camp of Judah	186400	201300		
2. South side	46,500	43,730	Reuben	Behold a son
	59,300	22200[154]	Simeon	Upright and devout
	45,650	40,500	Gad	was cut off
Camp of Reuben	151450	106430		
Center of camp	22,000	23,000	Levi	Joined in
3. West side	40,500	32,500	Ephraim	a double portion
	32,200	52,700	Manasseh	causing to forget
	35,400	45600	Benjamin	An oath of raised right hand
Camp of Ephraim	108100	130,800		
4. North side	62,700	64,400	Dan	To achieve justice
	41,500	53,400	Asher	Of an idol
	53,400	45,400	Naphtali	I have fought
Camp of Dan	157600	163200		
Total registered	603550	601730		

Nm 2:32 This was the census of the Israelites taken by ancestral houses. The total number of those registered by companies in the camps was six

hundred and three thousand five hundred and fifty. Nm 2:33, "The Levites, however, were not registered with the other Israelites, for so the LORD had commanded Moses. The Israelites did just as the LORD had commanded Moses; both in camp and on the march they were in their own divisions, every man according to his clan and his ancestral house."

The first census gives a description of how the camp was set up. Remembering that wording is exact so that the direction north is north and the direction east is east, so that north cannot mean northeast or northwest. The shape of the encampment was that of a cross. The tribe of Dan was to the north and Reuben to the south of the central camp. Both camps were about equal in size having about one hundred and fifty thousand men in each camp. The smaller camp of Ephraim was to the west of the central camp. The camp of Ephraim had about one hundred and eight thousand men compared to the largest camp of Judah to the east, which had about one hundred eighty thousand men. The populations of each arm of the camp was such that when the encampment was seen from above it was in the shape of a cross (See Diagram I). We can visualize the cross traveling across the desert toward the future.

This helps to explain the story of Balaam the prophet who spoke to God. He was not an Israelite; he was from Pethos on the Euphrates. Balak sent for Balaam with the message saying, "Please come and curse this people for us; they are stronger than we are. We may then be able to defeat them and drive them out of the country. For I know that whoever you bless is blessed and whoever you curse is cursed." Four times, Balak sent princes to appeal to Balaam to curse the Israelites. Each time, God told Balak not to curse the Israelites because they were blessed.37

Balaam was able to view the Israelites from the top of the hills. Balaam says to Balak, "How can I curse whom God has not cursed? How denounce whom the LORD has not denounced? For from the top of the crags I see him, from the heights I behold him. Here is a people that lives apart and does not reckon itself among the nations." 38

Balaam probably saw the encampment to be the shape of a cross and knew for certain that God blessed the Israelites.

Diagram I: The camp of the 603,550 Israelites formed a cross. See Numbers 2 chapter 2 and 3 that describes the encampment around the ark.

	North Dan ASHER NAPHTALI 163,200	
Ephraim and MANESSAH BENJAMIN WEST 108100	Merarites Moses Ark Aaron Gershonites Kohathites	Judah, Issachar & Zebulon <div align="right">East 186,400</div>
	RUBEN SIMEON GAD 151,450 SOUTH	

The camp of the Jews was a liturgical movement across the desert. When the Israelites camped, the camp was in the shape of a cross with the Ark in the center of the cross. The south arm of the encampment was broken with the death of the Simeonite people who drastically reduced the size of the camp in the south.

Balak seems to notice the arm of the cross was broken. He thought if Balaam would view the encampment from a different angle that he would see the broken arm and would be willing to curse the Israelites. Balak said, "Please come with me to another place from which you can see only some and not all of them, and from there curse them for me." 39 Balaam may not have perceived the broken arm because of where he was standing. The north arm would have appeared smaller than it actually was because it was farther away from the persons viewing the encampment from the south. Because the north arm was further away, the north and the south arm may have appeared to be the same size; thus the camp formed equal arms of a cross when viewed by Balaam.

This can be easily explained. When you are on top of a mountain, the further away car is or other object is from you, the smaller it seems to be. For instance, a car at the bottom of a mountain pass could appear to be the size of a matchbox when viewed from the summit of a mountain pass. A smaller car would appear larger than the car at the bottom of the mountain if the smaller car was one third of the distance from the bottom of the mountain.

Even, If Balaam knew the arm of the cross was broken, he would have known that God was protecting the Israelites. So, he could not have cursed them. The population in the Israelite encampment was so large that the cross-shaped encampment would have had to have been viewed from directly overhead to notice the broken arm.

The Second Census of the encampment in Nm 26:2 to 51 the south arm of the cross is broken.

	ASHER NAPHTALI 157,600	
Ephraim and MANESSAH BENJAMIN WEST 130,800	Merarites Moses Ark Aaron Gershonites & families Kohathites	Judah, Issachar & Zebulon 201,300 EAST
	RUBEN SIMEON GAD 106,430	

South arm broken

The south arm of the cross-formed by the camp is broken as a result of the deaths from the tribe of Simeon. The cross continued to march on through history. Of course, the march continued with a broken people until God offering Himself on the cross for all of our sins finally broke sin.

Chapter 7: The Book of Numbers (The 12 Tribes)

Covenants

The writers of the Book of Genesis start out slowly as they find an image for Deity. Then God was presented in an active role. Later, God passionately spoke through the Prophets. Eventually, God withdraws and leaves history to humans.

TANAKA is an acronym for the Books of the Torah, the Prophets, and the Writings of the Hebrew Bible. The books of the prophets are at the end of the Old Testament in the Christian Bible. The Prophet writings tell us about the Messiah and the writings lead into the New Testament. The Jews in the Alexandria Order set the Old Testament up in this sequence. Some Jewish scholars say that the Christians developed this order but Jews set the order even if it was during the patriarchal period.

Many people think the ordering of the books in the bible is important. They say that the Christian Bibles and the Jewish Bibles have effects that are different from each other because of the ordering of the books in the bible. However, this effect is apparent only if it is read from cover to cover like a novel. So, ordering of the books may not be important.

The Greek Alexandria tradition of the bible was called the Septuagint. The Greek bible did not enter into the present day Jewish tradition. But the Hebrew tradition of the bible had not initially been considered, because the Greek Jews were the active Jews. So, the Greek bible was the bible that was in use by the Israelites through 100 A.D. The Hebrew language has been recently revived and is a religious language. Aramaic is the language that was spoken during the second Temple period.

The Torah is essential and central to the study of the bible. The Torah has specific commandments and through narrative studies it tells the story of God's plan of salvation. The story is of a relationship between Yahweh and the human community through covenant love. God is, "I was who I was, I am who is, and I will be who I will be." God says, "I am"[155] and He is present to us. If God is real in your life, then you have belief.

Covenant (*Berit*)

Covenant is a cognate that has to do with binding (a fetter). When you are in covenant, you cannot do just anything that you want to do, there is a bond and the bond has requirements. A covenant is an agreement between two parties. Sometimes a covenant is an oath (Alah), like Holy Communion is a renewal of covenant.

God uses "things" to connect us with Himself. A grain sacrifice is a bridge between God and earth. The smoke is a visible bridge between man and the unseen Deity. Scripture further developed the concept to identify prayer to be the actual bridge. The story of Cain and Abel is a story of the tension that was present when there was a change from a pastoral society to an agricultural society. The name Abel (Heb. Hevel) means "breath, vanity, insubstantial, a meaningless and fleeting vapor". The name Cain (Heb. Ka yin) has a form of the word "kaniti" which means "acquired or gained." His mother named him Cain because she was excited and full of hope. Cain became a tiller of soil and Abel became a keeper of sheep.[156] The Lord warned Cain, "if you do what is right, will you not be accepted? But if you do not do what is right, sin is lying down at the opening; it desires to have you, but you must master it."[157]

This was a story of a way of life that was changing, and the change did not make sense to Cain. We live in a world where things happen naturally and they do not seem to be right. We have to realize that God has a good plan for the world, but it is not a narrow focus. God does good in the overall picture and consequently sometimes that means that things do not turn out for us like we think they should. God warned Cain to act properly to what happening in the world.

Names that end in the suffix "ite" are right stage people or desert people, and farmers are left stage people. The two groups always seemed to be in conflict with one another. The desert people were nomadic, so they did not think of what was left behind. The farmers were set and did not like how animals of nomadic people left behind refuge and destroyed the land.

We should never react to what happens in the world. We need to think things through, praise God, and act properly, or we will be in trouble because evil is laying in wait. If we do not have a plan, we will certainly die.

The Ten Commandments are the "ten utterances" or the "ten words". The Tablet of testimony and the Table of covenant became synonyms. The Hebrew word "Hendiboys" means that they were linked as if one. Genesis 21:6 comes after the annunciation of angels to Sara. Sarah then said, "God has given me cause to laugh, and all who hear of it will laugh with me. Who would have told Abraham," she added, "that Sarah would nurse children! Yet I have borne him a son in his old age."

Ancient oaths or covenants followed a pattern:[158] In the third millennium B.C., treaties were characterized by repetition of standard features, so that a stipulation and then a curse followed an oath. Then another oath was spelled out and then was followed by a stipulation and then a curse. This pattern was repeated several times. But in the west, at Ebla, a treaty had a prologue and a curse would be followed by a long list of stipulation, then more curses were invoked. Later treaties from the second and third Millennium follow the patterns of biblical covenants as listed below.

Known treaties are used to determine when Covenants were written. Early second Millennium Treaties from the late Second Millennium Hittite Imperial from Mari and Tell Leilan are comparable to treaties of the Sinai Covenant. The Patriarch treaties (1950 to 1700 B.C.) of Exodus are found in chapters 20 to 31, 34 to 35 & Lv 1 to 7, and 11 to 26.

Structure of Oaths
1. Often times there was an introductory oath at the beginning of a treaty. The title, or preamble (Ex 20:1) was part of the contract (Gn 21:23). There could have been a historical prologue to the oath (Ex 20:2).

2. An oath was asked for (Gn 21:23,26:28) and the stipulations were listed (Ex 20:3 to 17, 21 to 23, 25 to 31.
3. The oath was described or defined (Gn 21:24, 26:31, 31:53) and Ex 35, Lv 1 to 7, 11 to 25).
4. There were witnesses to the oath and then there was a recitation of the deposit of the treaty. Witnesses were sometimes physical (Ex 25:16and stood as a visible sign for future generations, or God could be the witness (Gn 21:23).
5. The treaty was concluded by spelling out a sanction or a curse that would result if either party broke the oath (Lv 26).
7. A celebration often followed the making of a treaty (Gn 21:33). There was a feast, a sacrifice, and a tree planting or exchange of gifts.
8. Blessings were also given (Lv 26).

Examples of early second millennium B.C. oaths were those between Abraham and God,[159] Abraham and Abimelech,[160] and between Jacob and Laban in Genesis 31. These pacts made by the Patriarchs were similar in order and pattern to treaties found in Mari texts and from the Tell Leilan dating to the early second millennium B.C. They differ from earlier treaties of the third Millennium B.C., and from treaties made in the middle part of the Second Millennium B.C.

There were seven parts to an early Second Millennium B.C. oath. First, an introductory oath may be present. Then the oath is demanded, and then the oath is given. Witnesses are usually present when an oath is made. Animals split in two are used as witnesses or warnings to seal the covenant between Abraham and God in Genesis 15. "He answered him, "Bring me a three year old heifer, a three year old she goat, a three year old ram, a turtle dove, and a young pigeon." He brought him all these, split them in two, and placed each half opposite the other; but the birds he did not cut up."[161] Agreements were sometimes made or ratified by both parties walking between the pieces of halved animals. The contracting parties invoked upon themselves a similar fate of the slaughtered animals if they did not keep their word.[162] God gave Abraham a covenant stating that his descendants would inherit the land from the River or Wadis of Egypt to the Euphrates River. This covenant was a gift of God to Abraham with nothing required of Abraham.

God was the witness of the agreement between Abraham and Abimelech.[163] Abraham agreed to respect Abimelech's rights for family succession. Abraham's right to water supplies were also stipulated.[164] "This is why the place is called Beer Sheba; the two took an oath there." God witnessed the contract as a warning to the two parties not to break the agreement. After the agreement is made, there is a ceremonial feast.

A mound of stones is the witness between Jacob and Laban. Gn 31:48 to 49, "Laban said, this heap of stones is a witness between you and me this day." That is why it was called Galeed and also Mizpah, for he said: "The LORD watch between you and me when one of us is concealed from the another.[165]

In the middle part of the second Millennium B.C., the pattern of the treaties changed to a title, followed by witnesses, and then the stipulations were listed. Finally the oath was made and the oath was followed by curses to the party who broke the oath. Treaties and covenants developed further in form and structure in the latter part of the second Millennium. Kitchen says, "Numerous Hittite imperial treaties from the fourteenth and thirteenth B.C. have been found that reflect an elaborate seven fold scheme."[166]

This seven part pattern was characteristic of the Sinai Covenant where God gave Moses the Ten Commandments which were the stipulations of the treaty.

The preamble of the treaty was in Ex 20:1, "Then God delivered all these words (commandments)": then a historical prologue was given in Ex 20:2, "I, the LORD, am your God, who brought you out of the land of Egypt, that place of slavery." The third part is the stipulations, which are the Ten Commandments[167] and the detailed regulations and rules concerning social life[168] and the conditions for the Tabernacle.[169] Services and social norms for the community were discussed further in Lv 1 to 7, and 11 to 25. The fourth part of the treaty described where to deposit or safeguard the covenant. Ex 25:16 says, "In the ark you are to put the commandments which I will give you." Then an altar was built and twelve pillars were erected as witnesses for future generations.[170] Finally, blessings and curses were outlined in chapter 26 of the Book of Leviticus.

This late second Millennium B.C. form for a treaty was also the pattern of the renewal of the Sinai Covenant found in the Books of Deuteronomy 1 to 32 and Joshua 24. Treaties from the First Millennium B.C. were different from the patriarchal treaties, and the covenant treaties, because these later treaties had only four major parts: title, witnesses, curses and stipulations

God is Love, and his covenants with us revolve around love. The Hebrew word used for love is Hesed which actually means "loving kindness" which is Covenant love. Hebrew and Christian covenants are both about Love. The love is Hesed (Alowl) Love with a contract. Contract relationships can be as broad as all humanity but it is Love in Contract. Hesed is not about feelings, it is love that is shown through actions and acting loyally. To love means to act well. God demands Hesed, which is a word that is interpreted to mean "mercy, goodness, loyalty, and kindness. Hesed implies that we have obligations to each other that arise out of friendship. So we should have active concern for others while walking with God.[171]

Covenants were present throughout the lands of the Mideast. We are able to compare the covenants of the bible to covenants of Mesopotamia, the Hittites, Armenians, and Phoenicians.

1. Vassal Treaties were concrete agreements that were made between powerful figures and subjects.

    A. A treaty could have grants to vassals such as land, protection, or grain.

2. Kings also made treaties with their subjects. 2 Sm 5 is a good example of a treaty between the people of Israel with King David.

All the tribes of Israel came to David in Hebron and said: "Here we are, your bone and your flesh. In days past, when Saul was our king, it was you who led the Israelites out and brought them back. And the LORD said to you, 'You shall shepherd my people Israel and shall be commander of Israel.'" When all the elders of Israel came to David in Hebron, King David made an agreement with them there before the LORD, and they anointed him king of Israel.

The contract was between a King and his subjects. The contract was between King David and other tribes in Hebron. Hebron is now in the occupied West Bank, and is central to Palestine autonomy. Hebron was a Davidic city before David established Jerusalem as the center.

The people always cut a covenant in the presence of Yahweh. God has convents with his people. The Israelites recognized one King so they yearly crowned God as King. The crowning implied that an earthly king could only be a vassal under God.

Rule by kings was a big change in history for the Israelites. God had a covenant with his special people the Israelites. At the end of the period of Judges, kings emerged. This was at a time of struggle of the Israelites with the Canaanites. Some scholars say that prophets, leaders like the poet Deborah, ad hoc and others emerged at times when needed by the Israelites. They say that kings were not needed by the Israelites and many say that a hierarchy is still not necessary. But scripture disagrees with these scholars, because the Jewish people continually fell into utter ruin before a leader emerged. For instance, a few women carried on the remnants of the people before Moses stepped forward.[172] A leader came but usually it was to revive the people, not to sustain them. Jesus came to form a covenant that he would be the invisible head and the Church would be his body. He is with the Church in every generation. This allowed the Church to continue through history, triumphantly.

Samuel was the last judge of the Israelites. Samuel resisted the concepts of an earthy king to rule the Israelites. He finally gave in to the wishes of the people and he essentially said, "you want a king, well you'll get one."

The Torah is at the very heart of Hebrew scripture. The Torah is also called the Pentateuch, which consists of the first five books of the Bible from Genesis through Deuteronomy. The Torah is considered a sacred kernel and everything refers back to it.

The Torah or Pentateuch has main Covenants between God and His people.

1. Deity and Adam and Eve had a covenant of marriage. Marriage is a stable and dependable relationship that is contracted. There are specific things spelled out in marriage. Marriage is also a major theme throughout the bible.

2. Deity and Noah formed a New Creation and a Noactic covenant of God promising not to destroy the earth. Humans were to be accountable for obvious rules that needed to be followed. Humans were accountable for bloodshed of animals and other humans, and we were to be protectors of the environment.

3. Deity and the Patriarch Abraham had a covenant that land would be given to his descendants. Abraham's descendants would be blessed, and the covenant from God said that Abraham's descendants would be as numerous as the sands in the sea.

4. Deity and People at Mount Sinai (Mt. Horeb in Deuteronomy) formed another covenant. The people were given commandments and codes to live by. These commandments of 10 words were radical and formed a right way to live. God said He would watch over all that obey His Laws and precepts.

Covenants mark critical junctures of a story. The covenants are critical turning points of history and there is a sign associated with each covenant. Examples are as follows:

Meaning of God's name   Covenant Sign (OT)
1. Yahweh   Adonai, Jews pronounce it as Lord. Seventh day
2. Elohim   Powerful God   Rainbow
                 (El comes from Canaanites)
3. Elshaddai

Powerful mountain God (God who protects) or circumcision.
Shaddai means "breasts or mountains"

Covenants are binding contracts between God and His people. The bible illuminates fully what the covenants mean. For instance, the giving of land to the descendants of Abraham is not as simple as some think. In Gn 12:1, the LORD induced Abraham to move. "Go forth from the land of your kinsfolk and from your father's house to a land that I will show you." But, God did not describe any real estate boundaries. God also told Abraham that He would make him a great nation and would bless him. The nations of the world would be blessed because of him.[173] God told Abraham that his descendants would be as numerous as the stars in the sky. Hebrews 15:8 and 1 Kings 4:20 say that Moses' descendants were as numerous as the sands on the sea and the stars in the sky. These descriptions refer to large armies, and great populations of the time.[174]

God then entered into a covenant with Abraham, and promised him the land from the Wadis of Egypt to the Great River (the Euphrates). According to Gn 15:20, this land was already inhabited by ten other tribes. In Gn 22:17 and 18 God once again told Abraham that he would bless him and make his descendants as countless as the stars of the sky and the sands of the seashore. God said that Abraham's descendants "shall take possession of the gates of their enemies, and in your descendants all the nations of the earth shall find blessing: all this because you obeyed my command." In Genesis 15, a covenant was made, but in this passage God is mentioning that the covenant was conditional and was based on Abraham's faith expressed through his actions. God's people must obey His commands.

God most importantly wanted the Israelites to know that he brought them to Himself. The Israelites thought God was speaking about land, but He spoke of much more. If the people kept God's covenant God said that He would make them special and they would be a kingdom of priests, a holy nation.[175]

One thing that gives the Bible an inner unity, unique of its kind, is the fact that later biblical writings often depend upon earlier ones.[176] These more recent writings allude to older ones, and develop new aspects of meaning sometimes quite different from the original sense. A text may also make explicit reference to older passages, whether it is to deepen their meaning or to make known their fulfillment. Thus it is that the inheritance of the land, promised by God to Abraham for his offspring (EX 15:7, 18), becomes entrance into the sanctuary of God (Ex 15:17),

> And you brought them in and planted them on the mountain of your inheritance, the place where you made your seat, O LORD, the sanctuary, O LORD, which your hands established.

Psalm 142:6 also described the land as a sanctuary or refuge of God, "I cry out to you, LORD, I say, You are my refuge, my portion in the land of the living."

The inheritance is further defined as a participation in God's "rest" (Ps 132:7 to 8) reserved for those who truly have faith (Ps 95:8 to 11; Heb 3:7; 4:11). The inheritance is ultimately entrance into the heavenly sanctuary[177] and eternal inheritance.[178]

The bible tells us that the covenants can be lost if we do not uphold our part of the bargain. For instance Jeremiah wrote that God would withdraw His promises if a covenant were not followed. Jer 2:9 says, "Therefore will I yet accuse you, says the LORD, and even your children's children I will accuse." Then Jeremiah referred to the binding of the covenant God made with Noah, which is a covenant to all of humanity.

> If you can break my covenant with day, and my covenant with night, so that day and night no longer alternate in sequence, then can my covenant with my servant David also be broken? So that he will not have a son to be king upon his throne, and my covenant with the priests of Levi who minister to me.[179]

If days and night no longer follow the normal sequence, it would be a sign that God is breaking the old covenant. The Gospel of Mark, described this type of occurrence, "At noon darkness came over the whole land until three in the afternoon."[180] The prophet Micah also warned of the covenant being lost. There were economic concerns during the time of Micah in the eighth century B.C. There was a wide gulf between the rich and the poor. So, Micah told the people that God was judging them and nature was the witness. God was accusing the people of breaking the covenants. "Hear, then, what the LORD says: Arise, present your plea before the mountains, and let the hills hear your voice! Hear, O mountains, the plea of the LORD, pay attention, O foundations of the earth! For the LORD has a plea against his people, and he enters into trial with Israel.[181]

Micah pointed out to the people that they had broken their covenant relationship with God. He wrote

> O my people, what have I done to you, or how have I wearied you? Answer me! For I brought you up from the land of Egypt, from the place of slavery I released you; And I sent before you Moses, Aaron, and Miriam. My people, remember what Moab's King Balak planned, and how Balaam, the son of Beor, answered him…from Shittim to Gilgal, that you may know the just deeds of the LORD.[182]

Micah told the people what God required from us was *Hesed*, which is Covenant love.

> "With what shall I come before the LORD, and bow before God most high? Shall I come before him with holocausts, with calves a year old? Will the LORD be pleased with thousands of rams, with myriad streams of oil? Shall I give my first born for my crime, the fruit of my body for the sin of my soul? You have been told, O man, what is good, and what the LORD requires of you: Only to do right and to love goodness, and to walk humbly with your God."[183]

Micah 6:9 to16 says that God was removing his protection from the people for breaking the covenant relation. "Hark! The LORD cries to the city. (It is wisdom to fear your name!) Hear O tribe and city council, you whose rich men are full of violence, whose inhabitants speak falsehood with deceitful tongues in their heads! Am I to bear any longer criminal hoarding and the meager ephah that is accursed? Shall I acquit criminal balances, bags of false weights? Rather I will begin to strike you with devastation because of your sins. You shall sow, yet not reap, tread out the olive, yet pour no oil, and the grapes, yet drink no wine. You shall eat, without being satisfied, food that will leave you empty; what you acquire, you cannot save; what you do save, I will deliver up to the sword. You have kept the decrees of Omri, and all the works of the house of Ahab, and you have walked in their counsels; therefore I will deliver you up to ruin, and your citizens to derision; and you shall bear the reproach of the nations."

Isaiah and Jeremiah also wrote that God could recall a covenant.[184] In the Gospel of John, the Pharisees even denied that God was their King. John 19:14 to 15, "It was preparation day for Passover, and it was about noon. And he said to the Jews, 'Behold, your king!' They cried out, 'Take him away, take him away! Crucify him!' Pilate said to them, 'Is it your desire that I crucify your king?' The chief priests answered, 'We have no king but Caesar.'"

Of course, God always picks us up on eagles' wings and brings us to Himself. Jesus gave us a new covenant for the forgiveness of our sins. Jesus is the new covenant and he gives us himself.

Jesus says in Matthew 26:26 to 28, "While they were eating, Jesus took bread, blessed it, broke it, and gave it to his disciples saying, "Take and eat; this is my body." Then he took the cup, gave thanks, and gave it to them. He said, "Drink from it, all of you, for this is my blood of the covenant, which is shed for many for the forgiveness of sins.

Paul described the new covenant in 1 Corinthians 11:23 to 29: 31. Paul passed on the tradition through his apostolic authority. The covenant was written like the early contracts.

1. There was a prologue that described the apostles as the witnesses to the covenant:
   "For I received of the Lord which I also handed on to you,
2. The stipulations were identified.
   That the Lord Jesus, on the night he was betrayed, took bread, and, after he had given thanks, he broke it and said, "Take eat; this is my body which is broken for you. Do this in remembrance of me." After the same manner also the cup, when he had supped, saying,
3. The Covenant was presented.
   "This cup is the new covenant in my blood. This do, as often as you drink it, in remembrance of me."
4. A blessing was presented.
   For as often as you eat this bread and drink the cup, you do show the Lord's death until he comes again.
5. A curse was identified if the Covenant was not maintained properly. Therefore whoever shall eat this bread and drink the cup of the Lord unworthy shall be guilty of the body and blood of the Lord. But let a man examine himself, and so eat of the bread and drink of the cup. For anyone who eats and drinks unworthy, eats and drinks judgment on himself.

The seventeenth Century was one seminal of Western Civilization. In the nineteenth Century the theories of Darwin were circulated and there was the emergence of modern biblical criticism. The two Protestant German scholars, Graff and Wellhausen began what is called biblical criticism. They developed what is called the documentary hypothesis. Their agenda was to discredit certain aspects of Jewish History. However, it can still be a good tool for studying scripture. There are certain inconsistencies, tones, and writing styles in the bible that suggests that different schools influenced the Old Testament. Within the Hebrew bible are various strata that are described as Higher Criticism from 1850 to 1860's.

1. The J (Y German), or Yahwist writers are identified as being from the southern part of Canaan. Hebrew is a dialect of Canaan. Abraham must have spoken Aramaic.
2. E (Elohist) are associated with the northern part of Canaan.
3. P (Priestly strand) was an ancient priest group who was interested in rituals. They included systematic organization for order, and they worked to preserve sacred sources. They can be described as artists who brilliantly wove together the various strands and formed them into books.
4. D (Deuteronomist) wrote the Deuteronomy and the prophetic books that established the covenant relationship as total Love.
5. Redactors (R) were editors in ancient Israel who wove together the strands of scripture. We do not know who they are, but editorial comments are evidence of their influence. For instance, in Genesis there is an editorial comment that the Canaanites were already in the land.
6. Holy Spirit was responsible for the bible being put together as a whole by. His signs are all through the bible.

The Books of Deuteronomy record the best and the worst of religion. The Deuteronomy Books consist of the books of Deuteronomy, Samuel I and II, Joshua, and Kings I and II. They were written before 700 B.C., which was time of the reign of King Josiah after the Northern Kingdom had been decimated in 722 B.C. They Deuteronomists resisted neo Babylonians and the book were composed in a self conscious form addressed on the plains to Israelites. The writings are pleadings to great leaders. The writings are both sublime and debased because they have both the highest spiritual norms interwoven with the worst decimation of the people.

Hebrew Scripture was written in an earthly manner with frank talk about sex. For instance, the story of Joseph with Judah and Tamar is a tale of misconduct. It is a tale of misconduct, sublime and earthly with humans woven into it. So the messiness of life is part of the Hebrew

Scripture. Even the genealogies have a beauty and artistry so they can be appreciated for generations to come.

The books of the Torah have different names in the Hebrew and in Christianity.

Genesis	In the beginning
Exodus	These are the names of the
Leviticus	And He called (God called Moses)
Numbers	In the wilderness of Sinai
Deuteronomy	These are the words Moses spoke to the Israelites

Most ancient texts are composites of many writings. The redactors may have edited and combined material during the fifth century B.C. The books of Ezra and Nehemiah describe the return from the Babylonian Exile and that the Israelites continued following God.

Orthodox Jews and many Christians say that Moses wrote the entire Torah. One reason is that the books of the Torah are a complete stand-alone source. Jesus also referred to the writings as being from Moses in John 1:45, and 5:45 to 46.

> "Philip found Nathaniel and said to him, "We have found him of whom Moses in the law, and the prophets, did write, Jesus, of Nazareth, son of Joseph."

> John 5:45 to 46, "Do not think that I will accuse you before the Father: there is one who accuses you, Moses, in whom you trust. For had you had believed Moses, you would have believed me, because he wrote about me. But if you believe not his writings, how shall you believe my words?"

The Torah was written tersely, it does not explain everything because it is full of holes and gaps. For instance the near sacrifice of Isaac is about a Father who is about to kill his son and yet, all the scripture says is that they walked together. It does not describe what was going on. The spaces were left in the text to allow for endless interpretation or what the Jews call Midrash, which is from the Hebrew root *DRSH* that means, "search out." The bible was written with few words yet they contain a lot of meaning. Midrash is the "creating" of new text. In the silence between the words is the place where God speaks to us.

Sacrifice was normal during the time of Abraham. The angel stops the action of Abraham with the knife and this is a revolutionary action. According to Jews, this signifies that the sacrifice at the altar was to be replaced by prayer. Justin Martyr thought differently, because sacrifices did not end with Abraham, in fact sacrifices went on until about the year 70 A.D. The binding of Isaac is called "Akedah" in Hebrew. It is written in Genesis 22:17 and 18,

> I will bless you abundantly and make your descendants as the stars of heaven and the sands of the seashore; your seed shall take possession of the gates of their enemies, and in your seed shall all the nations of the earth be blessed: because you have obeyed my command.

Then a ram caught in a thicket was offered instead of Isaac. And the ram was the reason for the shower, which is a ram's horn that is blown at the Jewish festival of Rosh Hashanah. We are reminded of God's promise when the shofar is blown. Abraham sees into the distance with his spiritual eyes. Gn 22:13, "As Abraham lifted up his eyes, he saw far off, and behold behind him a ram caught in a thicket by his horns: and Abraham went and took the ram, and offered him up for a burnt offering in the stead of his son."

Jews, today say that the Akedah scene signifies the binding of our faith is important and not Temple sacrifices. The synagogue became the new place of faith where prayer and scripture readings have taken the place of the centralized Temple cult. This theme is continued in the Book of Micah. Prayers are a form of sacrifice. But the prayers of Christians are sacrificial and not directly those of the Israelites.

Justin Martyr wrote that God anticipated all of the sacrifices we offer through the name of Jesus. These are the prayers that Jesus told us to offer.[185] God said to the Israelites, "Oh, that one among you would shut the temple gates to keep you from kindling fire on my altar in vain! I have no pleasure in you, says the LORD of hosts; neither will I accept any sacrifice from your hands,"[186]

The Eucharist with the breaking of the bread and the drinking of the cup of wine is the new offering that is presented by all Christians, throughout the world, and throughout time. The fact that an offering of the mass is continually being celebrated is proof that the offerings are pleasing to Him. This is confirmed with the words, "For from the rising of the sun, even to its setting, my name is great among the nations; And everywhere they bring sacrifice to my name, and a pure offering; For great is my name among the nations, says the LORD of hosts."[187]

Only in Christianity is this prophecy of Micah fulfilled. God speaks to the Jews with these words, "But you behave profanely toward me by thinking the LORD'S table and its offering may be polluted, and its food slighted."[188]

The full meaning of the Akedah or binding of Isaac is grasped when we understand that its purpose was to prepare our minds for the coming Jesus. God's testing of Abraham is often thought of as being horrible because Isaac was to be killed. There are always very important messages in the stories of the bible. Abraham was tested to show the world that he had faithfulness. It was through his only son Isaac that God's promise would come to past. The story first discussed that Abraham was righteous because of faith and then it described Abraham's test of Faith. This was done intentionally so that it would be revealed to us that we should also have faithfulness. This story also showed us how to visualize how Jesus would come as the Lamb of God. In Genesis 22:4 Abraham got sight of the place from afar and said to his servants, "Stay here…we will come back to you." Abraham had faith that they would both return even though he was told to offer Isaac as a sacrifice. Abram knew that God would find a way out of this seemingly impossible situation. Isaac knew that God's promise would be fulfilled that Abraham's line would continue through Isaac.

Jesus said the same thing to his followers that he would come back. These situations may not seem quite the same but more comes to light as the story continues. Genesis 22:6 continues, "Thereupon Abraham took the wood for the holocaust (sacrifice) and laid it on his son Isaac's shoulders, while he himself carried the fire and the knife." In John 19:17, a similar event took place. "So they took Jesus, and carrying the cross himself he comes out to what is named the place of the skull and in Hebrew is called Golgotha. There they crucified him."

Jesus had asked three times that the cup be taken from him if it was God the Father's will. In Genesis 22:7 when Isaac said to his father, Abraham, "Father?" "Yes my son?" Abraham answered. "The fire and wood are here." Isaac said, "but where is the lamb for the burnt offering?" Abraham answered, "God himself will provide the lamb for the burnt offering my son." In John 1:29, when John the Baptist saw Jesus he said, "Look, the Lamb of God, who takes away the sin of the world!" God did say that He himself would provide the lamb, in other words God was the lamb.

In Genesis 22:12, Abram had tied up his son Isaac and put him on top of the wood. The Lord's messenger told Abraham, "Do not lay your hand on the boy." A ram that had been caught in the bushes was sacrificed in Isaac's place. Later, just as Abram said, the lamb provided by God was offered for our sins. Jesus was the Lamb of God who took away the sins of the world and happy are we who come in his presence.

Through Isaac, Genesis 22:16 to 17 says, Abraham's descendants would be as countless as the stars in the sky, and through his seed all nations of the earth would find blessing. Jesus was the seed of Abraham that came through Isaac, Judah and David so that all nations would be blessed. Jesus was put on the cross-made of wood and sacrificed as a Passover Lamb and that is why Jesus was so meek while he was on earth. Lambs are roasted whole and they were formed with two spits in the shape of a cross and Justin tells us that the

Passover lamb is a type of Christ crucified. They anointed their houses in proportion to their faith with the blood of the Passover lamb. Justin tells us that Adam was a house for the spirit, which proceeded from God, and God only permits the lamb of the Passover to be sacrificed in where His name was named. The Temple sacrifice has ceased, and the whole lamb without blemish was a symbol of the suffering of the cross which Jesus would go through.5 Jesus became the sheep sacrificed at Passover for us all.

The blood of bulls, sheep, pigeons and doves could not do it, but the blood of Jesus was the perfect sacrifice for all of our sins. Now, none of us die because we have eternal life with Jesus. What is really great is that he died not only for people in California, Russia, Greece, Argentina and every point from east to west but for everyone in every age. Now, we praise him and everyone from east to west and age to age make a perfect thanksgiving to him. Scripture says that we were imprisoned in sin at no price, so that our heavy chains had to be removed at no monetary cost. The price for our salvation was the Son of God. This fulfills the prophecy of Isaiah 52:3, which says, "You were sold for nothing and without money you shall be redeemed." The yoke of Jesus is light and his way is easy and in him we find rest.[189]

Isaiah 53 says, "He (Jesus) grew up like a root out of dry ground. Surely he took our infirmities and carried our sorrows. But he was pierced for our transgressions and crushed for our inequities. The punishment that brought us peace was upon him, and by his stripes (wounds) we are healed." Isaiah 53 also describes why Jesus was rejected and why he suffered. In Psalm 22 it is written about his crucifixion. Jesus' first words on the cross were the first words in Psalm 22, "My God, my God, why have you forsaken me." Jesus' last words on the cross are also the last words in Psalm 22; "It is finished".

John 19:28 describes other details of his dying at Passover and dying without broken bones or other imperfections as was required of the Passover lamb described in Genesis 12:5. He was striped with a whip, carried his own cross, pierced with a spear and bled water and blood. He was crucified with the poor and sinful and his spirit left before the day was over, and he was buried in a rich tomb. Isaac carried the wood on his back and was later put on the wood. There is no other mention of Isaac until the servant brings Rebecca to Isaac her groom.[190] The servant represents the Holy Spirit bringing Rebecca who represents the Church. The Church is the bride, and Jesus is the bridegroom.

Through this scripture story, God told the people thousands of years ago that the sacrificial lamb would be provided by God. He would carry the wood of the cross and he would be put on it to be the perfect lamb sacrificed not only for our sins, but so that we could always be with Him. In the same way, we remember Him at every mass. And we ask Christ to cleanse our hearts, to create in us a new heart, so that he will continue to dwell in us.

A change in our heart is all that is needed for an incredible happiness. God will cleanse our hearts to purge ourselves of malice, competition, and bad thoughts.

Important Definitions:

Hebrew Word	*Definition*
Beirut	Covenant (Pact)
Edut	Testimony
Alah	Oath
Vassal Treaty	Treaty of powerful figure with subjects.
Royal Grant	Something given by King.
Covenant Love	Love with actions
Hesed	Covenant love

Shabbot is the Hebrew word for 'Sabbath'. Sabbath is a sign forever of the covenant between God and the people of Israel. Shabbot recalls the creation of the world where God rested and we join Him to be fully at rest with Him in our body and our soul".

Sub Section: Wisdom Literature

Chapter 8: Overview of the Wisdom Literature

Geographical context, historical context and the cultural context must be taken into account when studying wisdom literature. Context is a very important word in Christianity. The true meaning of a passage can only be understood when it is read in context. We are open to different ways of studying and reading the bible so that we can get to the real message.

Context helps us understand what we read. For instance, repeating the word hey with a different inflection and tone of the voice will give a different meaning each time it is repeated. First, it can be a means of getting attention or calling someone when there is a pause between each word. Second, it can be a means of expressing anger when the words are said loudly. When speaking the word in a nice manner it would express a question, or an exclamation. Another example of context is saying the word "you." When the word is pronounced it could have several meanings. It could be used in a sentence to refer to a certain person or it could be in reference to someone nearby. The word "you" could also be plural for both individuals. The true meaning could only be understood by seeing who the speaking is looking at or gesturing toward. We cannot hear the words or see the gestures of the original writer. So, we must understand the geography, the history, and the culture of a passage in scripture

The geographical context of the bible consists of the Holy lands and the areas surrounding them. The Holy lands are often referred to as the fifth gospels because walking in the holy lands makes the gospel more open and more near to us. Judaism, the Islamic faith, and Christianity come from this region. Israel is only fifty miles wide and one hundred and fifty miles in length. Israel has five geographical regions and yet most of the bible is written in this small region.

There are varieties in elevation ranges from 9200 feet Mt. Hermon to the Dead Sea 1300 feet below sea level. The Dead Sea is also ten times saltier than the ocean. There are also great varieties in climate because of the moisture differences. There are only three inches of rain a year in the south and west areas of Israel compared to forty inches of rain on Mt. Hermon. Parts of Israel have winds so strong that they can be described as darkening the world.

The vegetation is varied with trees having roots one hundred feet in length. The forests were destroyed during the Turkish period about four hundred years ago because the Jews were required to pay tax on each tree. They cut down most trees and only fruit bearing trees were kept alive. Many varieties of plants are peculiar to Israel. Studies of the Shroud of Turin described many plants that grow only in Israel.

Animal life has always flourished in the Fertile Crescent where Asia and Africa and the Modest come together. There are many varieties of sheep, goat, camel, and fish.

The geology includes the Jordan rift that extends from Turkey to Uganda in the African continent. Volcanic soil, chalk, silks, and other varieties of soil are present. The deserts are different in intensity, rock formation, and soil quality. Those who lived in the desert knew that life was not predictable. The climate and geology of the desert brought forth an exhausting life style. There are temperature differences of forty degrees a day, and nutrition is poor. Life is difficult, it is not easy, and hard work is required to survive in the deserts. These thoughts were instilled in their bones. Life was not predictable so the people who lived in the desert had to have a strong fiber of life.

Israel is the only land bridge between these three continents; consequently, there are over fifty-five recorded major invasions in this region.

The Spirit sent Jesus into the desert, and most of the Gospel took place near the desert and not the sea. An Agricultural way of life caused people to think in terms of life cycles, with ritual cycles of prayer and worship that provided a sense of being one with the Universe. There are still people whose government, religion, life style, and culture in these desert regions are almost identical to those of three thousand years ago. Today, Hebron is like a window into history. Many shops have been in families for hundreds or even thousands of years. There is a real sense of tradition in the region where the bible takes place.

The Cultural Context of Wisdom Literature:

Wisdom literature is one of the oldest literary forms known. There is wisdom literature that was written in Egypt over three thousand years ago. And we have the literary form that was written at least two thousand years ago in Mesopotamia.

Wisdom literature crosses cultural and religious boundaries. The writings are collections of sayings that were written for young men. Men were taught how to live. The head of the household was responsible for the entire household. So, the majority of the sayings are addressed to "my son." Wisdom and morality are not necessarily the same now, as they were when the literature was written. Wisdom literature says sometimes that the end justifies the means. Jesus even praised the manager who cheated his boss out of money. This is a different type of morality.

Wisdom literature began as oral literature. Many scholars think that it was in the post exile era when it was put into the bible. Wisdom has as the primary focus "life." It describes how to live life well and how to live life to the fullest. Tradition of One God was emphasized. Israelites took the feeling of the wisdom literature of others and fit them into their own culture.

There is a relationship between wisdom and the prophets. The prophets had a great respect in the tradition of Israel. Sayings influenced wise prophets on how to live their lives to God and this ultimately led to Wisdom Literature. The prophets also founded the Apoletic literature. They had an effect on other literature, as well. Cultic priests and wise teachers were also important.

Wisdom was oracular and the verses were easy to memorize one at a time, yet a person could spend a year meditating on one proverb. Wisdom literature teaches us the natural order of God in the world. Religion and literature is joined together in these writings.

Wisdom literature was also passed on in schools as well as from wise man to boys. Literature and teachings in the courts of kings were passed on to the wealthy, and eventually to the poor. Wisdom is our response to reality, dealing with what is. Reality was divided into natural occurrences of the sun, wind, crop cycles, and human interrelationships. Wisdom occupied a place in Israel and it influenced literature that influenced people. Wisdom touched, affected, and transformed people who did the same to the literature. Wisdom literature was not unique to the Israelites, however they brought Yahweh into it as not only the source of Wisdom but as Wisdom Himself.

The Cultural Context of Scriptures.
There were five elements to the culture during the time period described in the scriptures.
1. The people of the Mid East lived in harmony with nature. Some people want to give up their selves to nature as the Islamic people do. Some want to be master of and they want to subordinate nature to make it work for us, like most of the western civilization. People can live with nature and this concept is important in the culture of the Mid East
2. How we relate to each other is important. There are three ways to make decisions.
    a. The elders who have the only voice make decisions.
    b. Decision-making can be collateral where everyone has an opportunity to speak.
    c. Decisions can be individual or one voice as in America.
3. How we approach the way we do our activities. An approach to being can be one of seeing the moment as it is. Being can be thought of as becoming whole and it is in a process. This is part of the Mid East thought process. In North America, we are dynamic and most of us try to use every minute. We do not want to waste any time, so we are too busy.
4. Mid Eastern people see mankind as being basically good. The book of Genesis appealed to the good of the human heart.
    Some groups of people see human nature as bad or evil, and nothing is thought to be redeemable. Rulers try to get people to flip into their dark

sides instead of thinking in terms of peace and even tolerance. In North America we try to remain neutral with a balance of the other two groups.
5. How we view time will also affect our culture.
   1. Mid Eastern people remember people and events of the past.
   2. There are those who only live for now, they live for the moment. They work for a couple of hours a day and they spend much time in planning but they never plant crops for the future. People who live only for the present will plant only what they will eat for the coming season.
   3. The third group thinks of the future by planning ahead.

Aborigines spend seventy five percent of their day dreaming instead of working. Their outlook on life is that planning is the central importance of life. More cultures follow the Mediterranean cultures that dwell on the past.

We cannot read scripture from an individual mind set, because they were written from a community point of view. Christians and Jews are saved together and they sin together. Grace, when you are blessed then you can share the blessing and grace. Deconstruction offers no value to a Christian. We cannot say there is no difference when we read the bible literally.

Mid Eastern people have different ways of looking at ones cultural system than most American people. American Indians have many similarities to Mid Eastern Culture. Culture is a system of symbols, relating to and embracing people, things, and events that are socially symbolized or meaningful. The way Mid Eastern people live culturally is the way that the Christian community is supposed to live, or at least to read the bible.

Christians are gathered together not only by miracles and good, but also by suffering and oppression. We are to rise above family, politics, economics, and social systems. We are to plan and build for the Kingdom. We should rise above nationalism and look to God. We are to build our family, our governments and our social and economic concerns on the Divine call.

Table: Cultural comparisons of the United States and the Mediterranean Area.

U.S. Citizens	Mediterranean People
Egocentric identity having primary responsibility to ourselves and to the individual potential.	Group centric identity having primary obligation to others in support of common expectations.
Group membership results from a renewable contract and it promotes independence.	Group memberships results from one's inherited social and familiar place in society to promote in society to promote interdependence
Citizens view the parts	Citizens view the whole
Urge uniqueness of the individual. Seek autonomy to form social connection	Urge conformity for the common good by integration into social reality so the community is a save shelter.
Behavior is governed by rights and duties specified by one's personal goals. We do whatever we are not limited to.	Behavior is dictated by the group's causes and sanctions or the leaders authority.
Individual worth is based on individual achievements or individual possessions.	Individual worth is rooted in familial status, social position, class, or caste.
An individual strives for status. Individuals make their own decisions, even if they are not in the group's best interest.	Status is ascribed, and any personal decision is made in consultation with the group and often in obedience or deference to its will.
Achieving and competing are motivational necessities and are the norm.	Achieving and competing are disruptive to the group.
Equality is a key value	Hierarchy is the key value
Friendships are functional to help each other.	Friendships involve long term loyalties or commitments for common expectations.
Any group is viewed as only a collection of individuals formed for encouragement.	Any group is viewed as an organic unit, inextricably interlocked.
The individual is often viewed as an entity separate from the physical world and from other people so that there is planned achievement.	The individual self is viewed as organically connected with the physical world and with other persons. There is self-interdependent collaboration.
Private autonomy, usually with strong personal identity. But, many cultures do promote a strong family identity.	Corporate solidarity with strong familial identity.
Strong desire to be personally satisfied, we look forward to what is to come.	Strong desires to be interpersonally satisfied or satisfactory.

There were traditional peasant societies during the time of the Old Testament era. They found comfort in the status quo and their tradition was a safety net, a comfort. They got their protection from a God who cared. Society was stratified with upper and lower classes and it was thought that this was God's will.

A patriarchal society existed where even women oppressed other woman because they thought that everyone had to stay in their place. Roles were well defined so males and females knew what to do and what was expected of them. This attitude was a safe way to live because it was predictable.

The story of Mary and Martha is a story about Mary saying that she wanted to be a disciple, and Martha being ashamed because Mary wanted to be a disciple. Mary was breaking with the tradition. Jesus said that it was okay because males and females are equal.[191] Breaking bread together was an important step toward equality because men and women did not eat together. Jesus had them eat God's meal together and this was a great way to begin the change in the thinking of the time.

Tribal society was the dominant way of life. Everything was done for the family or kin and a person always redeemed his family's name. When Tamar was raped, they were ashamed because their family name was at stake.[192] The ultimate in human pain and suffering during the Old Testament times would have been to be ostracized from you family. They had a strong group mentality and they stuck together through both good times and oppression. It was rare for a person to be cast out from the family.

Stories were a way of holding on to concepts. Because society was so stratified, there were no major inventions except for the invention of chariots. The core Mediterranean value is honor and shame. A person wants more honor and as little shame as possible for your family. Loyalty is important and a person would give his life for the good of the group.

The Culture of Marriage

The culture of Marriage was also important. Men usually married by the age of eighteen and women married by early teens with an average age of about twelve and a half years of age. Bedouin tribes would put a flag up in their tents to let people know that they had an available daughter. If the family considered a woman to be inferior to the son, the father would make a public avowal. He would break open a piece of fruit in public and this would shame the woman. The betrothal usually lasted about one year. When the marriage day arrived, it was a tribal affair and a celebration that lasted one to two weeks and was very expensive. A fatted calf was prepared from the time of the birth of a child to be slaughtered for a marriage or an important event.

The wedding was ceremonial more than religious was. A pomegranate was broken up at the wedding celebration to symbolize that children were a blessing to everyone. Life was not just about the individual, but how an individual's actions influenced the community, or society. Song of Songs 1:7, says to love long in the name of tribe. It is about God speaking to His people. Paul wrote that marriage is an image of what happens between God and his people. There was always a vibrant, gut moving relationship between God and Israel.

Overview of the Wisdom Literature:

The English word Wisdom is *Hokma* in Hebrew and *Sophia* in Greek. Wisdom literature has an international flair (see Proverbs 30 & 31, and Job). There was a sharing of the Wisdom of Solomon with the people in the east.

1. The Temple was the center of worship and a place for the world to see the power of the Lord. Chapters eight and nine of 1 Kings described the righteousness that came as a result of Wisdom. God would dwell

in the Temple in Jerusalem if we would follow His Laws and precepts. The central worship also prescribed a liturgy to be followed.
2. Solomon's knowledge of plants and animals was described in Job 38, 1 to 31 (attributed to Solomon who knew plants and animals and their names).
3. Theological issues were addressed in Proverbs 8, & Sirach (Ecclesiastes). A message of Wisdom literature was experiential wisdom of the tribe or the family, collective praying, and responding to what was learned. This learning was passed on to other nations.

Each wisdom book has its own history because each clan had sayings that were wise. Later, court schools had more technical teachings, and eventually scribes were used teach the wisdom. . Chapters 44 to 50 of the Book of Sirach and the Book of Wisdom chapters 10 to 19 are the only exceptions to the standard wisdom literature.

Thee Psalms are credited to David, and Wisdom literature is credited to Solomon. It is doubtful that Solomon authored the three wisdom books that he is supposed to have authored. But the books claim his influence.

Egyptian and Mesopotamia literature had an influence on the writings of wisdom literature. The Egyptian Amen em Opet is an ancient wisdom book, and it seems that thirty chapters were adapted from it for Wisdom 22:17 to 24: 22. They put their own Palestinian influence on it and added Yahweh to the wisdom, but is thought to have been taken from the Egyptian work.

Types of wisdom included the Mashal, fables, riddles, and wise men that wrote proverbs.

I. A Mashal is a proverb or oracular saying used with different senses. It can be broken down into other units
1. Proverb had one line
2. Polished Aphorism

Proverbs 10:1 to 22 is an example of a Mashal and is as follows:

The Proverbs of Solomon: A wise son makes his father glad, but a foolish son is a grief to his mother.

Ill-gotten treasures profit nothing, but virtue saves from death.

The LORD permits not the just to hunger, but the craving of the wicked he thwarts.

The slack hand impoverishes, but the hand of the diligent enriches.

A son who fills the granaries in summer is a credit; a son who slumbers during harvest, a disgrace.

Blessings are for the head of the just, but a rod for the back of the fool.

The memory of the just will be blessed, but the name of the wicked will rot.

A wise man heeds commands, but a prating fool will be overthrown.

He who walks honestly walks securely, but he whose ways are crooked will fare badly.

He who winks at a fault causes trouble, but he who frankly reproves promotes peace.

A fountain of life is the mouth of the just, but the mouth of the wicked conceals violence.

Hatred stirs up disputes, but love covers all offenses.

On the lips of the intelligent is found wisdom, (but the mouth of the wicked conceals violence).

Wise men store up knowledge, but the mouth of a fool is imminent ruin.

The rich man's wealth is his strong city; the ruination of the lowly is their poverty.

The just man's recompense leads to life, the gains of the wicked, to sin.

A path to life is his that heeds admonition, but he who disregards reproof goes astray.

It is the lips of the liar that conceal hostility; but he who spreads accusations is a fool.

Where words are many, sin is not wanting; but he who restrains his lips does well.

Like choice silver is the just man's tongue; the heart of the wicked is of little worth.

The just man's lips nourish many, but fools die for want of sense.

It is the LORD'S blessing that brings wealth, and no effort can substitute for it.

you will take up this taunt song against the king of Babylon: How the oppressor has reached his end! How the turmoil is stilled!

2. Ezekiel 10:1 to 17 is an example of an allegory that was used in Wisdom Literature. An allegory was a way of about a spiritual meaning through material forms

Son of man, proposes a riddle, and speaks this proverb to the house of Israel:

Thus speaks the Lord GOD: The great eagle, with great wings, with long pinions, with thick plumage, many hued, came to Lebanon. He took the crest of the cedar, tearing off its topmost branch, and brought it to a land of tradesmen, set it in a city of merchants.

Then he took some seed of the land, and planted it in a seed bed; A shoot by plentiful waters, like a willow he placed it,

To sprout and grow up a vine, dense and low lying, Its branches turned toward him, its roots lying under him. Thus it became a vine, produced branches and put forth shoots.

But there was another great eagle, great of wing, rich in plumage; To him this vine bent its roots, sent out its branches, That he might water it more freely than the bed where it was planted.

In a fertile field by plentiful waters it was planted, to grow branches, bear fruit, and become a majestic vine.

Say: Thus says the Lord GOD: Can it prosper? Will he not rather tear it out by the roots and strip off its fruit, so that all its green growth will wither when he pulls it up by the roots? (No need of a mighty arm or many people to do this.)

True, it is planted, but will it prosper? Will it not rather wither, when touched by the east wind, in the bed where it grew?

3. Job was described as taking up his own parable in Job 27:1.
II. Fables were used in Wisdom Literature.
II Kings 4:9 and Judges 9:8 to 15 are two examples of ancient fables that still survive.

8 The trees went forth to anoint a king over them; and they said to the olive tree, 'You reign over us.'

9 But the olive tree said to them, 'Should I leave my fatness, wherewith by me they honor God and Man, and go to be promoted over the trees?'

10 Then the trees said to the fig tree, 'Come; you reign over us!'

11 But the fig tree answered them, 'Must I give up my sweetness and my good fruit, and to go be promoted over the trees?'

12 Then the trees said to the vine, 'Come you, and reign over us.'

13 But the vine answered them, 'Must I give up my wine that cheers God and men, and go to wave over the trees?'

14 Then said all the trees to the bramble, 'Come thou, and reign over us."

15 The bramble said to the trees, 'if in truth you anoint me king over you, come and put your trust in my shadow: and if not, let fire come out of the bramble, and devour the dears of Lebanon.

III. Riddles were used in Wisdom Literature.
Wisdom Poetry or Didactic Poetry has a style found in Proverbs 9:1 to 6 is.
The Queen of Sheba came with riddles or hard questions to test Solomon's wisdom, but we do not have any examples of these writings. Perhaps Judges 14:12 to 17 is one example.

> Samson said to them, "Let me propose a riddle to you. If within the seven days of the feast you solve it for me successfully, I will give you thirty linen tunics and thirty sets of garments.

> But if you cannot answer it for me, you must give me thirty tunics and thirty sets of garments." "Propose your riddle," they responded; "we will listen to it."

> So he said to them, "Out of the eater came forth food, and out of the strong came forth sweetness." After three days' failure to answer the riddle,

they said on the fourth day to Samson's wife, "Coax your husband to answer the riddle for us, or we will burn you and your family. Did you invite us here to reduce us to poverty?"

At Samson's side, his wife wept and said, "You must hate me; you do not love me, for you have proposed a riddle to my countrymen, but have not told me the answer." He said to her, "If I have not told it even to my father or my mother, must I tell it to you?"

But she wept beside him during the seven days the feast lasted. On the seventh day, since she importuned him, he told her the answer, and she explained the riddle to her countrymen.

Judges 14:18, The men of the city said to him on the seventh day before the sun went down, "What is sweeter than honey? What is stronger than a lion?" And he said to them, "If you had not plowed with my heifer, you would not have found out my riddle."

IV. The Wisdom literature can be found in most of Job, and Proverbs 1 to 9, and wisdom Psalms 1 & 37.

The Wise Men and their Wisdom:

In Hebrew scripture there are different groups of people who are called wise.

I. Craftsmen whose wisdom was doing their jobs well were called wise. Weavers, stone cutters, and other craftsman were also in this category (see Ex 31:2 to 6). Women in mourning were professionals who were considered wise. Jeremiah 9:17 describes these professional mourners. Proverbs 9:36 describes both ants, and badgers as being wise.

II. Royal counselors with sound judgment and political savvy who gave council to Kings and elders are described as having wisdom. Not what you know but how you apply knowledge. Beginning with II Samuel 15:31 is an example of wisdom. Also, Judges 5:28 to 30 where Solomon is fit in is an example of shrewd native wisdom.

III. Occultist: Joseph's (Gn 40) ability to interpret dreams, as was Daniel is called wisdom. Daniel 1:17 says he had every manner and wisdom that was ten times better than others was Daniel.

IV. The wise men of Proverbs

Recorded, organized, and preserved saying that they wrote themselves and taught others. They had honor along with priests and prophets. How can the good life be achieved? Manual of good conducts (not a manual of morality that we understand today). Human centered, Loyalty, Honor are good. Laziness, drunkenness, etc. are bad. Reward or prosperity, honor, and long life are good for the whole.

If you do something bad against God's law, God will punish you. Job and the ecclesiastical writings are two books that question this. Fear of the Lord is described in Proverbs 1:7, 2:6, and 9:10. Ultimately Wisdom comes from God and He gives us the wisdom to live a worthwhile life.

Sirach or Ecclesiastes, theory of Justice is undying, Wisdom or Justice leads to life even beyond the grave.

The second aspect of Wisdom theology is Creation. Creation is the source of Wisdom. Experiences of the world were for Israel, always-Divine experiences as well. God's acts were always experience for Israel. Nature/Super Nature has no separation in Wisdom writings. They are one and the same.

Proverbs 1, 8, 9 & Wisdom 7 to 9. She threatens enemies, laughs at doom, and offers protects for those who follow her. Lady Wisdom is a personified communication of God through creation to human beings.

The Book of Proverbs is a book of Wisdom that was compiled and transmitted to others. First it is a collection of passages strung together. Second, the book followed Egyptian prototypes; this is especially true in Proverbs 1 to 9, and the Book of Ecclesiastes. Third, the proverbs are thematic with one central theme. An example is found in Proverbs chapter 31. This proverb deals with the qualities of a woman of God.

> Proverbs 31:10, Who can find a virtuous woman? For her price is far above rubies.

11 The heart of her husband does safely trust in her, so that he shall have no need of riches.

12 She will do him good and not evil all the days of his life.

13 She seeks wool, and flax, and works willingly with her hands.

14 She is like the merchants' ships, she brings her provisions from afar.

15 She rises while it is yet night, and gives food to her household, and a portion to her maidens.

16 She picks out a field and buys it; out of her own earnings she plants a vineyard.

17 She grits her loins with strength, and strengthens her arms.

18 She knows her merchandise is good; at night her lamp does not go out.

19 She lays her hands to the spindle, and her hands hold the distaff.

20 She stretches out her hands to the poor, and reaches forth her arms to the needy.

21 She is not afraid of the snow for her household; for all her household are clothed with scarlet.

22 She makes herself coverings of tapestry; her clothing are silk and purple.

23 Her husband is known at the city gates where he sits with the elders of the land.

24 She makes fine garments and sells them, and stocks the merchants with belts.

25 Strength and honor are her clothing, and she shell rejoice in the days to come.

26 She opens her mouth with wisdom, and on her tongue is the law of kindness.

27 She watches well the ways of her household, and eats not the bread of idleness.

28 Her children rise up and call her blessed; her husband, too, and he praises her.

29 "My daughters have done virtuously, but you have excelled them all."

30 Favor is deceitful and beauty fleeting; but the woman who fears the LORD shell be praised.

31 Give her of the fruit of her hands; and let her own works praise her in the gates.

Carefully thought out literary composition used only occasionally, individual creation of author such as the book of Job.
5. Wisdom literature tells us that you can't master life or control it.
6. There is a deep respect for nature in the wisdom writings.

A. Book of Proverbs:

I Kings gives the impression that the Book of Proverbs was from Solomon but it is thought that some proverbs were written 3000 years before Solomon and some proverbs were written after his death.
There are five sections to the Book of Proverbs.

I. Chapters 1 to 9 make up a collection of proverbs that sets the stage for the rest of the book. For instance chapter 3 gives the type of wisdom to be passed on to a son.

1. My son, forget not my teaching, keep in mind my commandments

2 Length of days, and long life, and peace, shall they add to you.

3 Let not mercy and faith leave you; bind them around your neck; write them on the table of your heart:

4 Then will you find favor and good understanding before God and man.

5 Trust in the LORD with all your heart, and depart from evil;

6 In all your ways acknowledge him, and he will make straight your paths.

7 Be not wise in your own eyes, fear the LORD and depart from evil;

8 This will mean health for your naval and marrow for your bones.

9 Honor the LORD with your substance, with first fruits of all your produce;

10 so shall your barns be filled with grain, and your presses shall burst out with new wine.

11 My son, despise not the chastening of the Lord; neither be weary of his corrections.

12 For whom the Lord loves he corrects, even as a father the son he is delighted with.

13 Happy the man who finds wisdom, the man who gains understanding!

14 For her profit is better than profit in silver, and better than gold is her revenue;

15 She is more precious than rubies, and all the things you can desire are not to be compared unto her.

This type of proverbial saying is an aphorism; the two lines play with each other to help us memorize them by new refrains.

2. Proverbs 10 to 22 are called the Proverbs of Solomon. Proverb 10:1 says, "The Proverbs of Solomon: A wise son makes his father glad, but a foolish son is a grief to his mother."

This is an example of straight Proverbs where good is lifted up and this is what you want to learn to be wise.

3. Proverbs are described as being sayings of the wise: See chapter 22:17 to chapter 24:22. For instance Proverb 22:19 says, "That your trust may be in the LORD, I make known to you the words of Amen em Ope." There was an Egyptian scribe named Amen em Ope and so it is thought that these proverbs are probably from Egyptian writings.

4. Chapter 24:23 to chapter 34 is a short section of verses. They may have been added from another collection of proverbs.

5. More Proverbs of Solomon are found in chapter 25 to chapter to chapter 29. Chapter 25:1 tells us that the men of Hezekiah, king of Judah copied these sayings down. Chapter 25:8 is an example of Wisdom discourse, "Do not go hastily to strife, for what will you do in the end, when your neighbor puts you to shame?

26:14 & 16 are descriptions of laziness being considered bad. Laziness was bad because it was so difficult to survive during those times but also for the reasons cited.

Proverbs 26:14, The door turns on its hinges, the sluggard, on his bed!

Proverbs 26:15, "The sluggard loses his hand in the dish; he is too weary to lift it to his mouth.

6. The Words of the Son are found in Chapter 30. The writings are attributed to Agur son of Jakeh who is said to have spoken the words to Ithiel and Ucal.

> 1 The words of Agur, son of Jakeh the Massaite: The pronouncement of mortal man: "I am not God; I am not God, that I should prevail.
>
> 2 Surely I am more brutish than any man, and have not the understanding of a man.
>
> 3 Neither have I learned wisdom, nor have I the knowledge of the Holy One.
>
> 4 Who has ascended up to heaven and come down again who has gathered the wind in his fists? Who has bound up the waters in a garment? Who has marked out all the ends of the earth? What is his name, and what is his son's name, if you can tell?"
>
> 5 Every word of God is tested; he is a shield to those who put their trust in him.
>
> 6 Add nothing to his words, lest he reprove you, and you be found a liar.

This is an example of an oracle, which is a prophecy or a revelation. Agur, like Job 38 to 39 wants us to know of man's insignificance in comparison to God. Ignatius tells us that the words in verse four are descriptive of Jesus as part of the Trinity.3 This is also a place in the bible where inclusive language would prevent the revelation to be understood.

7. The words of Lemuel, king of Massa are found in Chapter 31. In Chapter 31 is a beautiful passage of the ideal wife, it is quoted above in the section of thematic proverbs..

B. The Book of Sirach

50:25 My whole being loathes two nations, the third is not even a people:

26 Those who live in Seir and Philistia, and the degenerate folk who dwell in Shechem.

27 Wise instruction, appropriate proverbs, I have written in this book, I, Jesus, son of Eleazar, son of Sirach, as they gushed forth from my heart's understanding.

28 Happy the man who meditates upon these things, wise the man who takes them to heart!

29 If he puts them into practice, he can cope with anything, for the fear of the LORD is his lamp.

In 1896 part of the original Hebrew of Wisdom literature was found. This was the first time it was seen written in Hebrew. We have no information concerning the author of this book, but Sirach lived after 322 B.C.. About ninety percent of the population were peasants at this time, so in Jerusalem where Sirach lived, only ten percent of the people were living in wealth with one percent in the cities. So the author's emphasis is on wealth in his writings. For instance Sirach 6 talks about the importance of a friend, instead of writing about worldly goods.

5 A kind mouth multiply friends, and gracious lips prompt friendly greetings.

6 let your acquaintances be many, but one in a thousand your confidant.

7 When you gain a friend, first test him, and be not too ready to trust him

8 For one sort of friend is a friend when it suits him, but he will not be with you in time of distress.

9 Another is a friend who becomes an enemy, and tells of the quarrel to your shame.

10 Another is a friend, a boon companion, who will not be with you when sorrow comes.

11 When things go well, he is your other self, and lords it over your servants;

12 But if you are brought low, he turns against you and avoids meeting you.

13 Keep away from your enemies; be on your guard with your friends.

14 A faithful friend is a sturdy shelter; he who finds one finds a treasure.

In America, we are extroverts and many of us would feel poor if we only had one friend. But in this culture, one friend is considered great.

15 A faithful friend is beyond price, no sum can balance his worth.

16 A faithful friend is a life saving remedy, such as he who fears God finds;

17 For he who fears God behaves accordingly, and his friend will be like himself.

18 My son, from your youth embrace discipline; thus will you find wisdom with graying hair.

Sir 38:1 Hold the physician in honor, for he is essential to you, and God it was who established his profession.

2 From God the doctor has his wisdom, and the king provides for his sustenance.

3 His knowledge makes the doctor distinguished, and gives him access to those in authority.

4 God makes the earth yield healing herbs which the prudent man should not neglect;

5 Was not the water sweetened by a twig that men might learn his power?

6 He endows men with the knowledge to glory in his mighty works,

7 Through which the doctor eases pain and the druggist prepares his medicines;

8 Thus God's creative work continues without cease in its efficacy on the surface of the earth.

9 My son, when you are ill, delay not, but pray to God, who will heal you:

10 Flee wickedness; let your hands be just, cleanse your heart of every sin;

11 Offer your sweet smelling oblation and petition, a rich offering according to your means.

12 Then give the doctor his place lest he leave; for you need him too.

13 There are times that give him an advantage,

14 and he too beseeches God That his diagnosis may be correct and his treatment brings about a cure.

15 He who is a sinner toward his Maker will be defiant toward the doctor.

The writer says that real truth is found is Israel but he still brings in some Greek in verses 14 to 20.

14 Better a poor man strong and robust, than a rich man with wasted frame.

15 More precious than gold is health and well being, contentment of spirit than coral.

16 No treasure greater than a healthy body; no happiness, than a joyful heart!

17 Preferable is death to a bitter life, unending sleep to constant illness.

18 Dainties set before one who cannot eat are like the offerings placed before a tomb.

19 What good is an offering to an idol that can neither taste nor smell?

20 So it is with the afflicted man who groans at the good things his eyes behold!

Sirach also tried to join together Jewish and Greek thought on sickness and death. This can be seen in Sirach chapter 38. He added the perspective of Yahweh to his writings.

C. The Book of Ecclesiastes

The passages of the book are concerned with putting our lives into proper perspective. The book tells us that there is a divine plan, an appointed time for everything. Everything has a time, the answer is in our heart, but we can never seem to discover what it is. We are warned to be obedient, do not be a lover of wealth, and do not be worried about sinners but continue to fear God. Good will come to many bad men and bad will come to many good men. All is vanity of vanities that the writer applies to everything. When bad happens to you, you are to remember that God may be trying to get our attention, so that we can become focused on heaven. We are told that life is conundrum or paradox that is beyond our ability to solve.

If your life is troublesome and does not make sense, then you may relate to these passages. These passages are about life from a negative point of view. They remind us that this life does not compare to our rest we will have when we are with Jesus. The word Ecclesiastes is Greek for the Jewish word Qoheleth that means a collector of sentences, or a public speaker like a preacher. The introduction begins with the identification of Qoheleth. No passage was quoted in the New Testament. The introduction to this book is found in Ecclesiastes 1:1 to 11.

> 1 The words of David's son, Qoheleth, king in Jerusalem:
>
> 2 Vanity of vanities, says Qoheleth, vanity of vanities! All things are vanity!
>
> 3 What profit has man from all his labor which he toils at under the sun?
>
> 4 One generation passes away and another generation comes, but the earth abideth forever.
>
> 5 The sun also rises and the sun goes down; then it hastens to the place where it arose.
>
> 6 The wind goes toward the south, then toward about to the north, the wind turns again and again, according to its circuits.

> 7 All rivers run into the sea, yet the sea is not full. To the place where the rivers come, the rivers return again.
>
> 8 All speech is labored; there is nothing man can say. The eye is not satisfied with seeing nor is the ear filled with hearing.
>
> 9 What has been, that will be; what has been done, that will be done. Nothing is new under the sun.
>
> 10 Even the thing of which we say, "See, this is new!" has already existed in the ages that preceded us.
>
> 11 There is no remembrance of the men of old; nor of those to come will there be any remembrance among those who come after them.

Part 1, 1:12 to 6:9, investigates purpose, meanings, and values of life. We are to enjoy life, but we are to always thank God and honor Him

Part 2 Chapters 8 through 12:9 implies that God will punish the bad and reward the good. Ecclesiastes is incomplete without the New Testament.

Part 3 The epilogue (Ecc 12:9 to 14) seems to have been written by someone else.

This book offers a window on the clash of Jewish and Greek cultures. The book adopts Solomon as author, but the writer was probably a sage in the employ of a king. The cultural context was about 322 B.C. when the Greeks ministered Israel. Wine and oil were export items over sustenance foods. So Quolith wanted sustenance King. Ecclesiastes chapter 8 says:

> 1 Who is as the wise (man), and who knows the interpretation of a thing? A man's wisdom makes his face to shine, and the boldness of his face shall be changed.
>
> 2 I counsel you to keep the king's commandment, and in regard of the oath of God,

3 be not hasty to go out of his sight. Stand not in an evil thing for he does whatsoever pleases him.

4 Where the word of a king power, and who may say to him, "What are you doing?"

5 "He who keeps the commandment shall feel no evil things, and a wise man's heart discerns both time and judgment;

6 because to every purpose there is time and judgment. Therefore the misery of man is great upon him.

7 For he knows not that which shall be: for who can tell him when it shall be?

8 There is no man that has power over the spirit to retain the spirit, neither power in the day of death: and no discharge in war; neither shall wickedness deliver those that are given to it.

9 All this have I seen, and applied my heart to every work that is done under the sun: There is a time one man rules over another to his own hurt.

If Qoheleth is in the employ of the King, he is saying do not make waves, keep things calm. The writings were directed toward young men, with themes summarized in one line, receive the gift of God and enjoy it while you can.
1. Sensually: Eating, drinking, and resting.
2. Enjoy friends on conjugal life but don't lose sight of the everlasting.
3. Enjoy your vocation. Do what you have been created to do. If you are fortunate that your career and vocation are the same, it is the better.

Disillusionment is the start of a religious life. This book is not for those who want to smile through life. There are no guarantees for life, all is passing. Prepares us for the Pascal mystery, "Take up your cross and follow me." These words are directed toward twelve step programs, those in hard tasks of life. In frailties of life, we are to love it as it is. This book seems to have an anti type of wisdom, which would imply a Greek influence. There is no strong proof of this. Author moves beyond this and says that God is in control and everything is in His hands. Moves from self-preoccupation to moving beyond self. Qoheleth says that bearing the cross of old age takes wisdom.

Summary, fear God and keep His commandments, it is a posture of utter humility and utter. Fear is a sense of awe or deep reverence when you experience power and magnificence and your smallness at the same time. Fear of God is a stance of total humility. Social and political stability guarantees stability, and responsibility falls on whole tribe and not the individual. Qoheleth uses a word that means mist or breath, life is passing away like a mist or breath. A theme of Qoheleth is that God does not want us to make our home here, we are meant to be frustrated and Qoheleth says the more frustrated we are the more we long for God. Work was never meant to give us a spiritual satisfaction, so beware of working for the wrong reason.

In his writings he was addressing a group of young men who are addressing life and they could have been frustrated if they were not taught well. Ecclesiastes 5:2 (5:3) says, "For a dream comes through the multitude of business; and a fool's voice is known by multitude of words."

Qoheleth said that if you are caught in the vise of violence, you are better off dead. To live wisely is to know that our life is passing away. Ecc 12:7 says, "Then shall dust return to the earth as it was, and the spirit shall return to God who gave it. This is echoed in Ecclesiastes 3:20 and Job 34:15.

Questions:
Should we quote the bible? Of course, just beware of scripture and context. Some things are good to be quoted. Do not prove things with scripture by taking them out of context.

Most of humanity starts off with a desert side of life, one of frustration and hardship. The farmers and the herd people were always in conflict. Explain.

If God is in control, what happens to free will?

Fatalistic approach to life, why try? God wants us to use what he gives us.

Life spans of people in early Genesis are based on numerology. 120 means he was really blessed.

Chapter 9: Song of Songs (Solomon's Canticle of Canticles)

The Song of Songs is attributed to King David but it may have been composed and edited over a long period of time, perhaps as long as 900 years. Song of Songs is a collection of twenty-five love poems strung together with a theme of Love between a young man and his lover. It is a wonderful story passed on through ages of the way God seeks after, and woes the Israel peoples. It is a mystical text written in a manner that expresses a healthy view of sex.

There are colorful descriptions of the human body. These are traditional that praise the bride's or the groom's body. These views have always been part of Middle Eastern culture. Strong and healthy women were desired at the time this book was written. The Song of Songs takes place in the wild and remote nature, habitual countryside, interior space like halls or bedrooms, and the city streets. The songs are to be sung in a safe place in the company of extended family, so the newly married couple can be allowed to put their fantasies into practice. The book is a warm up of the marriage ceremony.

One interpretation of the book is that it was to lift up our sexual thoughts. Anytime a young man and women were alone, it was thought in the culture that they would give themselves up to their passions. Appearances were not separated from realities, so ones thoughts could be lifted up. A second interpretation is that the book is a love song between Yahweh and His people.

Song 4 is an example of the metaphoric beauty of a woman.

1. Behold, you are beautiful, my beloved, behold, you are beautiful! Your have doves' eyes within your locks.[193] Your hair is as a flock of goats that appear from mount Gilead.
2. Your teeth are like a flock of sheep that are evenly shorn, which come up from the washing. Every one of them bears twins, none barren among them.
3. Your lips are like a thread of scarlet and your speech comely: thy temples like a piece of a pomegranate within your locks.
4. Your neck is like the tower of David builded for an armory; A thousand bucklers hang upon it, all shields of mighty men.
5. Your two breasts are like two young fawns that are twins, which feed among the lilies.
6. Until the daybreak and the shadows flee away, I will go to the mountain of myrrh, and to the hill of frankincense.
7. You are all fair, my beloved, there is no spot in you.

Chapter 3 is even more mystical. You cannot understand the garden scene in the Gospel of John 20:11 to 17 without reading the parallel passage in the Song of Songs. The Garden scene of Jesus is sadder and it can be understood better when it is compared with the Garden scene in the Song of Songs. Both, John chapter, and Solomon's Song of Songs chapter 3 takes place in the early morning when it is still the end of the night.

Table: Comparison of the tomb scene in John's Gospel to a similar scene in the Song of Songs.

John's Gospel	Song of Songs
20.1 Mary came to the tomb early in the morning of the eighth day.	3.1 On my bed at night I sought him
Tomb is outside of the city	3:2 Goes about the city searching
20:12 Angels always watch	3:3 Watchmen came
20:15 Where have you put him?	3:3 Have you seen him

20:17 Stop holding on to me for I have not yet ascended to my father.	3:4 I took hold of him 'til I bring him to the home of my mother.
Jesus is from the desert and is the bridegroom who is coming to be married to the church that is his bride.	3:6 Coming up from the desert like a column of smoke
19:39 myrrh & frankincense and perfume	laden with myrrh, with frankincense and perfume.

Frankincense is used in a burial, which indicates that the love described in Song of Songs is pointing us forward to Jesus who was obedient to love. The Book of Wisdom speaks of the garden as being women. The sexuality of a woman is connected with the Garden of Eden, and they are both connected to the Garden of Gethsemane.

> You are an enclosed garden, my sister, my bride, an enclosed garden, a fountain sealed.
>
> You are a park that puts forth pomegranates, with all choice fruits;
>
> Nard and saffron, calamus and cinnamon, with all kinds of incense; Myrrh and aloes, with all the finest spices.
>
> You are a garden fountain, a well of water flowing fresh from Lebanon.
>
> Arise, north wind! Comes, south wind! blow upon my garden that its perfumes may spread abroad. B Let my lover come to his garden and eat its choice fruits.[194]

The remainder of chapter three in the Song of Songs described a procession of sixty armed men coming with him to meet his bride. Solomon makes the carriage. Solomon built the Temple to God's specification, and like the Temple, the carriage is made in a purposeful way. The carriage is made of wood that symbolizes humanity. The columns used for support are made of silver. Silver was used for redemption of a slave and more exactly Jesus. Jesus is our pillar and our redemption. Gold covers the carriage and gold represents Divinity that covers us. The seat is purple, which represents royalty (King). The Gospel of John describes Jesus being anointed with oils by Mary at Bethany, he carries humanity to the cross, and redeems us at no price to us, so that now we can get on our knees and ask the father to forgive our sins. Jesus is God and he is buried with an amount of myrrh and frankincense that is befitting of a King because he is King of Kings and Lord of Lords.

But Mary stood weeping outside the tomb. As she wept, she bent over to look into the tomb; and she saw two angels in white, sitting where the body of Jesus had been lying, one at the head and the other at the feet.

They said to her, "Woman, why are you weeping?" She said to
them, "They have taken away my Lord, and I do not know where they have laid him."

When she had said this, she turned around and saw Jesus
standing there, but she did not know that it was Jesus.
Jesus said to her, "Woman, why are you weeping? Who are
you looking for?" Supposing him to be the gardener, she said to
him, "Sir, if you have carried him away, tell me where you have laid him, and I will take him away."
Jesus said to her, "Mary!" She turned and said to him in Hebrew, "Rabbouni!" (which means Teacher).
Jesus said to her, "Do not hold on to me, because I have not yet
ascended to the Father. But go to my brothers and say to them, 'I am ascending to my Father and your Father, to my God and your God.'"[195]

The message of scripture is the message of a marriage between Jesus and the Church. It was God's plan to draw us into a marriage with him. In Ephesians, Paul talks about the union of man and wife, but then he says that he is talking about Christ and the Church. In this passage, it gets fuzzy whether it is about man and woman, or about the relationship of the Church and Jesus. The Song of Songs is written in a similar manner. In Ephesians Paul says,

> This is a great mystery, but I speak in reference to Christ and the church.

In any case, each one of you should love his wife as himself, and the wife should respect her husband.[196]

John Paul II wrote a theological work when he describes marriage as always being permanent.[197] He says that man gives a gift of himself to his wife, which she fully receives. He is accepted fully and the acceptance is transformed into giving. A woman gives a gift of herself to her husband, which he fully receives. This act is a replay of history. God gives the woman to man as a gift and she was fully accepted and welcomed. God wishes us to be accepted for our own sake. When a woman is accepted for her humanity and femininity in dignity she reaches the inner depth of her person and full possession of herself. God also gives us a gift of Himself, which we must fully accept.

In Genesis 2:23 to 25 the man and woman become a gift for each other for the whole truth of their own body in its masculinity and femininity. God willed a dignity for male and female, for our own sake. We participate in the eternal and permanent act of God's will when we morally participate in innocence of the heart. We grow spiritually when we exchange the gift of each other with the gift of God. In Genesis 2:24 we are told that man and woman were created for marriage. We enter a relationship of self-reproduction in procreation.

The fulfillment of our marriages occurs when we enter Jesus who is the resurrection, and we enter into the communion of saints in communion with the Communion of the Trinity. Heaven is the eternal marriage of Christ's Church with the Church. Jesus said there is no marriage in heaven because as John Paul II explains, "heaven is the rediscovery of a new and perfect communion of persons, redeemed and glorified in Christ, and consolidated by complete concentration on God himself." Our marriage is a sign and heaven is the reality. Heaven is where we want to be, and it is sad when someone leaves us, but it is joyous that he or she is in heaven where we want to be.

Moses only allowed divorces because of he hardness of the people's hearts. But Jesus says, "from the beginning it was not so." He says in Matthew 19:9, "I say to you, whoever divorces his wife (unless the marriage is unlawful) and marries another commits adultery." Jesus does not say that a person can marry again, instead he reminds us that it is considered adultery to marry someone who had once been married.

Chapter 10: The Book of Wisdom (of Solomon)

There are four principal divisions of the Book of Wisdom.

I: The key to life is Justice (Wis 1:1 to 6:21).

II: We are to seek Wisdom as wisdom came to Solomon, and recognize wisdom as being a gift of God (Wis 6:22 to 11:1). Wisdom comes from God through prayer and living righteously (Wisdom chapters 9 to 11).

III: We are to give praise to God who liberated the Jews from Egypt and was an aid to them during the Exodus (Wis 11:2 to 16, 12:23 to 27, 15:18 to 19:22).

IV: Wood is described as being used in salvation, and it was used to carve useless idols (Wis 13:1 15:17).

The writer of the Book of Wisdom identified himself with Solomon. It is thought to have actually been written in Greek about a century before Christ. The Book of Wisdom was a preparation for the teachings found in the New Testament. The prophecies brought a hope that Jesus fulfilled.

For instance, the coming of Christ was prophesied. The book also described what went through the minds of those who persecuted the just one, the Messiah. They were blinded by their own wickedness. Wisdom described the idolatry and the love of material things of the Jews. He writes not of punishment of the Jews, but the book shows us what happens when wisdom literature is not taught correctly.

Chapter one was an echo of Isaiah calling us to love Justice. We are reminded that we should not test God. He enters only those who believe in Him. Wisdom will not enter a soul that plans evil, nor will Wisdom remain in a soul that is in sin. Wisdom will flee deceit, withdraws from counsels not in agreement with God, and Wisdom reprimands injustice. God did not make death, His justice is everlasting. We can bring death upon ourselves, however. We are told that God fashioned everyone to have everlasting life. In summary, God's Holy Spirit will withdraw from us if we do not value life, and if we do not defend those who cannot defend themselves.

When we think life has no purpose, we can do one of two things. We can live for self-gratification, and even resort to oppression of others for our own material benefit. Or we can focus ourselves on eternal life with God. We must remember that the souls of the just are in the hand of God.

The first part of Wisdom chapter two is about the vanity of life, and in the second part it speaks of Jesus' suffering. First, chapter two parallels other wisdom literature in speaking of the fragile nature of life, and life is even described as nothing. Our lives shall pass away as the trace of a cloud. Our name shall be forgotten in time.

We are to be reminded of the meaningless of life on earth so that we can focus on living forever in heaven. If we are not correctly taught, we can focus too much on material things and live only for the present moment. The Book of Wisdom mentions those who filled themselves with things like costly wines, crowned themselves with flowers that withered, and they would strive for luxury. They wrongly thought that material things brought joy. Then verse ten gives a description of those who brought about oppression of the poor, the widowed, and the aged.

They relied on their own strength and then they called it justice. By first relying on themselves, it was natural that there would be those who rebelled against the Messiah (verse 12). The Book of Wisdom describes the suffering that is echoed in the Gospels passion narratives. The Book of Wisdom refers to the Messiah as the just one, and Luke describes Jesus as the just (righteous) man. Luke 23:47, "When the Centurion saw what was done, he said, Certainly this man is a just man."

The just one is obnoxious to his enemies because he sets himself as an example against them. Jesus said in John 18 that the reason for which was born was to give testimony as to the truth. Jesus presents himself for all time as an example of pure truth. A special man came into the world, and that person is truth. The righteous one says he knows God and calls himself the

Son of God in Wisdom 2:13. This is echoed in the Gospel writings. In Wisdom 2:16 and 18, "He boasts that God is his Father. For if he be the true Son of God, he will defend him, and will deliver him from the hands of his enemies." Matthew says at the crucifixion, "He trusted in God, let him deliver him now, if he will have him; for he said, "I am the Son of God."[198]

The thinking behind the crucifixion of Jesus is also alluded to in Chapter 2:19 to 20, "With revilement and torture let us put him to the test that we may have proof of his gentleness and try his patience. Let us condemn him to a shameful death; for according to his own words, God will take care of him."[199] Verse 21 says, "These were their thoughts, but they erred for their wickedness blinded them"[200] Paul also wrote in Romans 1:21, "Because that, when they knew God, they glorified him not as God, neither were thankful; but became vain in their imaginations, and their foolish heart was darkened."

Immortality was a concern of the people and the writer was giving the Hebrew interpretation of immortality. The Isis cult was popular in Greece and even Jews were attracted to it. When deities suffered pain or loss or death, the people were able to identify with them. They would share pain with them. The myth of Isis says that her brother died and was resurrected; she was a symbol of a Hellenistic Egyptian. She was seen as a real gift. However, Wisdom 6:11 21 tells the real gift is wisdom from God, because only God lasts forever.

> Desire therefore my words; long for them and you shall be instructed.
>
> Resplendent and unfading is Wisdom, and she is readily perceived by those who love her, and found by those who seek her.
>
> She hastens to make herself known in anticipation of men's desire; he who watches for her at dawn shall not be disappointed, for he shall find her sitting by his gate.

For taking thought of her is the perfection of prudence, and he who for her sake keeps vigil shall quickly be free from care;

Because she makes her own rounds, seeking those worthy of her, and graciously appears to them in the ways, and meets them with all solicitude.

For the first step toward discipline is a very earnest desire for her; then, care for discipline is love of her;

love means the keeping of her laws; to observe her laws is the basis for incorruptibility;

and incorruptibility makes one close to God;

thus the desire for Wisdom leads up to a kingdom.

If, then, you find pleasure in throne and scepter, you princes of the peoples, honor Wisdom that you may reign as kings forever.

Isis and child were idols that were present when Christianity was forming. Christians easily replaced the image with the Madonna and child and the transfer was easy for the people. They are not the same things. The religions are never to be considered comparable. The Gospel's are God breathed. Christians replaced many pagan things such as worship sites, and even the wedding ring to become Christian practices. The author of Wisdom, like the author of Job showed that same desire can be applied to one God, the God of the Jews. Incorruptibility can only be found in the One God.

"Now what wisdom is, and how she came to be I shall relate; and I shall hide no secrets from you, But from the very beginning I shall search out and bring to light knowledge of her, nor shall I diverge from the truth.

Neither shall I admit consuming jealousy to my company, because that can have no fellowship with Wisdom.

A great number of wise men is the safety of the world, and a prudent king, the stability of his people; to take instruction from my words, to your profit."[201]

The purpose of Wisdom literature is to change people. They turn Jewish people away from the Kingship tracts and turn them into worshipers of the Lord. The Catholic Church identifies Jesus as Wisdom. Christ ended the ancient philosophies because he is the completion of all wisdom. Love of Christ is love of Wisdom because Christ is Wisdom. Christ brought about the fulfillment of the prophets, theology, and religion. He also brought the light for our full enlightenment.

Wisdom 2:23 to 24 talks about sin entering the world, "By envy of the devil, death entered into the world, and they who are in his possession follow him and experience death." This complements the teachings of Paul on original sin. Paul writes, "Wherefore, as by one man sin entered into the world, and death by sin, and so death passed upon all men, for that all have sinned."[202]

For God formed man to be imperishable, the image of his own nature he made him.

24 But by the envy of the devil, death entered the world, and they who are in his possession experience it.

The book lifted up human immortality, it is raised to the Divine sphere. This is illustrated in chapter 3:1 to 3,

1 But the souls of the just are in the hand of God, and no torment shall touch them.

2 They seemed, in the view of the foolish, to be dead; and their passing away was thought an affliction

3 and their going forth from us, utter destruction. But they are in peace.

If we do not live our lives for God, we will pass away unnoticed. Chapter 5 says, that we will be like ships that pass through the water. With power we separate the water and create noise, but once we are gone there are no traces of us in the water.

Part II.

Royalty is told to seek wisdom, for she is easily found. Those in authority will be speedily judged in a severely and a horrible manner. Power comes from the Lord, and strength comes from God who searches out thoughts and examines works. God is not a judge of persons and God cannot be made to stand in awe of any man's greatness. God has made everybody. Wisdom is glorious and never fades. Wisdom is seen by those who love her, and found by those who seek her. The desire of discipline is to seek wisdom, and to care for wisdom is done by love. With love, you keep her laws and you earn incorruption. When you desire wisdom you are brought to the everlasting kingdom. Wisdom 22:22 beautifully says, "If then your delight be in thrones, and scepters, rulers of the people, love wisdom, that you may reign forever.

Chapter 7 says that Solomon preferred Wisdom before kingdoms, and thrones because riches are nothing in comparison to wisdom. Precious gems and gold are like sand and silver compared to wisdom. Wisdom is an infinite treasure to men, and by using wisdom, a person becomes a friend of God. God commends each of us for our discipline. Wisdom 7:16 to 21 lists the areas that were learned by Solomon. Wisdom is described as the brightness of eternal light, and the unspotted mirror of God's majesty, and the image of his goodness. "God loves none but him that dwells with wisdom," Wisdom 7:29.

Solomon prayed for wisdom to dwell with him because God had chosen him to build the temple. The Temple is described in 9:8 as a resemblance of thy holy tabernacle, which thou have prepared from the beginning.

Chapter ten of the Book of Wisdom is a wonderful summary of Wisdom saving mankind. This chapter is a synopsis of the salvation mentioned throughout the Old Testament. Wisdom is presented as a person of God, and is fully realized in Jesus Christ.

Verse   Chapter 10 Interpolation

1,2 Wisdom preserved Adam and brought him out of his sin and gave him power to govern all things.

3 Cain perished when he withdrew from Wisdom.

4 Wisdom saved Noah and his family when the earth was flooded. Wisdom plotted the course for Noah when he was on frail wood. Tradition says that Noah followed a course that was in the shape of a cross.

5 Wisdom kept Abraham, the just man blameless before God.

6 Wisdom saved Lot from Pentapois, the five cities.

7 Lot's wife was disbelieving and became a pillar of salt.

9 Wisdom saves those who love God. Wisdom 16:8 says that it is God who saves us.

10 Wisdom directed Jacob when he fled from his brother's anger. Jacob was shown the kingdom of God and was given knowledge of holy things, and was helped to make abundant the fruit of his works. In preserving Jacob, Jacob learned that devotion or piety, which is fear of the Lord and is the mightiest thing.

13 Joseph was not abandoned when he was sold, and God was delivered him from sin.

16 Moses was delivered from kings.

17 Wisdom led the people, the holy ones, out of Egypt as payment for their works. They were led by a wondrous road, and was shelter for them by day and a starry flame at night.

21 Salvation history is summarized, "The just triumphed over the wicked, they sang "O Lord" and they praised God. Wisdom opened the mouths of the mute, and give ready speech to infants."

Jesus repeated this thought, "I thank you, Lord and God because you have hidden these things from the wise and prudent, and given them to the childlike."[203] Jesus tells us in Matthew 10 and 11 that prophets came for our sake, and even miracles were worked in areas that were in special need of grace. He reminds us that those who turn from wisdom will be punished. Wisdom is justified by her children, and Jesus tells us that he reveals the Father to us, and that we only have rest for our souls when we comes to him.

Chapter twelve warns against abortion and killing of babies. Wisdom 12:5 to 7, "These merciless murderers of children, ...and parents who took with their own hands defenseless lives, You willed to destroy by the hands of our fathers, that the land that is dearest of all to you might receive a worthy colony of God's children."

However, God even spared those who murdered their own children. God is slow in judgment.[204] He punishes by degrees so that we can have a chance to repent. God could easily destroy evil people with his power, but he chooses not to. By being gentle, God shows us hope and turns us to repentance of our sins. His power is used to judge in tranquillity and he disposes us very favorably. God tries to spare everyone, because we are all His, and He is a lover of souls (Wis 11:27).

Sometimes, God punishes us so that we can see our wrong. This happened at the Exodus of Egypt. When the Egyptians saw that their punishment benefited God's people, they realized that they had sinned and turned to the Lord.

Wisdom chapter 14 continues with the theme of wood being used for our salvation. We are not only justified by frail wood but we can be doomed if we carve idols of wood to worship as gods. Noah was the hope of the Universe and he was saved by wood, the wood of a raft protected by God. Justice comes to all of humanity by wood, the wood of the cross of Jesus. Idols made by hands are cursed, even those made by non-believers. We are warned that sexual immorality follows the making of idols.

Worship of idols is an abomination to God and is the cause, and the beginning and end of all evil (verse 27).

Idols

What are idols? Wisdom 13:10 to 19 lists three things that were done with idols. Even though idols were carved or molded by their own hands, they considered idols to be gods. Then they made shrines for these carvings that were images of men or animals. The dead idols were prayed to about goods, or marriage, or children, and they even invoked the powerless idols for strength and for life. They also prayed to the idols for aid in travels and for profit in business.

Wisdom 14:12 to 31 lists five things about idols. First, Idols came about because of the vanity of men. Some people made idols of dead men and then worshipped the carving as a god, even though they are dead, and without a soul. The graven images were worshipped. Images of kings were also honored. Their acts were evil, and yet they called such evils peace. Sin always followed the worship of idols.

They took for gods, the worthless and disgusting among beasts, they had wandered so far astray that they were deceived like children.8

Romans 1:21 to 23 reminds us that we can see God in everything that He has made. We should not honor what the Creator has made, we should honor the Creator. "People became vain, and their bad reasoning caused them to be blind, and they became fools. Yet, they thought that they were wise. They made idols in exchange for the glory of God."

Chapter sixteen of Wisdom reminds us that God allowed images, but idols that were worshipped were not allowed. In Exodus 25, 18 and 19, angels were hammered out to be placed on top of the Ark of the Covenant. In Number 21:8, a serpent was made and placed on a bronze pole, and when a person was bitten by a serpent, he would look at the pole to be healed. Images were also made for the Temple of Solomon. The people in the desert were not saved by what he saw, but by "the Savior of all."[205] Locusts and flies killed the Egyptians, but the children of God were saved even from the teeth of venomous serpents. It was the word of the Lord, which healed them, because only he has power over life and death. Jon 3:14 to 15 says, "And as Moses lifted up the serpent in the wilderness, even so must the son of Man be lifted up: that whoever believes in him should not perish but have eternal life."

Images were mostly prohibited in the time before Jesus came. The incarnate Jesus walked upon the earth and God was fully revealed to us. Images were not allowed because they were looking forward to the coming of Christ and had to try to envision a God they could not see except in His creations. Once, Jesus came we had an image of Jesus. We never worship a statute of a saint, we are reminded of their lives. Just as a nativity set reminds us of the story of the birth of Jesus, or a picture reminds us of someone we love.

The Book of Wisdom ends with a summary of salvation from Egypt. We are reminded that God magnified his people, honored them, and assisted them at all times and places. This book tells us of the fleeting life we have, but also how to direct it to God. The Egyptians gladly sent the Jews out of the land, but then they regretted their decision and pursued the Jews.

God then used nature to preserve His children unharmed. It was like creation was being made anew. Wisdom 19:4, "The cloud overshadowed their camp; and out of what had before been water, dry land was seen emerging: Out of the Red Sea an unimpeded road, and a grassy plain out of the mighty flood."

The water saved one nation that was in awe at the wonders of God. The same water was used to punish another people. Nature was changed and was even recreated by God for the protection of the people of His covenant.

Chapter 11: The Book of Job

The book was probably composed some time between the seventh and fifth centuries B.C. by an author who is not known. The book's literary form with speeches, a prologue and an epilogue were written according to a studied plan that indicates the purpose of the writing was didactic. The lesson is that even the just may endure sufferings and these sufferings are a test of their fidelity to God. They shall be rewarded in the end. Man's finite mind cannot probe the depths of the divine omniscience that governs the world. The problems we encounter can be solved by a broader and deeper awareness of God's power, presence (Job 42:5), and wisdom.

The Book of Job is divided into five parts as follows:

I: Prologue (Job 1:1 2:13) Job loses everything and three friends of his come to console him. "Your pain is our pain and your blessing is our blessing," is a tribal expression that they say to him. With the Jews, the tribe came first and the individual was second to the tribe.

II. Chapter 2:14 to 31:37:
III. Chapter 32:1 to 37:24 is the speech of Elihu.
IV. Chapter 38:1 to 42:6 the Lord's speech.
V. Epilogue (Job 42:7 17)

Job was responsible for the whole tribe. He had followed the conventional wisdom, and yet the evil had come upon him. Honor and shame hurt him because he knew that the rest of the people thought he was in a big sin. His friends were not convinced otherwise. Shame was the loss of honor. His friends said that if he had done something bad it was the reason for his problem. Sometimes pain is our best teacher because when we are in pain we have no choice but to learn. The culture was other centered and that is why his friends came to help him out. This is a Didactic lesson and is beautiful to learn from.

Two different stories are presented. One consisting of the prologue and it is told in Chapters 3 through 41. Job's friends told him to confess his sins because they thought bad things had come upon him as a result of his sins. However, Job was an example of a righteous man who does not sin. The three friends represented conventional wisdom, and Job represented unconventional wisdom that God confirms. God tested Job and then He restored everything back to him.

Chapter 38:1 to 10 is God's speech that put Job in his place. It is a speech that makes the reader realize the wonders of God. Who are we to question the creator of the Universe? Then again, the creator of the Universe calls us his children, and this is a wonderful thought.[206]

> The LORD answered Job out of the whirlwind. He said, Who is this that darkens counsel by words without knowledge?
>
> Gird up now your loins, like a man; for I will demand of you, and you are to answer me,
>
> Where were you when I laid the foundations the earth? Tell me, if you have understanding.
>
> Who has laid the measure thereof; if you know? Or who has stretched out the measuring line upon it?
>
> Where are the foundations of the earth fastened? Or who laid the corner stone,
>
> When the morning stars sang together and all the sons of God shouted for joy?
>
> And who shut up doors the sea, when it burst forth as if it had issued from the womb?

> When I made the clouds the garments of the earth, and thick darkness a swaddling band for it?
>
> When I set limits for it and bracketed bars and doors,

God never answered Job directly. Jesus responded with questions because he knew that we learn more this way. Spoon feeding answers is not a way to learn. Sometimes people suffer even when they are good.

> Job complained through out the book, yet after God spoke, Job only spoke four more lines:
>
> Then Job answered the LORD and said:
>
> I know that you can do every thing, and that no thought can be withheld from thee.
>
> Who is he that hides counsel without knowledge? Therefore have I uttered that I understand not; things too wonderful for me, which I knew not.
>
> Hear, I beseech thee, and I will speak: I will demand of thee, and declare thou unto me.
>
> I have heard of thee by the hearing of the ear: but now I have seen you with my eyes.
>
> Therefore I abhor myself, and repent in dust and ashes.[207]

Job is a representative of the universal struggle of suffering. He struggled like Jacob wrestled with God. The struggles allowed Job to relate to God. Jesus taught us that we are always to love, even if bad events happen to us. We take what Love really means and respond in that manner.

God demanded a holocaust from his friends and told Job that he must make the prayer. Job was taught that he is to forgive his friends and is to act as the redeemer.

Having wisdom is being able to see the underlying.
a. We should seek counsel from God and from others.
b. We need to reflect on God's word (2 Tm 2:15).
c. We need to associate with the wise (mentors) Prov (30:20).
d. We need to stay in close communion with the Lord like Job who had God with him and for him.

The gospel is the power of God for our salvation. Romans 1:17, "For there is where the righteousness of God is revealed from faith to faith: as it is written, the just shall live by faith." Paul wrote in Romans 2 that the unrighteous will be punished but God will protect the righteous. God's kindness and patience is meant to lead us to turn away from sin. "God will render judgment to each of us according to our works. God gives glory, honor and peace to every man that does good works. For those who persevere by continuing to do well by seeking glory, honor, and immortality, will receive eternal life."3

Wisdom 3:1 to 4 says, "The souls of the just are in the hand of God, and no torment shall touch them. They seemed in the eyes of the foolish to be dead; and their passing away was thought of as an affliction, and their going forth from us, utter destruction. But they are in peace."

Finally, Jesus said in Matthew 13:43, "Then the righteous will shine forth like the sun in the kingdom of their Father." Also, Psalm 14:6, "God is with the company of the just."

Chapter 12: The Book of Hosea

The Book of Hosea reminds us that the bible is not just a body of truth, but God himself who makes known his love for his people through nature, mighty acts and words. We see that the result of sin and unbelief is the breaking up of a marriage and even the break up of a nation. The covenant with God can be broken when we continue to sin and when we refuse to turn to Him. Discovering and obeying our loving God will lead us to a life of righteousness and justice.

The Book of Hosea tells us that the empire where God reigns is shifted from rulers to individuals. It was thought that the King was obedient to God and that he was held directly responsible to lead people in a Godly way. The people thought that they were then responsible to the King. Hosea teaches us that we are all directly responsible for our actions.

The Book of Hosea was written from the reflections of Hosea's words. One half to two thirds of the words in the Book of Hosea come from the prophet Hosea. Someone who had lived in the northern kingdom of Israel before the northern kingdom was destroyed probably edited the books. The editor seemed to have lived in the southern kingdom of Judah because of the way he wrote about the kings of Northern Israel. Mentioned first were Uzziah, Jotham, Ahaz, and Hezekiah who ruled the Southern Kingdom of Judah from about 783 to 697 B.C.. Mentioned next were Jehoash, and Jeroboam II who were rulers of the northern kingdom (Israel) from about 802 B.C. to about 748 B.C.. Jeroboam died about 748 B.C., and reigned in the years 787 to 748 B.C.. The writer did not mention the last six Kings of Northern Israel who ruled for a total of only twenty years and were described as unfaithful in Kings II.

The writer referred to the creation in Genesis by opening with the words, "In the beginning." Hosea wrote in this book of God going all of the way back to the creation of the world to bring His people back to Him. Hosea is a book about the covenant relationship between God and His people. When Jesus was told by the Pharisees that divorce was allowed by Moses, Jesus said it was because they were so hard hearted, but it was not so from the beginning. God made man and woman and they are one and are not to be separated. Hosea 1:4, 5 wrote of the bow of God's covenant,

> Then the LORD said to him; call his name Jezreel, for yet a little while, and I will avenge the blood of Jezreel upon the house of Jehu And bring to an end the kingdom of the house of Israel;
>
> It shall come to pass at that day I will break the bow of Israel in the valley of Jezreel.
>
> "I will break the bow of Israel," the Hebrew word `abrek is the same word used for the bow that God put in the sky (Gn 9:13) to remind us of His covenant. God's people had been unfaithful to Him and they had not taken care of the poor, so God is essentially saying that He is going to break this covenant.

The Book of Hosea is about this lawsuit that God brought against the people. The people were not obeying Him, so He is saying that they are to be punished.

Throughout the bible there is an image of the Lord as the Groom and Israel or the Church as the Bride. The first three chapters in the Book of Hosea described this marriage with the language progressing from God speaking in chapter one to a language that is personal in chapter three. Chapter one is written in the third person and it about an unfaithful marriage and we are told what God was planning to do. The marriage of the people to God was not a covenant marriage and was represented by the writer's marriage to Gomer who had offspring named Lo ruhama, and Lo ammi. The names respectfully mean "she is not pitied" and "not my people". The names were used to let us know that God no longer loved Israel as shown by his lack of pity, and by saying that the Israelites were no longer His people.

Chapter two was written in the second person with God speaking to Israel about its unfaithful marriage relationship with Him. God told Israel that because she was unfaithful to Him that He would strip her naked, by taking away the grain from her, and the wine, and the wool and flax. Hosea used this imagery to let us know that God will take Israel backward in time, back to the desert experience where there was no food, no drink, no clothing. They will find God in the desert because nothing was in the desert except for God.[208] By going back to the promised land, Israel will see God. Hosea 2:14 (2:16), "Behold, I will allure her; I will lead her into the wilderness and speak comfortably unto her." This is language used in Exodus 19:4, "tell the Israelites: You have seen what I did unto the Egyptians and how I bare you on eagle wings and brought you unto to myself."

Hosea said that God would take His people back to the time of creation, back to a time when there was chaos, and then He would give them a New Creation. A New Creation was mentioned in Hosea 2:20 (18). God said, "On that day I will make a covenant for them with the beasts of the field, with the fowls of the heaven, and with creepy things of the ground. I will break the bow and sword and the battle out of the earth, and I will make them to lie down safely."

The flood in Genesis was a new creation that resulted in a covenant. Now, God was once again calling for everyone to come to Him with all his or her hearts, and He would give a new covenant. Not a covenant with 613 commandments that were given after the people made a golden calf while Moses was on Mt. Sinai. This covenant is with the living creatures and is a covenant of the great day of creation. The people would once again be married to God and the qualities of the new people would be that they would know right and know justice, in both love and mercy. God gives gifts to the bride just as Rebekah was given bridal gifts.[209] Rebekah represented the Church coming to her groom Israel at the well of life. The well of Genesis 24:62 was named "the spring of the living water seeing me".[210] The Book of Hosea says, God will say, "You are my people," and the people will say "My God!"[211]

Finally, in the third chapter of Hosea, the language was shifted to the third person singular so that the reader does not know whether it was God speaking or Hosea talking. Chapter 1 is out there somewhere, then Hosea integrates it, so that the reader is being involved, and then to God being involved. Marriage is a covenant between a man and a woman, and God. God reversed the names of his people so to brothers He says, you are "My people" and to sisters, "You are pitied (loved)".

> Hosea chapters 4 through 7:16 are about Israel's punishment and call to repentance for their infidelity. In chapter 4 God presented a covenant lawsuit in which He brought about because the Israelites were not keeping the commandments:
>
> Hosea 4:1, Hear the word of the LORD, you children of Israel, for the LORD has a controversy with the inhabitants of the land: There is no truth, no mercy, and no knowledge of God in the land.
>
> Hosea 4:2, By swearing, lying, killing, stealing and committing adultery! they break out, and blood touches blood.
>
> Hosea 4:3, Therefore shall the land mourns, and everyone that dwells in it shall languishes with the beasts of the field, the fowls of the heaven; yea, the fish of the sea shall be taken away.

Because the commandments were not being followed, God took the people backwards and away from creation. He took his bride from the sixth day of creation to the fifth day of the creation of the creatures of the sea and the birds, and even further back in time to the third day of creation. There in the chaos is where all would perish in the darkness. God was concerned about the lack of knowledge of Him caused by the rejection by the priests and prophets attitude of not knowing God. The winds are described at the end of the fourth chapter. The winds represented the chaos which were present at the time of the winds on the first day of creation. Hosea 4:19, "The wind has bound her up in her wings; they shall be ashamed because of their sacrifice."

Divorce is contrary to marriage and is sometimes misunderstood. Matthew also wrote about marriage. Like Hosea, Jesus referred us back to the beginning, back to the creation of man and woman. Pope John Paul II wrote about marriage, saying that we need to go back to Genesis so that we will give ourselves totally to our spouses. We are also to receive our spouses completely so that the two of can become one flesh. In Matthew 19:3 to 8, Jesus says that from the beginning, divorce was not allowed.

> The Pharisees also came to him, tempting him, saying to him, "Is it lawful for a man to divorce his wife for any cause?"
>
> He said in answered and said to them, "Have you not read that He who made them from the beginning made them male and female,
>
> for this reason shall a man leave father and mother and shall cleave to his wife, and the two shall be one flesh'?
>
> Wherefore they are no longer two, but one flesh. Therefore, what God has joined together, let none put asunder.
>
> They said unto him, "Why did Moses then command to give a writing of divorce, and to put her away?"
>
> He said to them, "Moses, because of the hardness of your hearts suffered you put away your wives, but from the beginning it was not so.
>
> Matthew 19:3 to 8

What does it mean, in the beginning it was not so? Jesus orders us to return, in a way, to the threshold of our theological history. Pope John

Paul II in his theological work, *The Theology of the Body*, wrote about the theology of the body, beginning with the creation of Adam and Eve, progressing to their nakedness. It is a total vision of man. His writing is based on the Book of Genesis in the bible. He describes how everything God wants to tell us on earth about the meaning of life is contained somehow in the meaning of the human body. Mostly through the call of male and female to become "one body" in marriage. After all, the message of scripture is the message of a marriage between Jesus and the Church. It was God's plan to draw us into a marriage with him.

In Ephesians chapter 5:21 to 32, Paul wrote about the union of man and wife, but then he says that he is talking about Christ and the Church. In this passage, he is conveying a dual marriage, it is about man and woman, and about the Church and Jesus. We men are told to love our wives as Christ loves the Church. Jesus died for the Church to sanctify her.

> This is a great mystery, but I speak in reference to Christ and the church.
>
> In any case, each one of you should love his wife as himself, and the wife should respect her husband. (Eph 5:82)

Would we not want Christ to separate from us? We should not want to separate from our spouses. An Evangelical friend once told me, "If we have married again, we should treat our present marriage as a sacramental marriage. We must ask forgiveness of our past mistakes and with our correct understanding of the gift of marriage, we must be fully committed to our marriage for life."

The Pope wrote, "In our marriage, we love and our bodies become a gift and by means of this gift is fulfilled the very meaning of being and existence." We men can only find ourselves by making a gift of ourselves. Love is the source of God's creation being a gift. So that in a woman's body, creation is repeated.

A man gives a gift of himself to his wife, which she fully receives. He is accepted fully and the acceptance is transformed into giving. A woman gives a gift of herself to her husband, which he fully receives. This act is a replay of history. God gives the woman to man as a gift and she was fully accepted and welcomed. God wishes us to be accepted for our own sake. When a woman is accepted for her humanity and femininity in dignity she reaches the inner depth of her person and full possession of herself. God also gives us a gift of Himself, which we must fully accept.

In Genesis 2:23 to 25 the man and woman become a gift for each other for the whole truth of their own body in its masculinity and femininity. God willed a dignity for male and female, for our own sake. We participate in the eternal and permanent act of God's will when we morally participate in innocence of the heart. We grow spiritually when we exchange the gift of each other with the gift of God. In Genesis 2:24 we are told that man and woman were created for marriage. We enter a relationship of self-reproduction in procreation.

The fulfillment of our marriages is when we enter Jesus who is the resurrection, and we enter into the communion of saints who are with the Communion of the Trinity. Heaven is the eternal marriage of Christ's Church with the Church. Jesus said there is no marriage in heaven because as John Paul II says, "heaven is the rediscovery of a new and perfect communion of persons, redeemed and glorified in Christ, and consolidated by complete concentration on God himself." Our marriage is a sign and heaven is the reality. Heaven is where we want to be, and it is sad when someone leaves us, but it is joyous that he or she is where we want to be in heaven.

Moses only allowed divorces because of the hardness of the people's hearts. But Jesus says, "from the beginning it was not so." He said in Matthew 19:9, "I say to you, whoever divorces his wife (unless the marriage is unlawful) and marries another commits adultery." But Jesus never said that a person could marry again.

Marriage to God (Romans 7:1 to 13)

The Gospels are easy to follow compared to the writings of Paul. Paul was a man educated under the greatest Rabbi alive, Gamaliel, at the time. Paul's writings are hard to understand because he incorporates the Old Testament, and the customs of the time into his writings, which are very concise. He was a master of sublime language in that he could describe the heavenly in human terms.

Peter wrote in 2 Peter 3:16 to 17 that some of Paul's writings are difficult to understand. "And consider the patience of our Lord as salvation, as our beloved brother Paul, according to the wisdom given to him, also wrote to you, speaking of these things as he does in all his letters. In them there are some things hard to understand that the ignorant and unstable distort to their own destruction, just as they do the other scriptures."

Paul taught that we could have a new birth of our lives. God will give us a new heart so that with our new heart, we can follow Jesus and have our souls be his. An example of Paul's writings is Romans 7:1 to 13. Verses 1 through 3 contain a lot of information, but they can be construed in the wrong way if they are not understood properly.

> Are you unaware, brothers (for I am speaking to people who know the law), that the law has jurisdiction over one as long as one lives?

> Thus law binds a married woman to her living husband; but if her husband dies, she is released from the law in respect to her husband.

> Consequently, while her husband is alive she will be called an adulteress if she consorts with another man. But if her husband dies she is free from that law, and she is not an adulteress if she consorts with another man.

To understand these three verses we must look at the context of the passage by also reading verses 4 through 13. We must understand the Old Testament scriptures he is speaking of, and we must understand to whom he is speaking. We must properly understand what Paul means by consort and what he means by the law having jurisdiction over us.

The term, consort means marry or live with another. This concept can be understood by reading and understanding the story of the Samaritan woman at the well. In John 4:17 to 18, "The woman answered and said to him, "I do not have a husband." Jesus answered her, "You are right in saying, 'I do not have a husband.'

For you have had five husbands, and the one you have now is not your husband. What you have said is true."

Jesus was bringing a woman back to the fullness of God. He does it by speaking to her personally, but in a way that signifies much more. Her understanding of his statement is brought about because he was able to touch her soul. The ancient Jews lived in two countries. The Northern Kingdom was called Israel and the Southern Kingdom was called Judah, and Judah is now where the country is located that is named Israel. At the time of Jesus, people who had replaced the Israelites who had been sent into exile inhabited the Northern Kingdom.

The Jews had adopted the ways of the people who they lived with. The Israelites were supposed to have changed the people but instead the people in the surrounding countries changed the Israelites. They were no longer keeping God's commandments and statutes as spoken through the prophets. The Jews were "stiff necked"[212] and did not listen to God. They went back to the worship on high places instead of the central worship established by God in Solomon's Temple. They worshipped false gods, and they did not keep the commandments which prescribed a way of living that was different from they way other people lived. The countries of both Israel and Judah practiced these superstitious rites.

The Northern Kingdom was led by Jeroboam, and he led the Jews into their own destruction. They were conquered and an unusual thing was done to them. The Israelites, especially the learned people, and the leaders of the people were exiled to Assyria. Then the king of Assyria brought people from five other countries "and settled them into the cities of Samaria in place of the Israelites."213

The King of Assyria essentially told the people from these five countries that they were the new Jews and had to venerate the Lord. These people had worshipped idols (false gods), so they did not have a real relationship with God. In other words, they were married to five other gods, and not to the true God. The king first had lions kill those who did not worship God, then he sent them one of the exiled priests and he "taught them how to venerate the Lord."214

But these people were not married to God; they were just living with him. The Babylonians were married to Marduk; the men of Cuth were married to Nergal; the men of Hamth were married to Ashima; the men of Avva were married to Nibhaz and Tartak, and the Sepharvaim were the worst since they even sacrificed children to these images. "But, while venerating the LORD, they served their own gods, following the worship of the nations from among whom they had been deported."215

So, Jesus was not only speaking of the woman's own personal life. He was also speaking about the history of her people. She understood him and she changed. Just like the woman, the people of Samaria had five husbands and they were living with the Lord but they were not married to Him.

So, the people had to die so that they could marry again. Paul meant that when we die to ourselves that we change into a new person in unity with God. Paul was equating idolatry with adultery. He said that a woman's husband must die if she is to marry again. Paul told us, "In the same way, my brothers, you also were put to death to the law through the body of Christ, so that you might belong to another, to the one who was raised from the dead in order that we might bear fruit for God."216 Paul had just written in Romans 6:4 that when we are baptized we are baptized into his death, so that we can be raised from the dead and live a new life, a life in marriage to Christ. So now when we walk in our flesh, we are walking away from Grace.

What did Paul mean that we are released from the law? He said that the law is not sin, but it is a way to let us know what sin is. Everyone has a conscience that they must follow, but we have a way of living that is given to us through the law. Paul said that he once lived outside the law, and as a child he did. Then sin came alive through the knowledge of the commandments. Because, he sinned, he died. "For sin, seizing an opportunity in the commandment, deceived me and through it put me to death."[217]

Paul said that the law was holy, and the commandments are holy and righteous and good. Because it did what it was supposed to do and that was to put him to death. It used to be that we were bound to the law because it did not save us. Now, we die, we see that we are dead, we ask God for His forgiveness and we can become alive in a new birth. Paul was not so much emphasizing that we are powerless to keep the commandments, inasmuch as he was saying that there is now a way to become saved from our sins and that is through a life in Jesus.

St. Clement is thought to have learned from Paul, he was a direct hearer of the Apostle. He wrote in a manner like Paul. In his Letter to the Corinthians, Clement tells us how we can become saved, so that we can be counted among those who are Christians awaiting Jesus. "If our understanding be by faith toward God, and if we earnestly seek the things which are pleasing and acceptable to Him. To be saved, we must also do the things, which are in harmony with His, blameless will. We must follow the way of truth, casting away from us all unrighteousness and inequity, along with all coveting, strife, evil practices, deceit, gossiping, and evil speaking, all hatred of God, pride and haughtiness, vain glory, and ambition."[218]

All Church Fathers believed in perseverance as part of our salvation. We have a faith that produces love. Paul said that we must have obedience to faith.[219] When we do works that are good, St. Clement tells us that Jesus will give us his unlimited graces so that we can taste of immortal knowledge.

CHAPTER 13: ISAIAH

The Book of Isaiah is one of the two most important Old Testament books for both Christians and Jews. Isaiah was the liturgy that the early Jews spoke, and both Psalms and Isaiah were taught every week. Isaiah is a story of a community that was released from an oppressor. Isaiah uses imagery of the wilderness story from Exodus, and he wrote of the promise of the restoration of the Davidic kingship with a people of Mount Zion.

There are six Major Divisions in the Book of Isaiah.

Chapters 1 to 5 Part one began during the reign of King Jotham. Isaiah issued Oracles against the nations of Israel and Judah There was moral breakdown of the people and God promised rewards if the nation would ask for forgiveness.

Chapters 6 to 12 Isaiah told the people that God will come and dwell among us, he will be a light to the darkness. These are called the Emmanuel prophecies. During this period, Isaiah was an adviser to the King. Isaiah asked the king to be strong for God would protect the nation, instead the king aligned himself with Assyria.

Chapters 13 to 18 Isaiah issued oracles against the Pagan Nations.

Chapters 24 to 27 This is a historical appendage. God will bring the nations to Mount Zion. The remnant of the Jews consists of the gentile nations (Christians)

Chapters 2 8to 32 Described the situation during the reign of King Hezekiah in 715 to 687 B.C.. Hezekiah began an important religious reform. He faltered and Isaiah demanded Judah back to faith in Yahweh. The leader of the Assyrians, Sennacherib, captured Judah. God promised that in Zion He would lay a tested stone that would be a sure foundation for those who put their faith in Him.

Chapters 40 to 56 During the Babylonian exile God promised he would rise up the remnant and make them a light to the nations so that His salvation may reach the ends of the world. He said He would continue to give us His covenant love. The glory of the Lord is in the liberation of Judah.

The Book of Isaiah is often thought to cover a period of about 200 years and many scholars think that Isaiah was written by at least four major authors. The first author was Isaiah who was probably a preacher. There was also a second and third author of Isaiah, and the person who did the final writings in the fourth century before Christ. Some scholars say that there could have been even more authors.

The text does not seem to cover a time period as long as two hundred-years, however. Isaiah received his call from God in 742 B.C. at the earliest, and he interfaced with Hezekiah who lived until about 686 B.C.. This time period was about fifty-six years. Isaiah probably received his call in about 742 B.C. while Israel, the Northern Kingdom was under the threat of Assyria as an invasion force.

Isaiah was wealthy, married, and had two sons. The year that Judah's King Uzziah died is the year that Isaiah received his call from God. His theology concentrated the holiness of God, with victory through weakness as a major theme. He wrote of Zion as the place of worship, not Mount. Horeb. Isaiah also wrote that King David's line would always be preserved. So, it was from David and not Moses that the line of the Messiah arose.

Luke followed the theme of Isaiah in his gospel and in Acts of the Apostles. Luke wrote that Jesus wants his people to come to the holy mountain of Zion. Jesus is the person who is the fulfillment of the prophecies of Isaiah. Jesus ushered in the Kingdom of David, and the Kingdom is found in the Church. Luke wants us to know that we can climb the mountain of God if we live in righteousness and in justice.

Reigning Kings of Israel and Judah during the life of the Prophet Isaiah:

Kings of Israel		Kings of Judah	
Jeroboam II	786 to 746	Uzziah (Azariah)	783 to 742
Zechariah	746 to 745	(Strength of Jah (God))	
Shallum	745		
Menahem	745 to 738	Jotham (Jehovah is)	742 to 732
Pekah	744 to 732		
Pekahiah	738 to 732	Ahaz (possessor)	732 to 715
Hosea	732 to 722		
		Hezekiah (fidelity of God)	715 to 686

    The names of the four kings of Judah provide a message, Strength of God is for the possessor of him who has fidelity of Yahweh. God praised King Uzziah and King Josiah for their adherence to the Passover celebration. King Hezekiah ruled the land and he reigned from the age of 25 to the age of 59. He loved God and brought the people back to worship God (Yahweh).

    King Hezekiah took to heart the words of God that were spoken to Solomon at the dedication of the Temple in Judah. The Temple on Mount Zion was chosen by God to be the central place of worship.

    2 Chr 7:14 and if my people, which are called by name, shall humble themselves and pray, and seek my face and turn from their wicked ways, then will I hear them from heaven and forgive their sin and heal their land.2 Chr 7:15 Now my eyes shall be open and my ears attentive to the prayer of this place.

    King Hezekiah brought the people into correct worship of God. A lot of division had come to Israel because the kings had not stayed loyal to Yahweh. King Solomon in his later years had accumulated gold, in fact each year he accumulated 666 tons of gold. This is one of two places in the bible where this terrible number is used directly. So there was reason for separation and protest. King Hezekiah brought back correct worship of the Passover celebration. The celebration had been neglected that was supposed to be celebrated annually at the Temple, the central place in Jerusalem approved by God. All of the Jews were to celebrate the sacrificial feast. All of Exodus 12 was devoted to the Passover eating of the unblemished lamb with unleavened bread as the central theme of the Old Testament.

Leviticus 23:5 and Numbers 9:2 are two of the many references stating that the Passover Feast was to be celebrated at a prescribed time on a yearly basis. Paul encouraged the early Church to celebrate the Passover feast with Jesus as our unblemished lamb in unleavened bread. Paul said, "For even Christ our Passover is sacrificed for us, therefore let us keep the feast."[220] The feast we keep is the Passover feast, which is a sacrifice.

All of the people of Israel were invited and those who came celebrated the Passover in Jerusalem at the Temple with those in Judah. "The whole assembly of Judah, the Levites, the priests, and those who had come from Israel to celebrate the Passover. There was great joy in Jerusalem, for not since Solomon son of David King of Israel there was not the like of it in Jerusalem. The prayers of blessings by the priests, reached heaven, God's holy dwelling."[221]

No king since David and Solomon had made God so happy. So, God sent His prophet Isaiah to King Hezekiah who assured him that Assyria would not occupy Jerusalem.

> The remaining survivors of the house of Judah shall again strike root below and bear fruit above. For out of Jerusalem shall come a remnant, and from Mount Zion, survivors. The zeal of the LORD of hosts shall do this. Therefore, thus says the LORD concerning the king of Assyria: 'He shall not reach this city, nor shoot an arrow at it, nor come before it with a shield, nor cast up siege works against it. He shall return by the same way he came, without entering the city, says the LORD.[222]

God always sends wondrous gifts to the separated. He needs to woo them back to Him. The heavens always say, "Come home." It is hard to imagine how the praises and happiness must have been in a span of time during the reign of Hezekiah. The Jews knew that the highest honor given to them was to bless the Lord (praise the Lord).

The early part of Isaiah is about how Isaiah tried to get the city to reform, but they did not. They were consequently taken into exile to Babylon where they remained until the Assyrians who set the Jews free defeated Babylon.

> Is 1:1 The vision which Isaiah, son of Amoz which he saw concerning Judah and Jerusalem in the days of Uzziah, Jotham, Ahaz and Hezekiah, kings of Judah. Isaiah1: 2 Hear, O heavens, and listen, O earth, for the LORD has spoken: I have nourished and brought up children, and they have rebelled against me.

> When God brings cases before us, they are always witnessed by nature. God summoned the heavens and the earth to hear of his judgment.

> Is 1:3 An ox knows its owner, and an ass, its master's crib (manger); But Israel does not know, my people has not understood.

Isaiah forms all of Christian scripture, so even unrelated passages are used to describe Jesus.

God had run out of options to deal with Israel. The last thing left was to send them into exile. We should never allow God to run out of options with us. The Jews saw what was happening around them and still did not think judgment would happen to them. They should have turned to God and healed their sores, but instead they continued revolting and turning more from God.

> Is 1:4 Ah! Sinful nation, a people laden with iniquity, a seed of evildoers, children that are corrupters: they have forsaken the

> Lord, they have provoked the Holy One of Israel unto anger, and they are gone away backward. Is 1:5, Why should you be stricken any more? You will revolt more and more: the whole head is sick, and the whole heart faint. Is 1:6, From the sole of the foot to the head there is no soundness in it: but wounds and bruises, and putrefying sores: they have not been closed, neither bound up, neither mollified with ointment.

The situation was so bad that Isaiah referred to Jerusalem itself as Gomorrah. God could not destroy everything, so he looked for the best that there was to offer. He found a remnant to carry on his plan. We are one body and no part can be separate from the whole. The ear is not separate from the heart or the foot. But at this time in history, the whole body was full of wounds and bruises. The people would not close up the wounds and move forward.

> Is 1:7, Your country is desolate, your cities burnt with fire; Your land, strangers devour it in your presence (a waste, like Sodom overthrown)
>
> Is 1:8, And daughter of Zion is left like a cottage in a vineyard, as a shed in a garden of cucumbers, like a besieged city.
>
> Is 1:9, Except the LORD of hosts had left us a very small remnant, we should have been as Sodom, and we should have been like unto Gomorrah?
>
> Is 1:10 Hear the word of the LORD, you rulers of Sodom! Give ear to the instruction of our God, you people of Gomorrah!

God found no pleasure in their worthless offerings. Worship is entering into God's presence, and He does not want worship that is not real. A person can bow in church, but we must not do so without first laying our lives before God. We must always be right with our lives before God.

Is 1:11, To what purpose is the multitude of your sacrifices to me? says the LORD. I am full of the burnt offerings of rams and the fat of fed beasts; I delight not in the blood of bullocks or of lambs or of he goats.

In the ancient world the most difficult stain to remove was blood. Red stains are all hard to get out, such as stains from pomegranates, beets, berries, and blood. These stains, and even stains that are permanent in our world, God can get them out. God does not look at our past, he looks only at our future. God dealt with Peter, not in the present but as the Peter in the Acts of the Apostles. God knows the future, so he does not look at the past, we look at the past because we do not see the future. God wanted the people to care for the marginalized people, and to know that the Lord would clean their stains. Isaiah 1:17 to 18 says that God will make our red stains be clean as snow.

> Learn to do well; seek judgment, relieve the oppressed, judge the fatherless, and plead for the widow. Come now, and let us reason together, says the Lord: though your sins are as scarlet, they shall be as white as snow; though they are red like crimson, they shall be white as wool.

The idea of feasting is common in Isaiah and throughout the Book of Revelation. Both books tell us the goodness of the Lord, but also warn us of consequences as written in Isaiah 1:19.

> If you be willing and obedient, you shall eat the good of the land: but if you refuse and rebel, you shall be devoured with the sword: for the mouth of the Lord has spoken.

In scripture, reference to adultery is reference to a foreign God. Also, the fatherless and widows could not go to court, because only those who made their Bar mitzvah could go to court. There were generous judges who would hear a case from the marginalized, a case that he did not have to hear. People who do the minimum become bitter, we have to reach out to everyone.

Visual images are powerful. A plow is powerful, long and curved and you could convert it into a sword by straightening the plow. A pruning hook could similarly be made into a spear. Micah 4, tells us, as does Isaiah that God always had plans to gather up all of the remnants of His people. The remnants were so dispersed and interbred that they are actually the gentile people.

Isaiah tells us in Is 2:3 that many peoples shall come and say: "Come, let us go up to the mountain of the Lord, to the house of the God of Jacob, and he will teach us of his ways, and we may walk in his paths." For out of Zion shall go forth instruction, and the word of the LORD from Jerusalem. Is 2:4, He shall judge among the nations, and shall rebuke many peoples. They shall beat their swords into plowshares and their spears into pruning hooks; Nations shall not lift up sword against nation, nor shall they learn war anymore.4

John 10:16 also tells us that God wants everyone to be one, "other sheep I have that are not of this fold. Them also I must bring, and they will hear my voice, and there will be one fold and one shepherd." When people come to the knowledge of their safety, they lose fear. Fear is the cause of wars.

Isaiah spoke to God about the lives of the people of Judah. They were not looking to God for their strength, and they were not in a right marriage relationship. They were living lives filled with sex, and riches, and were turning to idols to worship and to be replenished.

> Is 2:5, O house of Jacob, come, let us walk in the light of the LORD! Is 2:6, You have forsaken your people, the house of Jacob, because they are replenished from the east, and are soothsayers like the Philistines; they please themselves in the children of strangers.

> Is 2:7, Their land is also full of silver and gold, and there is no end of their treasures; their land is also full of horses, and there is no end to their chariots. Is 2:8, Their land also is full of idols;

they worship the work of their hands, that which their own fingers have made. Are 2:9, And the mean man bows down, and the great man humbles himself: therefore forgive them not.

The prophet was speaking to God, and mentioned that the people would worship their wealth. Idols were also worshipped. When people accumulate wealth, it is easy to end up worshipping the wealth. Isaiah says that we must go to the rock of our salvation, fear the Lord, and remember that heaven is only a breath away.

Is 2:20, In that day a man will throw his idols of silver, and his idols of gold, which they made for himself to worship, to the moles and the bats.

Is 2:21, They go the clefts of the rocks and into tops of the ragged rocks, for fear of the LORD and for the glory of his majesty, when he arises to shake terribly the earth. Is 2:22, As for you, let man alone, in whose nostrils is but a breath; for what is he worth?

In the U. S., necessities are very inexpensive. Food and necessities are extremely valuable, and yet they are easy to obtain in the United States. In a time of famine, our material valuables will become useless. If we cannot figure out what is valuable, then God will create a situation to make it easy for us to be able to do so. Sometimes, we settle for our material things instead of what is really important. We think of a material gift that we posses, when we could have the only gift that is important. We could have God. Sometimes we forget that heaven is close, it is closer than we think. It is only a breath away.

A Beatitude is present in Is 3:10, "Happy the just, for it will be well with them, the fruit of their works they will eat."

The sin will punish the person, if a person sins, he does not get punished outside, he gets punished by the sin.

If you are God, your judgment does not depend on reality, reality depends on your judgment. This is true when Jesus says "Get up and walk," or "This is my body." His judgment is what forms us. Isaiah 4:4 implies that baptism will wash away our filth.

> Is 4:3, And it shall come to pass that he that is left in Zion and he that is remains in Jerusalem shall be called holy: every one that is written for life in Jerusalem.

> Is 4:4, When the Lord shall have washed away the filth of the daughters of Zion, And shall have purged the blood of Jerusalem from their midst by judgment and the spirit of burning?

Jeremiah 2:13 echoes the theme of baptism. Jesus is a living fountain, and they had dug cistern to hold water. They did not rely on God, but dug manmade cisterns instead of drinking the water that He provided.

> "Be astonished O heaven, and let the earth tremble still more at this, because the people hath committed two great evils: they have forsaken Me, a living fountain, and have hewn out for themselves cisterns. Is my holy hill Zion a desolate rock. For ye shall be as the fledglings of a bird, which fly away when the nest is removed."

Chapter 5 of Isaiah is a story about the vineyard. Wild grapes are not useful for wine. God said, I crown you with grapes, you crown me with thorns. He searched and could not find justice, so God took the stuff away from us. Isaiah 5:5 says, "Now, I will let you know what I mean to do to my vineyard: Take away its hedge, give it to grazing, break through its wall, let it be trampled!"

If God gives us gifts, we have the responsibility to use them wisely. If we do not meet our responsibilities with the gifts He gives us, God will take them away from us.

Isaiah described people who were so wealthy that they bought adjoining houses as the previous owners moved away. Today, we are living in a society where people are choosing to be alone. In ancient times, friends came over, today we choose to be alone in front of things like computers and televisions. Isaiah 5:8 warns us, "Woe to them who join house to house, that lay field to field, Till there be no place, that they are left to dwell alone in the midst of the land!"

We often do not use our strength to join one to another but to dissipate. Discretionary time and income are not used well. Isaiah tells us to change our ways.

The Emmanuel prophecies of Isaiah told of a time when God would dwell amongst us. There was a cloud in the eyes of the people that was blocking their view of God. Isaiah wanted us to know that God is present even if a cloud is blocking our view of His holy mountain. First Isaiah describes his own call in Chapter 6.

The structure of the call of Moses influenced the text of Isaiah with the following theme:

1. God initiates the call.

2. There is a setting of mystery / Holiness

3. Resistance of Moses (Isaiah, like Moses, thought he was not sufficient).

4. Reassurance of God

5. Commission of God: Now go do as I have told you.

This same structure of composition can be recognized in Isaiah chapter 6:
First, God initiated the call. Isaiah was in the Temple and he saw the Lord seated on a high and noble throne. Then, there was the setting of mystery/ holiness

> Is 6:2 Above it stood the Seraphim; each of them had six wings: with two he covered his face, with two he covered his feet, and with two he did fly.

Is 6:3 And one cried unto another, and said "Holy, holy, holy is the LORD of hosts: The whole earth is full with his glory!"

Is 6:4 The posts of the door moved at the voice of him that cried the house was filled with smoke.

Isaiah resisted the call because he thought he was not worthy.
Is 6:5 Then said I, "Woe is me, I am doomed! Because I am a man of unclean lips, and I dwell among a people of unclean lips; for my eyes have seen the King, the LORD of hosts!"

Reassurance of God:
Is 6:6 Then flew one of the seraphim to me, having an live coal in his hand, he had taken with tons tongs off of the altar.

Is 6:7 And he laid upon my mouth and said, "Lo, this has touched your lips. Your iniquity is taken away, and your sins are purged."

Commission to go speak the word of God:
Is 6:8 Then I heard the voice of the Lord saying, "Whom shall I send? Who will go for us?" "Then said I, here I, send me!"

Is 6:9 And he replied: Go and tell, you hear indeed but understand not; and you see indeed and perceive not.

Is 6:10 You are to make the heart of this people fat, and their ears heavy, and shut their eyes; lest they see with their eyes and hear with their ears, and understand with their heart and convert and be healed.

Isaiah mixed both images of joy and images of how lowly we are. God looked at his future, and the coal indicated to him that his sin was purged. Who will go for us? He saw the image that devastated him, and then volunteered, "send me." This is similar to Peter's story of being a believer.[223]

1. God initiates the call of Peter:
   There are two boats and of course, one of them belongs to Peter. Jesus gets into the boat belonging to Simon, and asks him to put out a short distance from the shore.
2. Setting of mystery / Holiness:
   Jesus tells Peter to go out further and to lower his nets. A miraculous catch of fish causes even the nets to tear, and they were all astonished.
3. Resistance of Peter who thought he was not sufficient:
   Peter fell down at Jesus' knees saying, "Depart from me, for I am a sinful man, O Lord."
4. Reassurance of God:
   And Jesus said unto Simon, "Fear not, from henceforth, you shall catch men."
5. Commission: Now Go…:
   And when they had brought their ships to land, they forsook all, and followed him.

If we want to do something great, we must make mistakes. In the Jewish way of looking at God, Isaiah said, "I am going to preach and no one is going to listen, but I am telling you this ahead of time." We, too will stand before God successful, because we spoke the words that he wanted us to speak. Our success is in God's hands. God does not have want us to teach to just the people in front of us; we teach to the Church which is in all time, past, present and future. When we enter into a relationship with God, we have a role in history.

Is 7:3 "Then the LORD said to Isaiah: Go out to meet Ahaz, you and your son Shear jashub, at the end of the conduit of the upper pool, on the highway of the fuller's field."

God knows the King will be by the pool, because water is important to life. Is 7:4, "and say to him: Take heed, be quiet, fear not; neither be fainthearted for the two stumps of smoking fire brands for the fierce anger of Rezin with Syria and with the son of Remaliah."

We have to show our strength, we cannot show our doubts even if they are present in our hearts. We can speak to one another about our doubts and fears, but our faith must always show forth to others. Rejoicing in the Lord must be our strength, so we can do the works that He needs done. God is always with His people, even during defeat. Isaiah's son is named Shear jashub, which alludes to a meaning of a remnant, shall return.

God can give a sign to a person but through another person, a confirming sign will also follow it. Isaiah, speaking for God, told King Ahaz to ask for a sign from God. King Ahaz knew he should not go beyond natural means to speak to God. So, he refused to ask God for a sign. St. John of the Cross wrote that we couldn't pass beyond the limits that God has chosen for our governance. King Azah knew that to attain to anything by supernatural means was going beyond the limits that are natural. God is offended by all that is unlawful, so it does not please him.[224]

> Is 7:10 to 12 "Moreover, the LORD spoke again to Ahaz saying, Ask for a sign from the Lord your God; ask for it either in the depth or in height above! But Ahaz said, I will not ask! Neither will I tempt the LORD!
>
> Is 7:13 Then he said: Hear now, O house of David! Is it small thing for you to weary men, but will you weary my God also?
>
> Is 7:14 Therefore the Lord himself will give you this sign: Behold, the virgin (bthuwlah) shall conceive, and bear a son, and shall call his name Immanuel.

The religious leaders of Jesus' time did not understand prophecy, and the natural order. They wanted a sign. Matthew's gospel says, "Then a certain of the scribes and of the Pharisees, answered, saying, Master we would see a sign from thee?"[225]

The leaders of the Jews were exceeding the limits that God has chosen for our governance. Jesus responded by calling the people an adulterous and evil generation who were seeking a sign from him. Then, Jesus said that only the sign of Jonas would be given to them. Jonas was in the whale's belly for three days, and Jesus was foretelling that he would rise from the abyss of death in three days. There is no comparison of Jesus to Jonas, yet the people of Nineveh repented when Jonas preached to them. The people should not have been asking Jesus for a sign. Yet, a sign was given to the Pharisees and the scribes, however they did not understand the sign that was given to them.

The people did not understand the sign given by Isaiah. It was a sign of hope, because the prophecy was not fulfilled until Jesus came. The name given to the Messiah is Emmanuel, in English it means God (El) among us. This passage in Isaiah is an important prophecy that points to the greatest work in history of the Holy Spirit. God told His people that he would send a great sign, and Matthew 1 tells us that this passage was fulfilled in Jesus. Jesus came into the world, and touched history for a span of about forty years. He is eternally Emmanuel, God with us. Matthew tells us that Jesus will be with us always.[226]

Our name is a description of which we are. Indians used verbs for names, and they changed their names during their lives. They knew that we do not know who we are until we have finished living out our lives. We change, and the description of who we are also changes. Thomas Moore told his daughter, "I am not a person of whom martyrs are made." And he spoke the truth, but he became that person and was able to be a martyr. Jesus named Peter *Rock*, because God saw him as He always sees us as what we will become. Jesus did not see Peter denying him, he saw Peter in the future as the man described in Acts of the Apostles.

The prophet Isaiah's testimony described in chapter 8 was of a terribly frightening darkness and distress that was about to descend upon the two nations of Judah and Israel. First, the wife of Isaiah gave birth to a son of whom was given the symbolic *name Maher shalal hash baz* which means speedy is prey, speedy plunder to describe what the Assyrians were to do to the countries of Samaria and Damascus, and it was even a warning to Judah

After King Ahaz and his people rejected the word of God and rejected it completely (Is 7:1 to 12 & 8:6), Isaiah 8:17 declared that God would hide from them to show His distaste. Isaiah wanted the people to not look at the past; instead to change because there was no hope for them in the way they were living and worshipping God. Chapter 8 ended on a dire note in verse 22, "And they shall look into the earth; and behold trouble and darkness, dimness of anguish; driven to darkness."

Isaiah 9:1 to 6 is dated to a time shortly after the Syro Ephraimite crisis that had Israel and Aram aligned against Judah. Assyria defeated both Aram and Israel, and made things easier on Judah. Chapter 9 of Isaiah addressed the anguish of the Israelites in Zebulun and Naphtali that suffered greatly during the invasion of the Assyrians. Many of the Israelite inhabitants were taken into exile, and the region was populated with people from other Assyrian providences. This is why it is called Galilee of the Gentiles in Isaiah 8:23 (9:1). Chapter 9 of Isaiah was about the hope of a great light, in contrast to Chapter 8 of Isaiah, which spoke of darkness.

Chapter 9 of Isaiah is also important in the foretelling of Jesus as Emmanuel. Isaiah 9:1 tells us that light would come to the lands of Zebulun and Naphtali described in Isaiah 8:23. This passage was used by Matthew to describe that this prophecy had been fulfilled when Jesus left Nazareth and went to live by the sea in Capernum in the region of Zebulun and Naphtali.

> Is 9:1, The people that walked in darkness have seen a great light; they that dwell in the land of the shadow of death, upon them has the light shined.9
>
> Is 9:2, You have multiplied the nation and not increased the joy: they joy before you according to the joy in the harvest, and as men rejoice when they divide the spoils. Is 9:3, For your have broken the yoke of his burden, and the staff of his shoulder, And the rod of his oppressor, as on the day of Midian. Is 9:4, For

every battle of the warrior is with confused noise, every garment rolled in blood, but this shall be with burning as fuel for flames.

Then following verses of Isaiah 9:5 to 9:6 described a child and the child is Immanuel.

For unto us a child is born, for unto us a son is given; and the government shall be upon his shoulder. ; And his name shall be called Wonderful, Counselor, The Mighty God, The everlasting Father, The Prince of Peace. [Is 9:6] Of the increase of his dominion and peace, there shall be no end. Upon the throne of David, and upon his kingdom to order it and to establish it with judgment and justice, now and forever. The zeal of the LORD of hosts will perform this!

This is the same child Isaiah wrote about in Is 7:14, 9:1 & 2, and 11:1.

This chapter described the inability to prevent the destruction of war. But more important, Isaiah taught that death would be removed when Jesus came. A child thinks everything is possible, and the fear of death is easy to remove. Jesus said everyone could be forgiven, Jesus said that we can live in peace. We think it cannot be done, because we have tried; but we have to remember that just because we tried and did not succeed, it does not mean that Jesus cannot do it. Old people may not bring new ideas but have much experience to contribute, and children may bring no experience but have new ideas. The two must come together. Pope Pius the XXII prayed each night that he did the very best for the Church that day, but it is our Church so he slept without worry. He allowed the Church to contribute to Her own needs and Her own growth.

When we are in a disaster, we do not just need to cleanup and continue on, we must reform. There must be a fundamental and radical change within us. Syria (Aram) and the Philistines had the Jews surrounded, and they still did not call out to the Lord.

Is 9:11 to 12, Aram in front, and the Philistines behind and they shall devour Israel with open mouth. For all this, his anger is not turned away, and his hand is stretched out still! The people do not turn to him who struck them; neither do they seek the LORD of hosts.

Jeremiah, Ezra, and Nehemiah were the leaders of the people when they returned from the captivity of the Babylonians. They prayed for release from captivity, but in their prayers they would not give up the past. Jesus can do anything, but we never expect what we have not seen before. We must rejoice in God's plan, even when we do not understand the plan. The Jews did not undergo a s radical change that God expected of them.

The captives in Babylon prayed for a new Moses, but they did not understand God's plan. As Cyrus came near, the Jews grew terrified of him. As Cyrus came even closer, they feared him even more because they thought that if he could destroy Babylon, surely he would have no pity on a nation of slaves. They still thought of themselves as a nation but they did not hear God coming to rescue them. To their surprise, Cyrus delivered them from Babylon and gave them money to start again. He was responsible from the rebuilding of the second Jewish Temple.

Sometimes, we are afraid of the wrong things. Many people are more afraid of not having knowledge than of being afraid of God. Cyrus was probably from the nation of the descendants of Ishmael. So, God always returns by a circular route so that the beginning and the ending are hard to distinguish from each other.

Isaiah chapter 10 warns us against the consequences of social injustice. God used Assyria to punish Israel, but Assyria was later be punished for raising a hand against His anointed people. God waited until after the people of Judah stop leaning on the Assyrians, "but lean upon the Lord, the Holy One of Israel, in truth. A remnant will return, the remnant of Jacob, to the mighty God" (Is 10:20 & 21). The word for remnant is the name of one of Isaiah's sons. This is a prophecy of God rebuilding his nation.

Isaiah wrote that a Messiah would come forth and from him a nation would grow. The spirit would rest on the Messiah. He shall bring justice, and Isaiah used imagery in his description of the Messiah to describe the new Kingdom that would grow from the shoot of the root of Jesse. Chapter 11 of Isaiah described the rule of Emmanuel. [Is 11:1] There shall come forth a rod out of the stem of Jesse, and a Branch shall grow out of his roots.

The word Hebrew word *neser* was used for branch and it is the word that is used in Isaiah 11:1 to describe Emmanuel from Nazarene. The rising light of Matthew's Gospel that the Magi followed used the same root word. Isaiah 49:6 also described this light.

> Is 11:2 to 3, And the spirit of the LORD shall rest upon him: a spirit of wisdom and of understanding, the spirit of counsel and of might, the spirit of knowledge and piety: and fear of the LORD. And shall make him of quick understanding of the fear of the LORD. And he shall not judge after the sight of his eyes. Neither reproves after the hearing of his ears.

The passage says that the Spirit rested on the Messiah, who is Jesus. Jesus did not need gifts of the Spirit so they were not given to him because he was in need of them. He was already filled with the powers of the Holy Spirit. The gifts rested on him, and the gifts are accomplished in him. He was the last of the prophets. The spirit rested forever upon Jesus. All prophets had gifts of the spirit, but after Jesus there were to be no more prophets like Elijah, Moses, and Daniel, and others of the Old Testament.

We cannot have a prophet who would contradict scripture, and a prophet cannot give new revelation. We can prophecy, but the gift is through Jesus, so prophets are different from the Old Testament prophets. He imparts to believers what he determines that we are worthy of. Joel 2:28 also wrote that the Messiah would pour out his spirit on all and that we would prophesy through his gift. All of this was fulfilled in the baptism of Jesus that is described in the Gospels. They also fulfill the words spoken in Psalm 2:7.

Isaiah 11 ends with the beautiful imagery of a wolf lying down with a lamb, and a lion with a child. Isaiah described a nation that would sprout from the branch of the Messiah. This is in agreement with Jeremiah 33 who said that God would make the bud of justice to spring forth unto David, and he shall do righteousness and justice in the earth. Jeremiah says that there will always be a man from house of David to sit on the throne of Israel.10

Isaiah in the following verses describes the beauty of God's holy mountain. Mount Zion is used throughout Isaiah as the mountain of God, the mountain of the Messiah. All of the remnants shall be gathered from the nations of the world.

> Is 11:4 to 11, But he shall judge the poor with justice, and decide right for the land's afflicted. He shall strike the ruthless with the rod of his mouth, and with the breath of his lips he shall slay the wicked. Justice shall be the band around his waist, and faithfulness a belt upon his hips. Then the wolf shall be a guest of the lamb, and the leopard shall lie down with the kid; The calf and the young lion shall browse together, with a little child to guide them. The cow and the bear shall be neighbors, together their young shall rest; the lion shall eat hay like the ox. The baby shall play by the cobra's den, and the child lay his hand on the adder's lair. There shall be no harm or ruin on all my holy mountain; for the earth shall be filled with knowledge of the LORD, as water covers the sea. On that day, The root of Jesse, set up as a signal for the nations, The Gentiles shall seek out, for his dwelling shall be glorious. On that day, The Lord shall again take it in hand to reclaim the remnant of his people that is left from Assyria and Egypt, Pathros, Ethiopia, and Elam, Shinar, Hamath, and the isles of the sea.

Isaiah 22

Isaiah 22 is important is describing the concept of succession which was a necessity in the Old Testament. Eliakim is made first in command after the king, and verse 21 says, "he shall be a father to the inhabitants of Jerusalem, and to the house of Judah." This is the same succession that Peter is given by Jesus.

Isaiah 22:21 to 24	Matthew 16:18 to 19
And I will clothe him with thy robe and strengthen him with my girdle I will commit thy government into his hands.	That thou art Peter (Rock) upon this rock I will build my church.
And the key of the house of David will I lay upon his shoulder;	And I will give unto thee the the keys of the kingdom of heaven;
so he shall open, and none shall shut; and he shall shut,	and whatsoever you shall bind on earth shall be bound in heaven: and whatsoever you shall loose on earth
and none shall open.	shall be loosed in heaven.

Isaiah 66 is also an Old Testament verse that speaks of continuation or succession. God says that he will be as the one whom the mother cares for, He will comfort us. "For as the new heaven and the new earth, which I will make, shall remain before me, says the Lord. So shall your seed and your name remain."11 Jeremiah also speaks of continuation of the line of David. There will never be a lack of a successor, "For thus says the Lord, David shall never want of a man to sit on the throne of the house of David."12

The Lord dwells on high, and he promised to fill Zion with justice and righteousness. The Lord is the sure foundation who has riches of salvation, wisdom, and knowledge. The fear of the Lord is the key to this treasure.13

Isaiah Chapter 33:14 to 15 described how we can see the king in his beauty, to dwell with devouring fire, and an everlasting burning. The man of justice will climb the mountain of the Lord. He who speaks truth, does not oppress, does not receive bribes, and does not listen to murderous plots, or look at evil. This man of justice will ascend to the mountain of God, and he will receive the Bread of Life, and the waters of baptism.

Second Isaiah

The second main section of Isaiah consists of chapters 40 through 55 and is called second Isaiah. It is thought by some that perhaps second Isaiah was written by a community that had followed Isaiah and interpreted him for future generations. Second Isaiah consists of a series of prophecies.

The first eight verses of chapter 40 are an introduction to this section. God's words are always words of comfort. If they do not come as comfort, either you were not the correct messenger or else the person is not ready to receive the message. You have to deal with what the person needs. Jesus never does the obvious, to the blind he asks, "What do you want?" God wants to bring comfort to us.

Isaiah 40 tells us that a voice will call out into the desert that the Messiah has come. The voice will cry out into the desert for us to prepare the way of the Lord. We are told to make straight the way for the Lord to come, and in the wasteland, a highway for God. The words we are to shout are words of God that stand forever. We must tell the world, "Behold your God."

Is 40:1, Comfort, give comfort to my people, says your God. Is 40:2, Speak of comfort to Jerusalem, and cry unto her that her warfare is at an end, her iniquity is pardoned for she has received at the Lord's hand; double for all her sins. Is 40:3, The voice of him cries out: In the wilderness, Make straight in the desert a highway for our God! Is 40:4, Every valley shall be exulted, every mountain and hill shall be made low; The crooked shall be made straight, and the rough places plain. Is 40:5, The glory of the LORD shall be revealed, and all flesh shall see it together; for the mouth of the LORD has spoken. Is 40:6 The voice said, "Cry out!" I answer, "What shall I cry out?" "All flesh is grass, and all their goodness is like the flower of the field.

Is 40:7, The grass withers, the flower fades because the spirit of the LORD blows upon it. Surely, the people is grass.

Is 40:8, The grass withers and the flower wilts, but the word of our God stands forever." Is 40:9, O Zion that brings good tidings Go up onto a high mountain, O Jerusalem that brings glad tidings; lift up your voice with strength, lift it up, do not be afraid. Say unto the cities of Judah, Behold your God!

These passages not only proclaim the coming of the Messiah, but the words are a message for us today. It is our responsibility to prepare the way of the Lord; it is God's who decides when to come. We must prepare the way by preparing ourselves to be the audience. He comes when He is ready. We cannot make Him come, or tell Him when He will come. As we get older, we recognize the foolishness of the material things that we chased after. The earlier in life we realize this, the better off we are because we can live our lives more fully. The less valuable things are for us, the more valuable relationships become for us. Even in creation, God did not say, "It is good," when he created man. Only when He created man and woman was it good. Communities in the Church are like a vow of poverty. We are fragile like dry grass, but our God is power, so we should not be afraid of the wrong things. We should not be afraid to cry out. God has power that can be exhibited in nature, and God has chosen not to use that power. God wants to have a relationship with each of us, and that is why he is gentle as a lamb rather than exhibiting power.

Isaiah 41:

Jesus and the Apostles dealt with a blind man. The Apostles looked to the past, and Jesus looked to the Kingdom of God. We do not see the future, He does not see the past. We speak about yesterday, He speaks about tomorrow. On Pentecost Sunday, Peter realized that even Herod and Pilate set the stage for the resurrection. He realized that there is only one plan, and that is the plan of God.

Isaiah 42 is an invitation for us to come completely into God.

Jesus with the woman at the well, talked about a lot of things until the subject of the woman's husband was brought up. We often think that we are the only decent people who can save a person, but we do not realize that we are not the only one. We must remember that God is the one who converts. We cannot look to the past, but to the future of God's plan. Is 8:19 tells us to seek our God. "And when they say to you, "Seek of them who have familiar spirits and wizards who chirp and mutter!; should not a people seek their God? For the living to the dead."

The Israelites did not know how to pray correctly when they were in captivity in Babylon. They wanted to get strong so they could destroy their captives. Instead of a powerful leader emerging from the Jews, God used Cyrus as his instrument to free the Jews. They also prayed too small. God saw their prayers as not being enough, He wanted them to be the light to the whole world, but they prayed only for their freedom. God's plans are always massive. At the annunciation,14 Mary knew that only the Ark of the Covenant could be overshadowed by the Holy Spirit. The educated think they know that a child cannot be born to a Virgin. God works beyond our knowledge, beyond our expectations. The Holy Spirit had the role of bringing about the incarnation (God coming into our history).

God used the rite of marriage to thwart Satan. There were two parts to the marriage. The first step was the betrothal and the second part was the groom coming for the bride and taking her into his home. The couple was legally married at the betrothal. Even Satan did not recognize this plan of salvation. He did not think that a married woman would be the virgin described by Isaiah, and this fact hindered him.

Yet, Mary says, "Because not impossible will be every word with God." With her verbal assent, salvatiosn was able to continue forward. Luke 1:35, And the angel said to her in reply, "The Holy Spirit will come upon you, and the power of the Most High will overshadow you. Therefore the child to be born will be called holy, the Son of God."

God said, His servant would prosper. When a person recedes from earthly things, he ascends into things of faith. The Pascal mysteries began with the arrest of Jesus and continue to his ascension. The Pascal mystery is a single event, and is called the incarnation.

Scripture study concentrates on the text with intensity of some sections. Justin the Martyr presented the second part of Isaiah as God giving his Kingdom to Christians.15

In Isaiah 42:6 continued the message of the conversion of Gentiles. He will enlighten the Gentiles and He will give a new covenant. "I the Lord have called you in righteousness, and will hold your hand, and will keep you, and will give thee for a covenant for the people, for a light of the Gentiles."

Isaiah continued speaking of Christians in Isaiah 42:16, "I will bring the blind by the way they knew not, I will lead them on paths that they have not known: I will make darkness light before them, and crooked things straight. These things I will do for them and not forsake them. To open the blind eyes, to bring out the prisoners from the prison, and them that sit in darkness out of their prison houses."

Justin tells us that if the law were able to enlighten the nations and those who possess it, there would have been no need of a new covenant. But God announced His intentions in advance that He was sending a new covenant and an everlasting law and commandment. Justin says that Isaiah 42:6 could not be about the old law and its proselytes, but of Christ and His proselytes. God has illumined us Christians.

In chapter 49 of Isaiah, he continues in verse 6 of foretelling us that to gather all of the people. "It is a light thing that you should be my servant to raise up the tribes of Jacob and to restore the preserved of Israel. I will also give thee to a light for the Gentiles, that thou may be my salvation unto the end of the earth. He said in verse 8, "Thus says the Lord, in an acceptable time I have heard you, and in a day of salvation have I helped you. I will preserve you and give you for a covenant of the people, to establish the earth, and to cause to inherit the desolate heritage."

Chapter 49 tells us that there will be a light to the nations and a gathering of all the tribes. The dispersed Jews had become part of the people of the nations. They were not a separate people at the time of Jesus. God sent Paul and the early Church out to the Gentiles and the dispersed Jews. The early Church had to go out to the Gentiles to gather them from beyond Judea and Samaria. Had the early Church not been persecuted, they may not have gone to gather all of the people beyond Judah and Samaria.

The Hebrew word *neser* is used for light or branch and is the word that is used to describe Emmanuel from Nazarene in Isaiah 49:6 as it was in Isaiah 11:1. The rising light of Matthew's Gospel that the Magi followed uses the same root. Isaiah 49:6 described this light that is to make the Gentiles the salvation for all people. The word neser is also used in Isaiah 60:21 for branch or bud, "Your people shall all be righteous, they shall inherit the land forever, the branch of my planting, the work of my hands that I might be glorified." This thread was mentioned in Isaiah 53:2, "he grew up before him like a tender shoot, like a root out of dry ground." This branch or shoot is of Jesse and finds it's fulfillment in Jesus. The word used for light, star, and branch means ruler, as in prince or king.16

Justin Martyr wrote that these words of light do not refer to the stranger and the proselytes, but to Christians who have been illumined by the light who is Jesus. Justin says that Christ would have been a witness even to them, but the Jews had become twofold. Christ's inheritance is the nations. Christ is the covenant of God, the covenant to establish the earth. Psalm 2:7 to 8 clarifies that Christians are the inheritance, "I will declare the decree, the Lord has said to me, thou art my son, today I have begotten thee. Ask of me and I shall give thee the heathen for your inheritance, and the uppermost parts of the earth for your possession."

Proselytes and Jews already had a covenant, and they both shared the same covenant. Christians possess the new covenant and are the true Israel. So, these verses did no refer to them, because God spoke of a new covenant. Isaiah 14:1 referred to Christians attaching themselves to the house of Jacob, because if the passage referred to proselytes it would not be logical. Why would the eyes of proselytes be open and not the eyes of the Jews. He would not have referred to Jews as blind and deaf while referring to the proselytes as being enlightened.

Luke in Acts 13 makes reference to Isaiah 49:6.

> For so has the Lord commanded us, I have set thee to be a light to the gentiles that you should be for salvation to the ends of the world. And when the gentiles heard this, they were glad and glorified the word of the Lord: and as many as were ordained to eternal life, believed. And the word of the Lord was made known throughout the region.

The nations of Jacob and Israel were named after Jacob. Jacob was surnamed Israel and from his two names came the names of the northern country of Israel, and the southern country of Judah. Christ begot Christians into God and we keep the commandments of Christ.

Isaiah also spoke in terms of kingship. We need to understand that Christ is the everlasting King. In Isaiah 43:15, God tells us that He has "made known Israel your King." Justin tells us that Jacob was not a king so scripture could not have been speaking about his son, Isaac, or Isaac's son. Nor is Jacob the patriarch in whom we should trust as described in Isaiah 42:1 to 4. Christ is whom we should trust. Christ is the Israel and the Jacob, and we are the Israeli race that Isaiah speaks of. Justin says that we Christians have been quarried out from the bowels of Christ.

Isaiah wanted the Jews to find true liberation by returning to the roots of the past. He called for the Jews to turn from their sins and to turn to God. Isaiah said that those who pursue justice, who seek the Lord should look to Moses. "Look to rock from which you were hewn."17 And those of justice should pursue to their ancestors, ""to the pit from which you were quarried."18

The song of Isaiah 53 is called the suffering servant song.

Isaiah 53 is the great song of the suffering servant. Christians see Jesus' passion in these passages. It is a chapter that should be memorized by both

Christians and Jews. The first verse, is an echo of Isaiah 11:1 that speaks of Jesse's root.[227] Is 53:1; "He grew up before him, like a tender shoot, like a root out of dry ground."

Only the Father saw the servant, yet in verse 4 Isaiah wrote, 'But surely, he takes our infirmities and carries our sorrows."

1 Peter 2:22 reminds us that Jesus did not sin, neither was guile found in his mouth, and this parallels the description in Isaiah 53:9. Peter continues that we were healed by his stripes as in Isaiah 53:5, "He was wounded for our transgressions, he was crushed for our inequities and the suffering that brought us peace was upon him, and by his stripes we are healed."

Isaiah 53:6, "We all like sheep have gone astray, each in our own way, and the Lord has laid upon him the inequities of us all." Compare to 1 Pt 2:25, "For you were like sheep going astray, but are now returned to the shepherd and bishop of your soul."

Isaiah 54 tells us of the new Zion that is created out of God's love. Verses 8 and 9 tell us that God promised us that he would not be angry with us. "But with enduring love I take pity on you." The love mentioned is Hesed love, which is covenant love. "For this is as the waters of Noah to me; I have sworn that the waters of Noah should no more go over the earth; so have I sworn that I will not be wroth (angry) with thee, nor rebuke thee."

Noah rode the waters of the flood with his son's Ham, Japeth, and Shem, and their four wives. There were eight in all, and the number eight signified revelations. The eighth day is revelatory and points to Christ appearing from the dead, forever the first in power. Justin wrote that Christ being the first born of every creature became the chief of another race. We Christians are regenerated by Himself through water, faith, and wood, containing the mystery of the cross; even as Noah and his household was saved by wood as they rode over the waters.

When Isaiah said, "I saved thee in the times of Noah," he is addressing a certain people. A people who are equally faithful to God, and who possess the same signs. The water rose above all the mountains so God's words are not to the land but to the people who obey Him. The Great flood had the symbols of water, faith, and wood. Those who are baptized in Jesus, and who repent of their sins shall escape from the adverse judgment of God.

The third major section of Isaiah begins with Chapter 56. Some scholars think that another scholar or a school of followers of Isaiah wrote this section.

To know what we are to fear, we must observe. We observe and then do. Observation is an art, and an artist sees details of their surroundings. God asks us to really look at things. Is 56:1, "Thus says the LORD: Keep your judgment (righteousness), and do justice; for my salvation is near to come, my justice (righteousness) is about to be revealed."

As a Christian we must make sure that others and we have a chance to worship. We cannot do anything that interferes with worship. It is not for us to decide whether or not someone goes to Church.

> Is 56:2, "Blessed is the man who does this, the son of man who lays hold to it; Who keeps the Sabbath free from profanation, and his hand from doing evil." We should not let foreigners feel left out. As Catholics we pick up things by experience. We express the trinity in signing others and ourselves, we genuflect, we put our hands in holy water, and we light candles. We need to be careful that we always keep the Sabbath. If we do not keep the Lord's Day, we will lose our connection with the past.

We remember that if someone is in Church that it was God who brought him there. Justin tells us that those who were selected out of every nation have obeyed His will through Christ who He calls also Jacob, and names Israel. God allots His inheritance to the nations but when he calls them Gentiles, it is to reproach the Jews.

The largest practicing religion in England is Catholicism, the second largest is Islam and the third is the Church of England. We do not go to Church for the priest, we go to Church for the encounter of the liturgy. Mormons put too many burdens on the choir; Baptists put too much emphasis on the minister's sermons.

In removing stumbling blocks we do what God wants. We need to remove the stumbling blocks for Protestants to come into the community. We did away with Latin in the mass, with statues, and we make other changes; some of us resist these changes and that is why it is taking a longer time getting Protestants to come in. The largest religious group in the U.S. is Catholic, the second largest group is composed of fallen away Catholics. Many of these Catholics fell away from the Church because they did not want to change, so that we could welcome others into the Church. Protestants are pouring into the Church and we need to speed this process up even more.

Isaiah 57:14 to 16 says that when we clear a path into the Church, we make it easier for people to enter.

> And shall say, cast thee up, cast thee up, prepare the way, take up the stumbling block out of the way of my people. For thus says the high and lofty one, that inhabits eternity, whose name is Holy: I dwell in the high and holy place, with him also of a contrite and humble spirit, to revive the spirit of the humble and to revive the heart of the contrite ones. For I will not contend for ever, neither will I always be angry; for then the spirit of man shall fail before me, and the souls I have made.

God made us, so he cannot be harsh forever, because we are whom God made.

The theme of Zion as the mountain of God comes up again in Isaiah 59.20 Isaiah tells us that the Messiah or deliverer will come out of Zion. He will save them from their sins. Paul tells us that God is ingenious and will save the gentiles and then Israel. All of Israel will be saved, He wants twelve tribes and not just two tribes. The Jews are beloved because of the call of the Patriarchs, and Paul says that God's call is irrevocable.21

Isaiah closed his book with a beautiful imagery of God who like a nursing mother will never abandon us. God tells us in Isaiah 66:7 to be patient because a new people is to birth forth. "Before she travailed, she brought forth, before her pain came she was delivered of a man child. Who ever heard of such a thing, or saw the like?"

We are told in this passage that God will joyfully beget a new people. This is the meaning of before she travailed. Like a mother who does not come to labor before giving birth. This passage also hints at the birth of Jesus through a virgin. She delivers a man-child, but not in the usual way because it is before she comes into labor. The word travailed is also descriptive of a birth as a midwife who helps with birth. A midwife has a gift to preserve and to protect life. Without a midwife, anything could go wrong during childbirth. Midwives encourage us, and even more, we are encouraged in the begetting or birth of a new nation.

Verse 11 tells us "That you may suck and be satisfied with the breasts of her consolations; that you may nurse and be delighted with the abundance of her glory." The Lord is going to give us comfort and prosperity at the breasts of our mother Israel.

God then said, "As one, whom his mother comforts, I comfort you: and you shall be comforted in Jerusalem."[228] He then says that He will come and gather every nation to come and see his glory. He will make a new heaven and a new earth, and as they remain so shall the seed remain of those who are gathered to Him.[229] In Revelation 21:1 John saw this New Kingdom coming down and he is told that God is Emmanuel and that He is now dwelling among us.

A mother carries her child in her womb. When the baby is born, the mother holds her child to her breast and says, "Take, eat and drink, this is my body." This is what Jesus says to us, "When he had given thanks, he broke the bread, gave it to his disciples and said, 'Take, eat, this is my body which is broken for you. Do this in remembrance of me.'"[230] The realities of heaven, comes to earth and are given to us, this is the meaning of the word remembrance. That is why John saw Jesus as the lamb that was slain and was standing at the altar surrounded by the heavenly creatures and the elders.[231] He asks us to come, take, eat, and drink of his body.

BIBLIOGRAPHY

Confessions, Saint Augustine, translated by RS Pine Coffin, Dourest Press, NY, 1986.
Critical Meaning of the Bible, Raymond E. Brown, Paulist Press, NY, 1981
Divino Afflante Spiritu, Pope Pius XII 1943
Erasing History, The Minimalist Assault on Ancient History, Baruch Halpern, Bible Review XI, 6.
History of the Jews: How a Tribe of Desert Nomads Changed the Way Everyone thinks and Feels, Thomas Cahill, Doubleday.
Lex Talionis and the Rabbis, Jacob Milgrom, Bible Review, XII, 2.
Models of the Church, Avery Dulles, Doubleday Publishers, NY, NY, 1987.
A New Look At An Old Earth, Don Stoner, Foreword by Dr. Hugh Ross, 1992, Schroeder Publishing Co.
Outline of History, H.G. Wells, Garden City Publishing, Garden City, NY, 1931
Reading the Old Testament, An Introduction, Lawrence Boadt, Paulist Press, NY, NY, 1984
The Theology of the Body (Human Love in the Divine Plan), John Paul II, Pauline Books and Media, 50 St. Paul's Avenue, Boston, MA02130, 1997.

NOTES

1 See also Gal 3:26, Gal 4: 6-7, Ephesians 1:51, and John 3:2.
2 John 6:51 & John 6:54 to 56; Mark 14:22 to 26; Lk 22:19 to 20, Mt 26:26 to 30, 1 COR 11:23 to 25.
3 Mt 6:19 to 21
4 1 Cor 12: 26 If a part suffers, all the parts suffer with it; if a part is honored, all of the parts share in its joy.
  1 Cor 2:9, But as it is written: "What eye has not seen, and ear has not heard, and what has not entered the human heart, what God has prepared for those who love him."
5 1 John 3:1 and 2, See what love the Father has given us that we may be called children of God. Yet so we are. The reason the world does not know us is that it did not know him. Beloved, we are God's children now; what we shall be has not yet been revealed. We do know that when it is revealed we shall be like him, for we shall see him as he is.
6 Heb 12:22, No, you have approached Mount Zion and the city of the living God, the heavenly Jerusalem, and the countless angels in festal gathering.
7 Romans 8:29, also see Rev 1:5
8 From the Apostles' Creed
9 Mat 22:32, "I am the God of Abraham, the God of Isaac, and the God of Jacob'? He is not the God of the dead but of the living."
10 Revelation 5:1 to 8, When he took it, the four living creatures and the twenty four elders fell down before the Lamb. Each of the elders held a harp and gold bowls filled with incense, which are the prayers of the holy ones. Also see Revelation 8:2-8, and Isaiah 29:11.
11 Mk 10:18
12 Hebrews 6:12, and 18 to 20.
13 Hebrews 9:15
14 1 Timothy 3:15

[15] Col 1:24

[16]

[17] 1 Cor 5:7

[18] John 17:21, so that they may all be one, as you, Father, are in me and I in you, that they also may be in us, that the world may believe that you sent me. Also see John 14:20 to 21.

[19] Acts 9:4 Saul was on a road when he was knocked to the ground when he encountered Christ. Saul was persecuting the Church when Jesus asked, "Saul, Saul, why persecutes thou me?"

[20] John 1:42

[21] John 17:17 to 18.

[22] John 17:23

[23] Isaiah 6:3, "Holy, holy, holy is the Lord of hosts!" Also see Revelation 4:8, etc..

[24] John 15:5

[25] John 6:56

[26] Cyprian, 251 A.D., "The Unity of the Catholic Church".

[27] "Didache" also called "Teaching of the Twelve Apostles" 160 A.D., 15:1.

[28] "Letter to the Corinthians", 42:13, Clement of Rome 80 A.D.. (See also 44:2 to 3 on Succession and 47:6.)

[29] Mt 16 5 to 12

[30] Mt 16:13 to 20 (See also Mk 8:27 to 30)

[31] Matthew 16:18, the gates of hell will not prevail against it. Also, see Luke 22:31 and 32.

[32] Matthew 17:24 to 27

[33] Acts 2:38, 2:41, men and women 8:12, Samaria 8:16, Eunuch 8:36 & 8:38, Paul 9:18 & 10:48 Gentiles baptized by Peter, 16:15 Lydia and her household, 18:8 jailer and his household & Corinthians, disciples of John 19:5, Paul 22:16.

[34] Luke 1:38, "May it be done to me according to your word." *Rema* is the word used for word, and it is the word of God that creates.

[35] Luke 1:37 & 38.

36 John 15:17, Revelation 12:17, Wisdom 6:18, John 5:3, and 2 John 6.
37 Romans 16:20
38 Ephesians 5:25
39 Ephesians 5:32
40 Galatians 4:26
41
42 Justin the Martyr: dialogue with Typho the Jew, Chapter 134.
43 Gospel of John 19:13
44 Hebrews 8:13 and Jeremiah 31:31 to 34.
45 John 20:22, He breathed on them, and said receive the Holy Spirit. Then Jesus gave them power to forgive sins
46 Revelation 1:3, Blessed is the one who reads aloud the words of the prophecy, and blessed are those who hear and who keep what is written in it, for the time is near.
47 1Cor 11:23 to 30, also see 1Cor 5:7, Lk 22:17 to 20, Mt 26:20 – 30 and Mk 14:17 to 26.
48 Martin Luther, "Collected Works," Number 7 page 391 in speaking of the many Fathers of the Church believing that the body and blood are really present, "But they are all of them unanimous." See also Ignatius of Antioch, "Letter to the Philadelphians" (4:1), and his "Letter to the Smyrnaeans" (7:1). See Justin the Martyr, "First Apology" Chapter 66, and Cyril's Lecture 19:7, 22:2,3,6 and 22:9.
49 "Interpretation of the Bible in the Church by Biblical Commission".
50 Vatican Council II, Chapter IV, paragraph 16 of *Dei Verbum* (Divine Revelation), Costello Publishing Company, Northport, New York, 1975.
51 Leviticus chapter 1 to 7 and Leviticus chapters 11 to 15
52 Psalm 139
53 Matthew 6:23 and 33.
54 1 Cor 6:4
55 Genesis 2:23, "for out of her man, this one has been taken." Also, Gn 3:16, "Yet your urge shall be for your husband and he shall be your master."
56 Genesis 1:27, "male and female created he them."

57 Genesis 3:1 to 3:7.

58 Jeremiah 29:17

59 Hosea 2:14

60 Genesis 3:21

61 Matthew 21:18 to 22, "When they were going back to the city in the morning, he was hungry. Seeing a fig tree by the road, he went over to it, but found nothing on it except leaves. And he said to it, "may no fruit ever come from you again." Mark 11:20 to 25 and Matthew 21:18 to 22 are in agreement with the prophecies of Jeremiah and Ezekiel.

62 Genesis 3:15. Genesis 3:13 also says, "Thorns and thistles shall it bring forth to you." This is a subtle illusion to John 19:1 where the Messiah is described as wearing a crown of thorns to end this curse.

63 Luke 2:7, Matthew 1:25, and other passages of the bible.

64 Revelation 12:5 and 12:9

65 Jeremiah 23:24

66 'Adam means man or mankind

67 Cain derived from the Hebrew word *qayin*, which means produced, acquired or created with the help of the Lord (begot).

68 Irad is from the Hebrew word *Irad* which means wild ass, onager (also cane huts) The Bible Anchor Dictionary) defines it as fleeting.

69 The root of lament is *lamech*, which means despairing. Strong's concordance defines the name as powerful.

70 Jabel or Jabal is from the Hebrew word *miqneh*, which means possessions. Probably tent dwelling traders. The root *ybl* means to bring, and El is short for Elohim (al is short for Yahweh) and combining *ybl* and El, the names means to bring and Elohim leads (in procession) (The Bible Anchor Dictionary).

71 Jubel's name was spelled Jubel or Jubal and was the brother of Jabel (Jabal). His name comes from the Hebrew word *yubel*, which means father of the lyre. A fuller meaning is rams horn from the Hebrew *yobel*, which is blown to proclaim special days, seasons, etc.(The Bible Anchor Dictionary).

72 Tubalcain is from the Hebrew name *Tubal* meaning creates, and *cain* that means acquire. Tublacain's sister's name was Naamah, the Heb *n'm* which means the playing of music (The Bible Anchor Dictionary).

73 The flood came when Noah was 600 years old. Methuselah lived 782 years after giving birth to Lamech and Lamech was 182 years of age when Noah was born. (782 minus 182 equal 600 years).

74 Seth means God has granted, given compensation, or appointed.

75 Enosh means frail or mortal, and the name also means dedicated.

76 Jered in Hebrew is *yrd* (yered or yared) that means descend and the name appears in W. Semitic personal names. Jared can also mean rose in Hebrew, and servant but servant is an uncommon personal name (Bible Anchor Dictionary).

77 Methuselah means Elohim's (God's) death shall bring. Strong's concordance defines it as *man of the dirt*.

78 Lamech is from the root word for lament, but it also means powerful: so a great cry or lament.

79 Genesis 6:5 to 6:7

80 Genesis 9:4 to 9:6

81 Genesis 9:6 referring to Genesis 1:26. Also see Lv 24:17, Nm 35:33, and James 3:9.

82 Genesis 6:5 to 6:8

83 Genesis 9:12 and 13

84 Genesis 8:22

85 1 Peter 3:20 to 22

86 Ex 25:2, "Tell the Israelites to take up a collection for me. From every man you shall accept the contribution that his heart prompts him to give me.
Ex. 25:3 These are the contributions you shall accept from them: gold, silver and bronze.

87 Number 21:9, Moses accordingly made a bronze serpent and mounted it on a pole, and whenever anyone who had been bitten by a serpent looked at the bronze serpent he recovered.

88 Dt 8:9 a land where you can eat bread without stint and where you will lack nothing, a land whose stones contain iron and in whose hills you can mine copper.

89 Samuel 27:7 In all, David lived a year and four months in the country of the Philistines. Samuel chapter 27 and 28 spoke of David living with the Philistines, being given a city to rule, and being part of their military.

90 Erasing History The Minimalist Assault on Ancient History by Baruch Halpem (Bible Review XI, 6). Some scholars say the reference is to a village that is not yet known.

91 The *Outline of History*, H.G. Wells, page 256, Garden City Publishing Co., Garden City, NY 1931. Also, see the book *Ancient Near Eastern Texts*.

92 See Wisdom chapters 10 and 14, especially Wisdom 10:4 and Wisdom 14:6 to 7.

93 Deuteronomy 15:12 to 18

94 *Lex Talionis* and the Rabbis by Jacob Milgrom, Bible Review, XII, page 16.

95 ibid.

96 Matthew 5:38 to 5:45

97 2 Cor 1:21 and 22.

98 1 Peter 2:2 to 5.

99 1 Peter 2:9 to 11.

100 1 Cor 3:16 and 17.

101 2 Cor 1:20 to 22.

102 Of course Russia and Israel still have problems with using military means for killing in the name of what they call national security and also they call it "justice."

103 Matthew 19:7 to 9

104 Gn 4:14 to 15 describes God protecting Cain. "Since you have now banished me from the soil, and I must avoid your presence and become a restless wanderer on the earth, anyone may kill me at sight." "Not so!" the Lord said to him. "If anyone kills Cain, Cain shall be avenged sevenfold." So the Lord put a mark on Cain, lest anyone should kill him at sight.

105 Gn 2:12, looking about and seeing no one, he slew the Egyptian and hid him in the sand.
106 1 Chronicles 22:8
107 Luke 4:17 to 19 and 4:21
108 Ezekiel 34:22 to 31
109 Joshua 10:1 to 15 describes the defeat of the five Amorite kings.
110 Joshua 11:3
111 Genesis 11:9, the story of Abraham immediately followed the story of the Tower of Babel.
112 Daniel Smith Christopher lectures in Southern California, 1998 with his former professor.
113 Joshua 24:15
114 Joshua 24:18 to 21
115 Joshua 3:14 to 17
116 *History of the Jews: How a Tribe of Desert Nomads Changed the Way Everyone Thinks and Feels*, Thomas Cahill, Doubleday, 1997.
117 *The gifts of the Jews: How a tribe of Desert Nomads Changed the Way Everyone thinks and Feels*, Thomas Cahill, Doubleday, 1997.
118 *The Substance of Things Hoped For: A Memoir of African American Faith* by Samuel DeWitt Proctor, pg. xxi, Putnam's Sons, New York, 1995.
119 Genesis chapter 49
120 Hebrew *re'uben*, Arabic "substitute (for another), *r'b* "to restore", most common meaning is, Behold an upright and devout man
121 Simeon is from the Hebrew *sam'a*, which means "has heard." Another variation of Simeon is *sim'on* which is an obscure name but may refer to an animal like a hyena.
122 Levi, from the Hebrew word *Lewi* "to be joined" but the meaning of the name is uncertain. It can mean "to coil or twist," and the Arabic is *lawa*.
123 Judah comes from the Hebrew word *yehuda* that means ravine or canyon, *hyr yhd* are mountains of Judah *yhd* and *yada* "to give thanks or praise."
124 Zebulon, Heb. Zebulun. *Zbl* means "dwell", *zebadan* means "God has given me, a good gift" (*zebed*) The name comes from two sources.

[125] Issachar, Heb. *Yissaakar* means, Hire, recompense. *Q. yissaskar* means "I have surely hired you *(sakor sekartika)*, my compensation (sekar). Kin of Issachar are often called "men for hire."

[126] Dan, Heb. *Dan*, to achieve justice. From Heb. Root *dn* "to judge." From the *Dictionary of Proper Nouns and Places in the Bible.*

[127] Gad from Heb. *Gdd* derivation means to cut off. Cut off means "killed." Although, in Genesis 30 Gad means good fortune.

[128] Asher Heb. *'aser*, eighth born to Jacob "happy one" or "righteous one". Name could also mean the name of a god, the male form of the goddess Asherah.

[129] Naphtali Heb. naptali formed from the base Nip`al of part 1, a verb means "to twist" or "to wrestle" with wrestling, Gn 20:8. "I have fought".

[130] Joseph Heb. yoser son of Rachel. ysp is a Hebrew verb "he adds" or "may the Lord add."

[131] Benjamin, Heb. Binyamin son of the right hand, symbol of strength, Is 62:8, Dn 12:7, Rev 10:57 "oath with uplifted right hand. The name can be defined as "child of happiness or fortune."

[132] Gn 31:32

[133] Numbers 25:4 and 14, and Dt 4:3.

[134] Nm 3:7 to 10

[135] Nm 3:12 and 44

[136] Nm 16:2 to 13

[137] 1 Pet 2:9, But you are "a chosen race, a royal priesthood, a holy nation, a people of his own, so that you may announce the praises" of him who called you out of darkness into his wonderful light.

[138] See Mt 5:13 to 16, Mk 4:21, Lk 8:16 and 11:33, and Jn 5:35.

[139] Nm 6:22 to 27.

[140] Nm 16:15

[141] Lk 1: 78, A rising light from on High will visit us to shine on those who sit in darkness, & to guide us. Matthew speaks of a rising star in Mt 2:2 & 9.

[142] Nm 12:1 to 15.

143 Nm 13:3
144 Nm 13:33, also see Gn 6:4
145 Mt 19:21, the woman actually touches the hem of Jesus' garments
146 Luke 23:34
147 Nm 21:1
148 Nm 20:12
149 Lv 11:45
150 See Nm 21:9 and 2 Kgs 18:4 where King Hezekiah smashed the bronze serpent because it was being used as an idol.
151 Nm 21:9 discussed in Jn 3:14 to 15 and in Wisdom 16:5 and 6.
152 Nm 21:16
153 See Nm 25, especially verses 1 to 4 and 9.
154 See Numbers 24:9, 24000 men were killed
155 I am in Greek is *ego eimi*, see John 8:28, John 18:5 and 8. I am, is Hebrew is *ho on*, see Genesis 3:14, Dt 32:39, and Is 43:10.
156 Genesis 4:2
157 Genesis 4:6 and 7
158 Biblical Archaeology Review, Volume 21, # 2, pages 52 to 56 "The Patriarchal Age, Myth or History" by Kenneth A Kitchen.
159 Genesis 15:1 to 20
160 Genesis 21:22 to 31
161 Genesis 15:9 and 10
162 New American Bible footnote for Jer 34:18, World Bible Publishers, Iowa Falls, Iowa, 1970 to 1986.
163 Gn 21:23 and 25, Therefore, swear to me by God at this place that you will not deal falsely with me or with my progeny and posterity. You will act as loyally toward me and the land in which you stay as I have acted toward you." Abraham replied, "I so swear."
164 Gn 21:25 to 31, "Abraham, however, reproached Abimelech about a well that Abimelech's men had seized by force." I have no idea who did that," Abimelech replied. "In fact, you never told me about it, nor did I ever hear of it until now. "Then Abraham took sheep and cattle and

gave them to Abimelech and the two made a pact. Abraham also set apart seven ewe lambs of the flock, and Abimelech asked him, "What is the purpose of these seven ewe lambs that you have set apart? "Abraham answered, "The seven ewe lambs you shall accept from me that thus I may have your acknowledgment that the well was dug by me."

165 Genesis 31:44 to 52

166 Biblical Archaeology Review, Volume 21, # 2, pages 52 to 56 "The Patriarchal Age, Myth or History" by Kenneth A Kitchen.

167 Ex 20:3 to 17

168 Ex 21 to 23, and Ex 25 to 31

169 Ex 35

170 Ex 24:4 8

171 See Gn 5:24, "then Enoch walked with God"; Gn 6:10, "for Noah walked with God" ; and [Micah 6:8] You have been told, O man, what is good, and what the LORD requires of you: Only to do right and to love goodness, and to walk humbly with your God.

172 Exodus 1:20 and 21

173 Genesis 15:5 and 18

174 See Joshua 11:4, Judges 7:12, 1 Sm 13:5, 2 Sm 17:11, 1 Mc 11:1, and Jer 15:8

175 Ex 19:4 to 6, tell the Israelites: You have seen for yourselves how I treated the Egyptians and how I bore you up on eagle wings and brought you here to myself. Therefore, if you hearken to my voice and keep my covenant, you shall be my special possession, dearer to me than all other people, though all the earth is mine. You shall be to me a kingdom of priests, a holy nation. That is what you must tell the Israelites."

176 "The Interpretation of the Bible in the Church" by Pontifical Biblical Commission, section III, Characteristics of Catholic Interpretation.

177 Heb 6:12 to 15, so that you may not become sluggish, but imitators of those who, through faith and patience, are inheriting the promises. When God made the promise to Abraham, since he had no one greater by whom to swear, "he swore by himself," and said, "I will

indeed bless you and multiply" you. And so, after patient waiting, he obtained the promise. Also, see Heb 6:18 to 20 describes the promise of the land as heaven.

178 Hebrew 9:15, For this reason he is mediator of a new covenant: since a death has taken place for deliverance from transgressions under the first covenant, those who are called may receive the promised eternal inheritance.

179 Jeremiah 33:20 to 21

180 Mark 15:33

181 Micah 6:1 and 2

182 Micah 6:3 to 5

183 Micah 6:6 to 8

184 See Jeremiah 2: 4 to 5, Listen to the word of the LORD, O house of Jacob! All you clans of the house of Israel, thus says the LORD: What fault did your fathers find in me that they withdrew from me? They went after empty idols, and became empty themselves.
See also, Isaiah 3: 13, The LORD rises to accuse, standing to try his people.

185 Dialogue of Justin the Martyr and Typho a Jew, paragraph 107

186 Micah 11:10

187 Micah 11:11

188 Micah 11:12

189 Mark 11:29

190 Genesis 24:62

191 Luke 10:38 to 41

192 Genesis 38:24

193 Behind your veil is a more recent translation.

194 Song 4:12 to 4:16

195 John 20:1 and John 20:11 to 17.

196 Ephesians 5:32 to 33

197 *The Theology of the Body: Human Love in the Divine Plan,* John Paul II, Pauline Press, Boston, 1997.

[198] Mt 27:43, Mk 15:20 to 47, Wisdom 17:20
[199] Wisdom 2:19 & 20 compared to the Gospels and James 5:6, "You have condemned and killed the just and he does not resist you."
[200] Wisdom 2:21 (NAB)
[201] Wisdom 6:22 to 25
[202] Romans 5:12
[203] Matthew 11:25. Also see Psalm 8:3 and Exodus 4:10 to 16.
[204] Wisdom 12:10 and 18 Also, see Sirach 5:4 (also called Ecclesiaticus 5:4).
[205] Wisdom 16:7
[206] See John 1:12, Romans 8, Gal 3:26, Phil 2"15, 1 John 3:1, 1 John 5:2, Wisdom 5:3, etc.
[207] Job 42:1 to 6
[208] Hosea 2:5, "I will strip her naked leaving her as on day of her birth; I will make her like the desert reduce her to an arid land, and slay her with thirst.
[209] Genesis 25:53
[210] *Lahairoi* or well of the living water (KJV).
[211] Hosea 2:25
[212] 2 Kings 17:14
[213] 2 Kings 17:24
[214] 2 Kings 17:28
[215] 2 Kings 17:33
[216] Romans 7:4
[217] Romans 7:11
[218] "Letter to the Corinthians, Chapter 35, St. Clement
[219] Romans 1:5 and 16:26
[220] 1 Corinthians 5:7
[221] 2 Chronicles 30:26-27
[222] 2 Kings 30:33
[223] Luke 5:1 to 11
[224] St. John of the Cross, "Ascent of Mt. Carmel," Chapter 21
[225] Matthew 12:38 forward

[226] Matthew 28:10 "Lo, I am with you always, until the end of the world."
[227] Also see Isaiah 49:6 and Isaiah 60:21
[228] Isaiah 66:13
[229] Isaiah 66:22 and in Revelation 21:1. John saw the new kingdom coming down and he described God as Emmanuel, He is dwelling with us.
[230] 1 Cor 11:25, also Mt 26:26, Lk 14:22, and Lk 22:19
[231] Revelation 5:6

INDEX

Aaron, 53, 106, 108, 133, 145, 147-148, 150-151, 168
Abel, 67, 120, 159
Abraham, 9, 19, 28, 42, 45, 47, 53, 55-56, 99, 129-130, 136, 160-162, 165-167, 171, 173-175, 222, 275, 281, 283-284
Adam, 6, 23, 42, 44, 52, 64-68, 70, 130, 143, 165, 176, 222, 235, 278
Adultery, 114, 146, 152, 215, 233, 236, 239, 247
Ahab, 141, 169
Ahaz, 230, 243, 245, 253-254, 256
Amos, 41
'Apiru, 89
Ark, 53, 56, 68, 70-71, 74-76, 80, 95, 133, 140, 155, 163, 224, 264
Assyrian, 256
Baal, 128, 135, 138, 152
Babylon, 44, 51, 82-83, 108, 141, 191, 245, 258, 264
Babylonians, 72, 171, 239, 258
Balaam, 154-156, 168
Boaz, 125
Branch, 76, 148, 192, 259-260, 266
Acts, Book of, 21, 24-25
Augustine, 28, 32, 36, 48, 273
Baptism, 5, 8, 12, 16, 18, 62, 75, 80-81, 250, 259, 262
Baruch, 41, 273, 280
Bathsheba, 141
Caesar, 29, 169
Cain, 52, 67-69, 120, 130, 159, 222, 278-280
Canaan, 86, 88-90, 92, 126-127, 129-131, 133, 135, 148, 171
Canaanite, 88, 126, 135-136, 138
Canon, 31-33, 38, 42, 44-45
Chronicles, 41, 44-45, 57, 281, 286

Church, 1, 3-9, 11-33, 36-38, 42, 46, 67, 71, 80, 96-98, 124-125, 131, 147, 150-151, 164, 177, 212-214, 220, 231-232, 235-236, 240, 242-244, 246, 253, 257, 261, 263, 266, 269-270, 273, 276-277, 284

Clan, 137-138, 154, 189

Clement, 22, 42, 240, 276, 286

Commandments, 4, 26-27, 68, 107, 124, 133-134, 149, 159-160, 162-163, 165, 198, 208, 232-233, 238, 240, 267

Commission, 34, 98, 100-101, 131, 251-253, 277, 284

Communal, 8, 13

Context, 47, 137, 181, 183-184, 206, 208, 238

Covenant, 5, 10, 25-26, 28-29, 41, 47, 52-53, 56, 65, 70, 72, 74, 77, 95, 98, 102, 107, 110-111, 113, 124, 133, 140, 148, 159-171, 177, 224-225, 230-233, 242, 264-266, 268, 284-285

Covenant Code, 110-111, 113

Creation, 3, 5-6, 40, 42-44, 52-53, 56-57, 60-61, 65, 70, 75, 126, 133, 149, 165, 177, 195, 197, 225, 230-235, 263

Criticism, 35, 46-47, 95, 170

Cross, 4, 7, 14, 29, 80, 95, 97, 149, 151, 154-157, 175-177, 207-208, 213, 222-223, 254, 268, 286

Culture, 39-40, 86, 89, 92, 102, 136, 138, 181-185, 188, 202, 210, 226

Cyrus, 258, 264

Daniel, 32, 41, 44-45, 136, 195, 259, 281

David, 23, 25, 41, 43, 77, 83, 89-90, 92-93, 102, 104, 118, 121, 125, 129, 139-140, 142, 163-164, 167, 175, 189, 205, 210-211, 242, 244, 254, 257, 260-261, 280

Davidic Kingdom, 43, 83, 139-140

Death penalty, 116, 118

Deeds, 40, 66, 97-98, 146, 168

Deutero Canonical Books, ix

Deuteronomic Code, 110-112

Deuteronomy, 41, 43-44, 52-53, 55, 92, 108, 112-114, 124-125, 143, 163-165, 171-172, 280

Diaspora, 31

Didache, 276

Dogmas, 16

Deuterocanon, 41-42
Ecclesiastes, 42, 189, 195, 204-206, 208
Egypt, 32, 40, 53, 67, 74, 82-83, 85-97, 99, 102, 105-107, 109, 123, 126, 130-131, 135, 150, 162, 166, 168, 183, 216, 222-223, 225, 260
Ekklesia, 26-28
Elijah, 22, 136, 141, 259
Elohim, 3, 45, 47, 51-52, 165, 278-279
Elohist Source, 51
Enoch, 69-70, 103, 284
Ephesians, 6, 27-28, 213-214, 235, 275, 277, 285
Eve, 6, 23, 64, 66-68, 70, 165, 235
Exegesis, 33
Exodus, 26, 40, 42-43, 51, 53, 55, 57, 82-83, 86, 91, 94, 96, 99-100, 102, 105-108, 111, 113-114, 124, 126, 129, 131-132, 136, 147, 160, 172, 216, 223-224, 232, 241, 244, 284, 286
Ezekiel, 41, 44, 65-66, 123-124, 191, 278, 281
Ezra, 15, 41, 44-45, 125, 172, 258
Family, 3, 5, 7-9, 55, 65, 70-71, 79, 96, 104, 109, 112-113, 121-123, 137, 142, 162, 185, 187-189, 194, 210, 222
Fig tree, 20, 64-66, 68, 193, 278
Figs, 64-65
Form Criticism, 46
Fundamentalism, 17
Galilee, 100, 128, 256
Genesis, 3, 27, 40, 43-45, 47, 51-53, 56-62, 64, 66-70, 75-76, 82, 120, 129-130, 133, 141-143, 149, 158, 160-161, 164-166, 171-176, 184, 209, 214, 230, 232, 234-236, 277-279, 281-286
Groom, 125, 149, 177, 210, 231-232, 264
Habakkak, 41
Hebrews, 9-11, 14, 42, 94, 103, 144, 166, 275, 277
Hebron, 127-129, 163-164, 182
Hezekiah, 55, 199, 230, 241-245, 283
Herod, 67, 96, 263
Hirem, 139

Historical Books, 41
Hittites, 128, 163
Holiness Codes, 110-111
Horeb, 47, 53, 165, 242
Hosea, 41, 57, 65, 108, 230-234, 243, 278, 286
Hyksos, 88-89, 91-92, 94-95
Isaac, 9, 19, 28, 47, 53, 99, 172-175, 177, 267, 275
Isaiah, 5, 19, 23-24, 41, 44, 68, 87, 100-101, 105, 107-108, 121, 125, 142, 169, 176, 216, 241-270, 275-276, 285, 287
Jacob, 9, 19, 28-29, 51, 55, 96, 99, 109, 141-143, 161-162, 222, 228, 248, 258, 265-267, 269, 273, 275, 280, 282, 285
Jamnia, 31
Jebusites, 128
Jeremiah, 22, 29, 41, 44, 65-66, 77, 97, 100, 167, 169, 194, 250, 258, 260-261, 277-278, 285
Jericho, 127, 137-138, 148
Jeroboam, 141, 230, 238, 243
Jerusalem, 28-29, 43-44, 65, 92, 104, 127-129, 140, 149, 164, 188-189, 201, 205, 244-246, 248, 250, 261-263, 271, 275
Job, 42, 47, 103-104, 188-189, 192, 194-195, 197, 200, 208, 219, 226-229, 286
Joel, 41, 259
Jonah, 41
Jordan, 133, 137, 139, 148, 152, 182
Jordan River, 133, 137, 148, 152
Joseph, 53, 67, 96, 109, 142-143, 145, 171-172, 195, 222, 282
Josiah, 55, 111, 138, 171, 243
Joshua, 41, 43, 83, 94, 104, 126-129, 131-132, 136-137, 148, 151, 163, 171, 281, 284
Jubilee, 69-70, 111, 121-123
Judges, 41, 43, 52, 82-83, 128-129, 137-139, 164, 192-194, 247, 284
Judith, 32, 41
Justification, 4, 67
Justin, 28-29, 36, 173-176, 265-269, 277, 285
Kingdom, 7, 19, 23, 25, 43-44, 63, 80, 83, 86-89, 135, 139-141, 149, 166, 171, 185, 219, 221-222, 229-231, 238, 242, 257, 259, 261, 263, 265, 271, 284, 287

Kings, 9, 12, 41, 43, 52-53, 55-56, 82-83, 85, 110-111, 118, 127-128, 135-136, 138, 140-141, 146, 163-164, 166, 171, 183, 188, 192, 194, 197, 213, 219, 222, 224, 230, 243, 245, 281, 286
Kingship, 220, 241, 267
Laban, 28-29, 143, 161-162
Lachish, 127-128
Lake, 71-72, 80
Lamb, 16, 18, 174-177, 244, 260, 263, 271, 275
Lamentations, 41
Law, 4, 26, 41, 43, 45, 82, 94, 96, 101-103, 108-115, 117-118, 124-125, 130, 172, 195, 197, 237-240, 265
Levites, 52, 56, 145-146, 154, 244
Leviticus, 41, 51, 53, 56, 114-115, 121, 163, 172, 244, 277
Literal, 37, 48
Literary Criticism, 35, 47
Maccabees, 32, 41
Malachi, 41
Manasseh, 137, 143, 145
Mari, 160-161
Mary, 25-27, 30, 67-68, 75, 77, 187, 211, 213, 264
Matthew, 7, 19-21, 23, 29, 80, 95-98, 100, 103, 147, 169, 215, 218, 223, 229, 234, 236, 254-256, 259, 261, 266, 276-278, 280, 282, 286-287
Mediterranean, 71-72, 85, 185-187
Messiah, 22, 25, 43, 67-68, 124, 140, 142-143, 158, 216-217, 242, 255, 259-260, 262-263, 270, 278
Micah, 41, 97, 168-169, 173-174, 248, 284-285
Midianites, 56, 96, 102
Moab, 139, 151, 168
model, 18, 26, 130-133, 140
Mother, 5, 28, 62-65, 67-68, 78, 95, 109, 113-114, 141, 159, 190, 194, 199, 212, 234, 261, 270-271
Moses, 26, 29, 39-41, 43, 51, 53, 56, 74, 82-83, 90-91, 94-97, 99, 102-103, 105-106, 108, 120, 124-126, 129, 131, 136, 138, 145-148, 150-151, 154, 162, 164, 166, 168, 172, 215, 222, 225, 231-232, 234, 236, 242, 251, 258-259, 267, 279

Mystery, 6, 9, 18, 27-28, 99-100, 207, 214, 235, 251, 253, 265, 268
Mystical body, 10, 22-23
Name, 12, 20, 24-25, 29, 51, 64, 68-69, 88, 93, 96, 99, 101-103, 124, 131, 140, 142-144, 147, 151, 159, 165, 169, 174, 176, 187-188, 190, 200, 217, 231, 243, 254-255, 257-258, 261, 270, 278-282
Naomi, 125
Nehemiah, 15-16, 41, 44-45, 125, 172, 258
Nineveh, 255
Noah, 53, 62, 68, 70, 74-76, 78, 80-81, 165, 167, 222-223, 268, 279, 284
Numbers, 16, 41, 51, 53, 56, 74, 114, 116, 125, 141, 143-147, 149, 152, 155, 158, 172, 244, 282-283
Oaths, 85, 160-161
Obadiah, 41
Omri, 169
Oral, 38-40, 46, 48, 53, 111, 183
Original Sin, 3, 220
Palestine, 53, 88, 90-92, 164
Pascal, 18, 207, 265
Passover, 18, 62, 76, 82, 106-107, 140, 147, 169, 175-176, 243-244
Pattern, 57, 63, 77, 100, 105-107, 160-163
Paul, 4, 6-7, 9, 14, 18, 21, 24-25, 27-29, 34, 102, 112, 120, 169, 188, 213-214, 218, 220, 229, 234-240, 244, 266, 270, 273, 276, 285
Pentateuch, 39-40, 43, 47-48, 51-53, 85, 100, 164-165
Peter, 4, 19-25, 29-30, 42, 80-81, 119, 124, 237, 247, 252-253, 255, 261, 263, 268, 276, 279-280
Pharisees, 31, 169, 231, 234, 254-255
Pharaoh, 87, 89, 92, 96, 99, 103, 105-107, 109, 126, 130
priests, 15-16, 20, 29, 52, 55-56, 88, 118, 133, 138-139, 145-146, 166-167, 169, 183, 195, 233, 239, 244, 284
Priestly Source, 55
Prophets, 14, 19, 21-22, 26, 41, 43-44, 52, 65, 101, 118, 135-136, 138-140, 146, 148, 158, 164, 172, 183, 195, 220, 223, 233, 238, 259
Proverbs, 42, 93, 110, 188-190, 193-195, 197-201
Psalms, 39-40, 42, 47, 189, 194, 241

Rachel, 29, 97, 143, 282
Ramesses, 86-87, 126
Redaction, 35, 48
Redactors (R), 52
Reed, 38
Remembrance, 8, 20, 170, 206, 271
Revelation, 10, 15, 27, 31, 36, 42, 67, 200, 247, 259, 271, 275-278, 287
Rehoboam, 141
Rhetorical criticism, 46
Righteousness, 4, 7, 63, 188, 229-230, 243, 260-261, 265, 269
Rock, 19-20, 23-24, 53, 142, 144-145, 150, 182, 249-250, 255, 261, 267
Ruth, 41, 125
Sacrifices, 56, 105, 107, 111, 119, 152, 173-174, 247
Sadducees, 31
Samaria, 141, 239, 255, 266, 276
Samuel, 41, 43, 52-53, 118, 136, 139-140, 164, 171, 194, 280-281
Sargon, 95
Satan, 19, 24, 27, 66-68, 103-104, 264
Saul, 41, 83, 118, 139, 141, 163, 276
Scientific, 37, 57, 61
Septuagint, 31-33, 158
Sex, 13, 171, 210, 248
Shechem, 201
Silver, 88, 91-92, 102, 191, 199, 213, 221, 248-249, 279
Sinai, 26-27, 47, 53, 55-56, 83, 85, 87, 89-90, 94, 97, 147-148, 160, 162-163, 165, 172, 232
Sirach, 32, 42, 189, 195, 201, 204, 286
Slave, 10, 29, 95, 99, 102, 111-112, 136, 213
Slavery, 14, 86-87, 94, 102, 109, 111-113, 123, 162, 168
Social Revolution, 130-131, 138
Solomon, 42-43, 56, 62, 121, 139-141, 188-190, 193-194, 197, 199, 206, 210-212, 216, 221, 224, 238, 243-244
Song of Songs, 188, 210-212, 214
Source criticism, 47

Spirit, 4-5, 13, 17-18, 21-27, 29-30, 62, 65, 67, 75-76, 101, 119-120, 123, 131, 134, 148, 171, 176-177, 182, 204, 207-208, 217, 250, 255, 259, 263-264, 270, 277
Teaching, 101, 198, 276
Temple, 13, 23, 25, 43-44, 52, 55-56, 62, 68, 118-119, 138-140, 158, 173-174, 176, 188-189, 212, 221, 224, 238, 243-244, 251, 258
Testament, 21, 26, 29, 31-32, 34, 36, 38-40, 42-43, 45, 48-49, 52, 74-75, 82, 100, 103, 108, 112, 118-119, 127, 132, 142, 150-151, 158, 170, 187, 205-206, 216, 222, 237-238, 241, 244, 259-261, 273
Text, 33-36, 39-40, 46-48, 93, 99, 115, 128, 130, 150, 167, 173, 210, 242, 251, 265
Tobit, 32, 41
Torah, 43, 96-98, 158-159, 164-165, 172
Tradition, 3, 12, 15, 22, 25, 32-35, 46, 48, 53, 74, 82, 94-95, 102-103, 106-108, 111, 121, 124-125, 136, 158, 169, 182-183, 187, 222
Treaty, 160-163, 177
Tribes, 56, 82, 128-129, 131, 137, 139, 141-142, 144, 147, 152, 158, 163-164, 166, 188, 265-266, 270
Tyre, 139
Universal Church, 18, 27-30
Uzziah, 230, 242-243, 245
Vulgate, 36-37
Wayfarers, 146
Wisdom, 3, 28, 32, 42, 47, 57, 93, 105, 107, 120, 140, 169, 179, 181, 183-184, 188-195, 197-203, 206, 208, 212, 216-227, 229, 237, 259, 261, 277, 280, 283, 286
Wisdom, Book of, 105, 107, 189, 195, 212, 216-217, 222, 225-226
Wisdom literature, 179, 181, 183-184, 188-189, 191-194, 197, 201, 216-217, 220
Womb, 30, 62-63, 67, 77, 100, 227, 271
Yahweh, 47, 51-52, 56, 67, 82, 90, 102-103, 110, 131, 135-136, 138, 142, 159, 164-165, 184, 189, 204, 210, 241, 243, 278
Yahwist Source, 51, 53
Zechariah, 41, 44, 243
Zedekiah, 141
Zion, 5, 24, 68, 241-244, 246, 248, 250, 260-261, 263, 268, 270, 275

About the Author

Jim McKeehan is a biochemist who has always been a student of Scripture. He is an avid painter of landscapes with oil. He is currently working as a teacher in Southern California.

0-595-20758-8

Printed in the United States
6145